ALLUSION
A LITERARY GRAFT

THEORY/CULTURE

Editors:
Linda Hutcheon, Gary Leonard
Janet Paterson, and Paul Perron

ALLAN H. PASCO

Allusion
A Literary Graft

UNIVERSITY OF TORONTO PRESS
Toronto Buffalo London

© University of Toronto Press Incorporated 1994
Toronto Buffalo London
Printed in Canada

ISBN 0-8020-0449-0

∞

Printed on acid-free paper

Canadian Cataloguing in Publication Data

Pasco, Allen H.
    Allusion : a literary graft

    (Theory/culture)
    Includes bibliographical references and index.
    ISBN 0-8020-0449-0

    1. French literature – 19th century – History and criticism.
    2. French literature – 20th century – History and criticism.
    3. Allusions in literature.
    I. Title. II. Series.

    PQ283.P37 1994   840.9'007   C94-930656-8

This book has been published with the generous assistance of a grant from
The Hall Family Foundation and The Kansas University Endowment
Association.

For Schuyler, Teague, Brandt, Chandar
who have brought light and joy to a life of study

Contents

Although 'intertextuality' has come to mean little more than the relationships between texts, it seems possible to distinguish three kinds of intertextualities: of imitation, opposition, and allusion. The latter device, allusion, occurs throughout literature, though it frequently escapes attention, resulting in misreadings and misinterpretations. Allusion calls on texts outside the work in the reader's hands, but it works internally, within and during the reading. A study of the device as it functions during the experience of specific texts highlights its dependence on metaphor and also casts light on other related devices – such as imitation, plagiarism, allegory, or parody – and on the way we read.

It is not enough for readers to invent irony. For irony to function with validity, the text must give sufficient indications of its presence. Flaubert's 'Un Cœur simple' offers a case in point, since critics have divided on whether the work should be read ironically. For those who see irony, the parrot's identification with God provides the touchstone. A careful look at the text of 'Un Cœur simple' and of *Trois contes*, however, reveals the striking fact that an ironic reading of the parrot has no consistent, textual support either in the story or in the incorporating cycle. The tale does, however, establish systematic allusions to the Beatitudes and to the legend of St Félicité.

Translation, imitation, and plagiarism are all different from allusion. The alluding author may attempt to replicate the preceding text, but he does so only to exploit it in his own creation. Anouilh, for example, announces his debt to the past in the title of his *Antigone*, summarizes Sophocles' version in the program, and repeats the summary in the first few minutes of the play. Thereafter the modern version, while maintaining remnants from the classical text, begins to deviate significantly. The ancient image remains in the reader's mind, however, and sets up a parallel with Anouilh's version. It also brings death to the fore and emphasizes the fact that Antigone must die.

Especially when allegory receives its traditional definition, its binary nature contrasts with allusion. Its figural sense remains distinct from the literal level, while allusion's external text combines metaphorically with the text in hand. Barbey d'Aurevilly's 'Le Rideau cramoisi,' for example, reminds knowing readers of Stendhal's *Le Rouge et le noir* through a parallel plot, themes, and images. It simultaneously stimulates affective patterns of a previous response and encourages the search for an explanation of Brassard's inexplicable cowardice. Albertine is more than a mere girl. The allusion encourages readers to become sensitive to the text's suggestions that she is satanic.

Beneath the surface of Proust's novel there exists an interwoven pattern of allusions that highlights the various thematic movements. I call this tapestry of allusions an allusive complex. Names, parallel plots, repeated imagery, and suggestive themes key allusions to 'Le Rideau cramoisi,' to the myth of Icarus, to the *Arabian Nights*, to *Swan Lake*, and to Parsifal and the Fisher King. The very length, complexity, and completeness of the various allusions in this sequence indicate a sustained effort to make the reader feel the hazards of the protagonist's quest, while insisting on Albertine's ephemeral charm, mystery, magic, and perhaps most important, her need for freedom.

6   **Oppositional Allusion:** *Electre, La Symphonie pastorale,*
    Eugénie Grandet   98
Allusions of opposition are distinct from satire, irony, or parody. Devices of the latter variety are rejective, while allusions are
integrative. A comparison of two recent versions of *Electre* helps
illustrate the difference. Giraudoux's play serves in addition to
show how an opposition can suggest that a modern *Electre* just
might end differently, and thus raise suspense. Gide's *La Sym-*
phonie pastorale provides a somewhat different example of oppositional allusion. The many echoes of the Bible include erroneous references, quotations out of context, and inconsistent
and faulty interpretations that insist on the pastor's hypocrisy
and moral blindness. In *Eugénie Grandet*, on the other hand,
Balzac focuses on a materialistic religion by opposing an
aborted 'second coming' to that suggested by the Bible. The
allusion creates a vehicle to play out the divine-human comedy
more fully than in any other of Balzac's works.

7   **Allusive Oxymoron:** *La Faute de l'abbé Mouret*   121
Zola's *La Faute* alludes to two different sets of allusive complexes that eventually come together, as does an oxymoron. On
one side, he deployed allusions to fertility goddesses and then
opposed them to allusions of (almost) equal strength to an inhuman god of spirit and mind. Cybele is set against Jehovah,
Désirée against Archangias, Paradou's tree of life against the
cemetery's tree of death, body against soul, nature against the
church. The opposing allusions then work together metaphorically to direct attention toward a third term or synthesis. Peace
is established and opposites marry. They produce, not a child,
but the vision of what it means to be a human being.

8   **Allusive Permutations:** *La Nausée, Les Gommes*   161
As preceding chapters have attempted to demonstrate, the essential relationship of allusion is straightforward, whether it
forms parallels, oppositions, or oxymorons. Of course, writers
may complicate the matter in a number of different ways. They
may allow related devices to 'slide into' allusion. Sartre's *La*
Nausée begins with an obvious burlesque of Proust's *A la re-*
cherche du temps perdu, for example, only to end by suggesting a
Proustian salvation through art. Or, like Robbe-Grillet in *Les*

Gommes, a writer may set up several sets of allusions without ever allowing them to come together to form a coherent 'complex.' The only limitation comes from ignorance. When readers have not read what is alluded to, or share no common tradition with writers, then allusions seeded in a text will produce neither plant nor fruit. Of course, their potential remains, and a reader may one day come with the background to permit a new efflorescence. When this happens, the bond takes and the reader's mind gives birth to a living text.

Acknowledgments

Colleagues at home and abroad will remember how often this long-standing project surfaced in our conversations. My debts to them are indicated wherever I could be specific, but I am also grateful for the many unnamed friends whose help was no less real, though it consisted for the most part in providing a sounding board in occasionally far-ranging discussions. David Lee Rubin made a number of excellent suggestions after reading early versions of several chapters. Dallas, my wife and partner, patiently and perceptively read, and often read again, as the manuscript took shape, and my entire family has shown incredible tolerance in putting up with what must on occasion have seemed an obsessive and interminable interest. They will be pleased for me to move on to something else. As with any project that has been long in the germination, the debts I have incurred are many and real.

I appreciate as well the encouraging and essential financial help I have received from various institutions. The University of Chicago provided several summer grants. Purdue University did also, and in addition awarded me a semester free from teaching and administration in their Institute for Research in the Humanities. Indiana University's Lilly Library generously gave me an invaluable summer with their collection. Finally, I especially want to thank the University of Kansas and the Hall Family Foundation for the endowment that gave me the time to finish this manuscript.

Portions of *Allusion: A Literary Graft* were previously published. An early version of the chapter on *A la recherche du temps perdu* appeared in *Romanic Review* 62 (1971): 113–26, one on 'Le Rideau cramoisi' in *PMLA* 88 (1973): 461–71, and two others on *La Faute de l'abbé Mouret* in

Forum for Modern Language Studies 14 (1978): 208–16 and *Nineteenth-Century French Studies* 7 (1979): 232–44. I am grateful for permission to reprint this material.

ALLUSION
A LITERARY GRAFT

1

Introduction

Since Julia Kristeva coined the term 'intertextualité,' considerable work has been done on the concept as it applies to literature. Kristeva began with an understanding of a text as a 'mosaic of quotations [where] every text is the absorption and transformation of another text.'[1] For her, literature constitutes that 'transposition of one (or several) sign systems into another.'[2] Add to this freewheeling conception Roland Barthes's conclusive demonstration that texts may be constructed of signs far removed from words, and we have been transported well beyond Tzvetan Todorov's view of a '[l]iterature . . . created from literature, not from reality, whether the latter be material or psychic; every literary work is conventional.'[3] For numerous critics, literature's only limit in the way it uses signs and texts is, as the Czech structuralists insisted, that while literature can never really be autonomous, it does exist within a system, within a society.

Since the inception of this kind of thinking about literature, what seems the infinitely expansible potential of intertextuality has rendered communication with the reader increasingly remote. Harold Bloom says, 'Poems are not things but only words that refer to other words, and *those* words refer to still other words, and so on into the densely over-populated world of literary language.'[4] As literature devolves into a series of mirrors, one is hardly surprised to find Barthes discovering Proust (1871–1922) in Flaubert (1821–80) and savoring 'the reign of formulas, the reversal of origins, the detachment which brings the anterior text from the ulterior text.'[5] Meanwhile, the reader shifts from one more-or-less interesting nebula to another, unable or unwilling to take firm positions about particulars, ready to comment only on what he or she, the reader as 'text,' becomes while partaking of the Gargantuan Text of all texts, the 'body' of literature.

The thrust is, of course, less in the texts than in the readers, who have recognized the all-too-obvious imprecisions, approximations, thus, imperfections of language as a means of communication. Proust's protagonist was also struck by his inability to express his joy before a bright, new day (he was reduced to 'Zut, zut, zut, zut'),[6] though he subsequently learned not only to appreciate his own feelings more fully but also to find ways to make language more aptly express them. Unlike this hero, however, post-structuralist critics have concentrated on the imperfections, inexactitudes, vaguenesses, and vagaries to such a degree that sign is not just distinguished but separated from signified, reference from referent, from allusion or – in brief – from meaning. As critics and readers, we become more aware of the proliferation of detail when we refuse to accommodate those conventions that guided authors in their creation. The attitude is perhaps described in the following quotation from Geoffrey Hartman: '[T]he more you load language with quotations or allusive matter, the more it subverts meaning. Puns, in which this load becomes an overload, are a special case of this subversion: however witty and explosive, however energetic their yield of meaning, they evoke in us a sense of leprous insubstantiality, of a contagion that might spread over language as a whole. We feel like the Cheshire Cat, who says to Alice: "You may have noticed that I am not all there." The literary nihilist is the Cheshire Cat of language. He is a mobile synecdoche. Language shows its teeth in an empty grin.'[7] There is no doubt that allusive overload exists – my favorite example is Eliot's *Cocktail Party*, with its polygenetic, polysemous, and polyvalent elements that, for me, never quite work together. The work's semantic chains are so numerous that one is not quite sure which are pertinent. Such loaded texts, however, are far from the rule. And even in Eliot, F.O. Matthiessen would argue that the very multiplicity of allusive reference 'can greatly increase the implications of his lines by this tacit revelation of the sameness (as well as the contrasts) between the life of the present and that of other ages.'[8]

Michael Riffaterre reminds us that though the reader may recall innumerable texts that more or less resemble the text in hand, one should distinguish those external texts that depend only on the reader from those that are specifically indicated by the text, where the 'intertext leaves in the text an indelible trace, a formal constant which plays the role of an imperative for reading and governs the deciphering of the literary message.'[9] Of course, such a reading requires accepting the conventions that give a semblance of order to signs and, moreover, defining literary texts as the words more or less firmly fixed in and limited to the written, sung, or recited forms considered definitive. In short, while there is no doubt that the reader must of necessity unify and illuminate (or 'create') the text, for this study I assume that the text has certain conventional imperatives that influence those readers willing to submit to the external textual authority. Although Walter Pforzheimer's point of view is acceptable when he says, 'I look at a book as a glass that is half empty. . . . You have to rely on your own personal knowledge of things,'[10] one needs to remember that the glass is also half full of material that restrains and directs the reader.

The emphasis on 'theory' and the voyage to the ultimate in universals, to the general, to the transcendent, has doubtless taught us to be wary of the arbitrariness of distinguishing text from text and was perhaps as rewarding as abstract art to another medium, but here I shall concentrate on a more limited, textual reality. However interesting, amusing, or malicious it may be to join a creative critic like Barthes in finding Proust in Flaubert, in truth, of course, he is not there. Such readerly 'discoveries' are at best ephemeral vapors that cannot withstand the sunshine of examination. While those who appreciate Barthes's creation are not overly concerned by the fact that inventing Proust's presence distorts the Flaubertian work considerably, I join Frank Kermode in his belief, '[T]he text to interpret is the one the author would have recognized as his own.'[11]

In setting aside the more unrestrained conceptions of intertextuality, I wish to retain the term, since it remains useful when carefully defined. I see intertextuality as any textual exploitation of another text. It would include satire, parody, pastiche, *imitatio*, *refacimento*, reference, allusion, modeling, borrowing, even plagiarism. Although the list is far from complete, its range of intertextualities may seem ungainly. On looking closely, one might nonetheless discern three distinct categories: of *imitation*, of *opposition*, and of *allusion*. In *imitation*, the author fits his text into a tradition and willingly attempts to use its means – whether styles, forms, lexicon, or devices – and its values to echo previous success. In *opposition* – whether irony or satire or even negative commentary and comparison – the signified images resist integration and emphasize disparateness. In *allusion*, different texts – both the one in hand and those that are external – are integrated metaphorically into something new.[12] To exploit the botanical analogy I have used in the title of this book, one might say that the author has grafted another text onto the root-stock of his creation. In an ideal environment, the two texts – plant and implant, stock and scion – bond to make a new creation, different from either of the component texts, quite different from what the text would have been without the external material, and, in addition, distinct from what exists outside the work in hand.[13]

I plan to concentrate on one aspect of the latter of these categories: on literary allusion, by which I mean simply allusion that occurs in litera-ture. By limiting and simplifying this study to but one area of inter-textuality, although I trust I will increase our grasp of the other two strategies of imitation and opposition, I am primarily engaged in at-tempting to understand allusion more fully and in proposing an ex-planation both of how it functions and of what it does as we readers recognize and interpret it. To this end, the following pages will consider allusion at work in specific texts and will use related intertextual devices to provide a contrast for allusion in its various manifestations.

I concentrate on literary allusion, not because it differs fundamentally from other allusions to history or dance or whatever, but rather because its literary use is generally complex, and thus offers frequent illustra-tions as I pursue an explanation of allusion. Important conclusions remain to be made about the way the device functions in specific texts and, moreover, in respect to allusive theory. I insist upon function, since allusion is not a genre, but is rather a mode, a strategy, a device that occurs in all genres.[14] Though little or no attention has been paid to allusion within the reading process when the external text is metaphori-cally grafted onto the internal image to create something new, the device encourages consideration of the information needed to interpret specific textual signs and of the process of interpretation that results. Perhaps because of literature's complexity, allusion has caused signifi-cant, interpretive problems through the ages, and its literary usage has provided marvelously instructive examples for someone who wishes to study the device. Perhaps such a study will lead to a new assurance in interpretation.

The main difficulty in understanding how allusion works may be the failure to consider the device in the light of the way we read. We know that as our eyes follow the words on the page our minds convert the signs into images in accordance with the conventions of the lan-guage. The reader's mind searches for ways to fit these significances into a conception, a mental image with history, context, color, depth, direction, weight, and velocity. We watch and apprehend Anouilh's

Antigone, for example, as she struggles with the circumstances that surround her. Not uncommonly, while continuing to complete the reader's conception, the text being read will recall a completely different conception (or text) from the reader's previous experience. When Anouilh recreated *Antigone*, he clearly hoped to raise a second image, since he summarized the Sophoclean tragedy in the program and since his Chorus clearly forecasts the girl's future in the first few moments of the performance. By raising the classical story, Anouilh insists metaphorically on the terrible destiny that draws Antigone toward death. Consequently, the modern play's portrayals of hope, purity, society, love, government, and so on, are all integrated into the theme of fate because of the allusion. In synoptic allusions,[15] like the reference to Ulysses in Du Bellay's 'Heureux qui, comme Ulysse . . .' and the consequent insistence on his own homesick yearning, the allusive significances are limited in number and are immediately integrated into the base conception; but with more extended allusions, the reader's mind may for some time maintain the two concepts side by side. Eventually, however, the reader may perceive the relationships between the two conceptions and may go through a process much like that explained by Coleridge in his reformulation of metaphor, creating a new image or conception while maintaining the individuality of the constituent images. In the course of experiencing Anouilh's *Antigone*, though the integrity of Sophocles' version persists, and though we recognize the specific events and coloring of the play being performed, we find that the allusive addition of Sophoclean fate adds extraordinary depth and power to the theatrical destiny. Without the addition of the classical tragedy to the modern performance, the play would be understandable, at least on some levels, but it would lose profundity and impact.

Because the device is widely used by writers to enhance the meaning of their works, we need to have a better grasp of alluding, allusion, and allusiveness. Allusion has been around long enough, almost since the beginning of communication. One might even argue that communication is impossible without some sort of allusion. Whether auditory, visual, olfactory, or tactile (to move into the Orwellian world of 'the feelies'), every sign is an allusion to something either physical or figurative. Allusion is even more universal than the omnipresent 'prose' that Molière's *bourgeois gentilhomme* speaks with such wonder, for it appears in poetry as well.

Even though I have limited my subject, it embraces an enormous corpus. Literature may allude to myth, as in Joyce's *Ulysses*, to archetypes, as in Melville's *Billy Budd* or *Moby Dick*, to historical events or persons, as in Dickens's *A Tale of Two Cities*, or to one or more elements of specific literary, religious, or philosophical works. The device may function significantly in masterpieces and in trash, from the *Satyricon*, which alludes to the *The Odyssey*, to *Valley of the Dolls* and its allusion to *Gone with the Wind*. I do not mean to suggest that every literary work uses allusion as I am now confining the term. To the best of my knowledge, *L'Histoire d'O* alludes to no recognizable text, though it does, of course, fit into the particular tradition of which it is a part.

It remains nonetheless true that the use of allusion by authors is very widespread and, in addition, that scholars and critics frequently recognize it. A medieval rhetorician would include the device in the category of *imitatio*, while concentrating on the overriding concern of imitating or, ideally, reproducing the perfect form. Literati through the ages have mentioned allusion in one way or another, whether they deemed it an ornament, a source, or the undeniable proof of either literary debt or that particular graft we deem plagiarism.

But although the term 'allusion' is a commonplace, and is, so to speak, on the tips of the tongues of enormous numbers of people interested in literature, very little attention has been paid to the way it works – to what it does for those who recognize and interpret it. Moreover, despite the fact that the device appears in the literature of all periods with which I have acquaintance, some of the clearest examples of allusion have been passed over.

Boccaccio's 'Tenth Tale of the Tenth Day' about the Marquis of Saluzzo, Gualtieri, and his wife, Griselda, provides a good example. Contemporaries like Chaucer apparently understood the obvious allusions to Job and Jehovah. According to Enrico de' Negri, however, later critics did not, and it became 'one of the most misinterpreted [tales] of the whole *Decameron*.'[16] Nonetheless, despite this limited appreciation, Boccaccio's tale was not deformed by the well-intentioned but misconceived ordering of an editor. Lope de Vega's *Rimas sacras* was not so fortunate. Lope's cycle of poems first appeared in 1614. Although it included a few poems written some years before, the majority of its verses were written specifically for this work, which parallels the imagery and development of the Mass. The reader's experience of the Mass heightens the affective force of Lope's creation. To destroy the inherent movement of the cycle and impose another is a risky enterprise, a fact that, of course, did not stop it from happening. Shortly after the publication of the *Rimas sacras*, an anonymous editor extracted thirty-two poems and added one *romance* from the *Pastores de Belen*.[17] He then rearranged these poems according to his own rather pedestrian conception of Christ's birth and Passion. The result, titled the *Romancero espiritual*, has little literary value. Cues that are meaningful in the *Rimas sacras* lead nowhere in the *Romancero espiritual*. This latter edition is perhaps responsible for a tendency to consider the *Rimas sacras* as a collection of individual poems, many of which are unable to withstand extraction. In isolation, the harsh judgments of such modern critics as E. Allison Peers and José F. Montesinos seem valid because even the more justifiable of Lope's hyperbole, puns, and dated conceits seem unprepared.[18] Granted, like most cycles, the *Rimas sacras* has dross, but I believe an exculpatory movement binds the whole work into a loose but cohesive unity of striking beauty. And the *Romancero espiritual* thus seems reprehensible.

Perhaps authors themselves should bear the responsibility for whatever distortion may occur when their allusions pass unnoticed. They, after all, must have chosen to weave their allusions into their works in such a way that they are often anything but obvious. Many allusions through the ages leave at least one element in twilight. Why do writers indulge in such subtlety? It is true that somewhere in the work the text usually, though not always, mentions the author or the creation it is alluding to. In cases like Proust, however, that reference may appear hundreds of pages farther on. Although some would doubtless suspect that the authors are ashamed of their debt to another work, that they have plagiarized, surely they are not involved in dishonesty, in the kind of literary thievery some would call graft. Plagiarism consists of equal, nonmetaphorical terms, and when it is successful, the text in hand does not suggest a source. Quite the contrary, because successful allusion *must* suggest something else, it must be recognized before it can add to the effect of the story.

Without running the risk of producing comedy, however, allusion cannot be so obvious as to suggest startling contrasts. Take, for example, Agatha Christie's *The Labors of Hercules*. There the parallels with the mythic strongman are patent; the author announces them in the title, and she reminds us of them with each chapter heading. In my opinion she has, however failed to create allusion, though she has produced a marvelously comic effect. As the reader's mind jumps back and forth between the mythic Hercules and Hercule Poirot, Mrs Christie's character seems more and more ridiculous. Still, I am not one of Hercule Poirot's admirers, and I am told by admitted fans that the adventures recounted in this particular book successfully portray the hero as a modern-day Hercules who triumphs not by brute strength and primitive cunning, but by his superior mind. As near as I can determine, they accept the Herculean backdrop and become involved in the story. They do not make continual comparisons, whereas I do; and what is for them allusion, the grafting of a scion to rootstock, is for me burlesque. Where it may be difficult to reach a final decision on that point, it does appear that Mrs Christie came dangerously close to pushing her allusion too far in the direction of parody.

Conventional wisdom would propose that this allusion errs on the side of explicitness. 'An allusion which is explained no longer has the charm of allusion. . . . In divulging the mystery, you withdraw its virtue,' says Jean Paulhan.[19] Recent students of allusion, such as Ziva Ben-Porat and Carmela Perri, would disagree. On looking at literature itself, rather than criticism or theory, they discover that authors allude overtly with great frequency and that explicitness does not necessarily vitiate allusion's effectiveness.[20] The French myth plays of the 1940s and 1950s provide numerous examples. I suspect Agatha Christie's problem (if problem there be) grows from the disparity between the ancient and the modern Hercules. For me, the two are so different in both time and character as to resist metaphoric conjunction, forming instead parodic disjunction. A noble head has been stuck askew onto a pathetic creature to make a sideshow freak.

When allusion is unnoticed or misunderstood, the blame should often fall on readers rather than on the writers and their occasional use of covert allusion. It seems that, however widespread the device and the term may be in primary and secondary literature, the cause can be traced to the scant attention that has been paid to the device itself, to the way it works, and to its importance in specific works of art. I think this is particularly true when, as is most often the case, allusion is categorized according to its functional thrust, on the one hand, or its external referent, on the other. When the reference to another text serves comic ends, as in such parody as Petronius's *Satyricon*, or involves 'literary criticism "in action,"' as Proust termed his pastiches, or functions to warn against any concessions to the 'beast,' as in the case of Vercors's allusion to the tragic death of Saint-Pol-Roux in the novella *Le Silence de la mer*, one might categorize the device in the light of its thrust, be it comic, critical, or didactic. Inevitably, however, such labels oversimplify, for the *Satyricon* is perhaps more didactic than comic, and Proust's pastiches are certainly as much comic as critical. Or one might follow a more traditional schema and, depending on whether an author alludes to current events, as Huysmans does in the last chapter of *Là-Bas*, or to recorded history, as Mme de La Fayette does in *La Princesse de Clèves*, or to literature, or to myth, classify the allusion according to the historical, mythic, or literary referent.[21] Given a certain amount of intelligence and perseverance, the adherent of such a system could easily become committed to the endless categorization that has plagued image studies. Florencio Sánchez's allusion to *King Lear* in *Barranca abajo*[22] would be theatrical or Shakespearian, and Zola's allusion to Saint Laurentius in *Thérèse Raquin* would, I suppose, become a saintly allusion. Though such analyses give some indication of a writer's proclivities for a certain type of comparison, they do little to help readers establish viable relationships with the works themselves. In such readings, the critics usually leave the work to focus on the external referent text.[23]

For the vast majority of us who want to understand, enjoy, and profit from literary works, the tendency would be to dismiss similar studies as trivial. The danger is that the device is likewise dismissed and thereafter ignored. Classifications imply and all too frequently impose methods of study and optics of reading. To choose to orient ourselves according to but one of the constituent elements, and one that moreover exists outside the text, is to run the danger of misunderstanding the mechanism of the allusion, of not noticing its presence, and of being incapable of passing valid judgment on those works that employ the device. Because allusion is a process that is internal to the reading experience, each example gains life only as it occurs within the relationship that exists between a reader and the relevant texts.

My insistence on the inadvisability of external classifications might seem too punctilious if literature were not dependent on the personal experience or discovery that occurs when a knowledgeable, sensitive person picks up a text and establishes a relationship between the self and the text. Good readers know that interpretation often results in the excitement of an aesthetic, encompassing understanding of the work, an experience of meaning or beauty or perhaps even what Eliseo Vivas terms 'intransitive rapt attention' upon an object. Unfortunately, acceptable readings are difficult to describe in the abstract and more difficult to stimulate in others. In addition, a description of what happens in us does not stimulate that experience in others. Perhaps that is why teachers of literature typically either present students with a model reading, in the hopes of encouraging them to do something similar with other works, or teach contiguous disciplines like biography, psychology, sociology, history, or whatever, which, though potentially interesting and important, are not literature. We seem to lack the means to teach that experience at the heart of literature, or even to describe it clearly. But one of the things we know is that it does not take place unless a reader is open to the movements, the interweaving denotations and connotations, and the patterns of technique of the work being read, and senses its unifying spirit. At any point the reader may realize that some portion of the text needs special attention or knowledge and be led outside the text. No work of literature is really autonomous. The Russian formalists claimed so for a while, though they rapidly recognized that the position was indefensible. As Valéry put it, 'A work is made by a multitude of minds and of events – (ancestors, states, accidents, earlier writers, etc.) – under the direction of the Author.'[24] We may need to know something the author knew. If so, the text will make us feel the lack. What must not be forgotten, however, is that once we have this information, we must once more let the text, the whole text, work its charm on us. Anything outside the work must be reintegrated into the work, for although not autonomous, it is dominant, and whatever resists integration has no importance for the text in hand.

Consequently, I prefer a definition of allusion that insists on the internal functioning of the device, on the way the grafted cutting becomes an integral part of the new stock. Only then does allusion's importance to meaning and understanding receive the proper emphasis. For me, and in the pages that follow, *allusion is the metaphorical relationship created when an alluding text evokes and uses another, independent text.* Neither the reference nor the referent, it consists in the image produced by the metaphoric combination that occurs in the reader's mind.

What I understand as a metaphor may be illustrated by the Gidian phrase 'riant de fleurs [laughing with flowers].' It comes from Gide's *La Porte étroite* and represents one of the rare examples of such limited metaphors in his work. Furthermore, it is a commonplace that Gide managed to revive and render newly evocative through his context. A word by itself has no meaning. Hung in the middle of the universe without being perceived by a sentient being, it would be nothing but a smudge of ink. When a human being perceives it, immediately it takes on a fuller life, because the perceiver adds meaning. For those cognizant of the conventions of the French language, *riant* (laughing) denotes a physiological reaction marked by an inarticulate noise that usually expresses amusement. But through association and metonymy, it connotes an enormous number of other things, a number limited only by the intelligence and background of the perceptor. 'Laughing' or *riant* might suggest associations as diverse as mockery, exultation, optimism, sneering, Momus, hyenas, crows, comedies, or specific writers like Rabelais, to mention but a few. For the reader of goodwill, however, its connotations are limited when it is put into a context – which is what happens when it is joined to *de fleurs* (with flowers). Immediately, the denotative significance is negated. To the best of my knowledge, flowers have never been known to laugh. We are consequently encouraged to seek a figurative meaning that makes sense. In the process, such associations as 'mockery, exultation, Momus,' drop aside. Some will doubtless read the phrase as a 'path where there are flowers' and thus lose much of the resonance, for both terms have meaning that is important to the text. And although 'flowers' has at least as many possible connotations as 'laughing' – ranging from *Le Sacré du printemps*, to the theme of *carpe diem*, to works by such painters as Van Gogh, to death and funerals, to spring and life in the sun – still the conjunction of the two words, or what the Liège Group ʊ calls an '*intersection* of the two terms,'[25] tells us what is pertinent and what is not. The reader of goodwill ignores the nonpertinent associations and understands the metaphorical combination to depict ephemeral flowers exuding joy. Succeeding images will reveal that this garden is protected from the world by hedges and walls. The metaphor, by its conjunction and because of the combination of the two terms that takes place in the reader's mind, further elicits and emphasizes a connotation that is present, I think, only peripherally in the isolated terms: a joyous aura of transitory youth and love. That is why Ricoeur is right to call it an 'event.'[26] Thus Gide described and at the same time prepared imagery alluding to the garden of Eden that becomes progressively more important through the rest of *La Porte étroite*. Simultaneously, he revived a metaphor that had become a cliché.

For our purposes, the example demonstrates an important truth of metaphor, and of allusion: in any metaphorical relationship there is the creation of an image that is distinct from any one of its constituent terms. If, as Michael Riffaterre has suggested, attention should be focused on what the external work adds to the alluding text,[27] one should recognize that allusion is more than the external term or intertext, indeed, more than the sum of the internal and external terms. It is a *relationship* between a minimum of two terms that, through varying degrees of parallels or oppositions, creates a new entity greater than any of its constituent parts. It is this metaphoric creation or 'event' that stands above the constituent texts, since it incorporates them. At least one of the terms must be explicit, and it must of necessity be in the text. The other term may be either explicit or tacit. Both Perri and Ben-Porat have rightly argued that it must be independent, by which they mean that the intertext (or referent or 'marked' or external text) must have a life of its own, with an intension and significance that is free of and not limited to the reference or 'marker' or alluding text in hand.[28] In cases of internal relationships, as for example with the Marcel/Albertine–Swann/Odette allusion in Proust's *A la recherche du temps perdu*, the referent text must have a context that is sufficiently distinct to permit the allusion to work its allusive magic.

Allusion does not encourage the reader's mind to jump from one term to another, as Leo Hickey believes;[29] rather we are encouraged to rise above the elements without negating them, to put them together, and to experience the resultant image. And I suggest that it is this metaphorical relationship, which is common to all allusive events, that permits us to distinguish allusion from other devices.[30] Not all critics would agree with the distinction I make. Ronald J. Christ took a somewhat different tack and suggested that Borges uses allusion 'in relentless, recurring demonstrations of his belief in the unity of the mind.'[31] By means of this device, according to Christ, Borges 'treats identical ideas as emanations of the same mind.' In other words, in Christ's view, the two constituent terms become one and the same. I would say that they retain their individuality, while at the same time producing something different from either. The Argentine writer perhaps shared the hesitation I feel before Christ's theory (I say *perhaps* since Borges was something of a Peck's Bad Boy of literature and is difficult if not impossible to pin down). At any rate, he said in the preface to Christ's study: 'I am neither a thinker nor a moralist, but simply a man of letters who turns his own perplexities and that respected system of perplexities we call philosophy into the forms of literature. The fact that in one of my stories the man is both a dreamer and the dream does not necessarily mean that I am a follower of Berkeley and of the Buddha.'[32] I would prefer to suggest that Borges uses Berkeley and the Buddha, combining their writings with his own text to make something additional: an approximation of his own understanding.

Most of the examples I have chosen to study are allusions that extend over a large portion or the whole of a literary work. Not that 'extended' allusions differ fundamentally from the briefer, 'synoptic' variety. In fact, though they may employ different means, and though in the detail there may be great variety, all allusions establish the same basic relationship. Extended allusion does have an advantage for my purposes, however. It makes use of an increased number of allusive elements and thus facilitates detailed study of how it works.

If I am correct in basing my study of allusion on the three-pronged relationship of text, external text, and metaphorical combination that I have discussed, we can easily dismiss a number of concepts that are often confused with it. Plagiarism, as I have already suggested, does not satisfy the requirements of allusion. For it to exist the text in hand and the external text must be identical, or different only in minor ways that in no way affect the meaning, and the intention must be to prevent their coming together. The author of plagiarism attempts to prevent the reader from seeing their identity and bringing them together, thus establishing the theft.

Nor is acknowledged paraphrase allusion. In paraphrase, the attempt is to remain faithful to the meat of the source, while rendering it in a somewhat different way. It involves stylistic changes. Consequently, it can never accurately communicate the true meaning of the original. For our purposes, however, the point is that paraphrase attempts to equal the significance of the original, without copying it.

Parody differs in that its two or more terms are different, the one constantly holding the other up to ridicule and judgment, constantly saying, 'I am not that other absurd thing.' Metaphoric integration is violently resisted. Source, as well, falls outside the realm of allusion. Although a source may be turned into an allusion, in itself it does not suggest the combination with another image (or text) that will permit the metaphorical relationship. The source is merely the material of which the fiction is created. In itself it does not function, it remains an element that can be isolated and needs no other text to exist. Allegory – by which I mean not extended metaphor but the device found in such works as Bunyan's *Pilgrim's Progress* or *Le Roman de la rose* – also resists integration of the two terms. In such works the explicit narration implies an abstract or spiritual story. Philip Wadsworth put it another way. For him, allegory is 'a type of composition in which specific persons, objects, and actions have two meanings. The literal meaning is accompanied by a second one which is abstract and often didactic.'[33] To this should be added one of Goethe's insights, that is, that the spiritual concept is 'completely contained, beheld, and expressed in the image.'[34] Again, allegory does not integrate the two or more independent terms;

the internal term (the basic, referring 'text' that is first created in the reader's mind) is rather subordinated to the other (a second, referent 'text' suggested by the first), although the latter, superior, spiritual term cannot exist independently of the other. In short, to return to the vocabulary of Ben-Porat and Perri referred to above, the referent text of allegory is not 'free' or independent.

Nor does allusion fall into the category of models. As an example, one might consider the medieval artist who wanted to recreate the ideal form by using the topoi, the structures, and the devices that had been consecrated to that purpose, by using, in other words, the materials at hand. He did not want to create something new; he wanted to attain the model that, theoretically at least, existed. References, on the other hand, normally do expand the text into something more, and thus have the potential for use in constructing allusion.

I should not leave the impression that everything is as clearly delineated as I suggest here. In most of these cases, there can be a fine line separating them from allusion, and indeed often they can be forced over the line. I think, for example, of Montherlant's *Les Célibataires*, which, by announcing a model, and indeed by repeating many of Balzac's character traits and narrational devices, would seem to make it but a variation of the model established in Balzac's trilogy *Les Célibataires*. In fact, of course, it quickly becomes clear that Montherlant uses those portraits created by Balzac allusively in order to insist on the futility and unhappiness of the lives of his heroes and in order to universalize his vision. Similarly, in the film *Jesus Christ Superstar*, it is evident that an enjoyment of the picture depends to large measure on a prior knowledge of the Christ story. The biblical version of Christ's divinity and the certainty of his ultimate crucifixion set up uneasy relationships with the filmic evidence of his petulant humanity, at least if one has the background to make sense of the movie hero's sparse statements. Although it is primarily but another version of the story of Jesus, it makes extensive use of allusion. Like all effective devices in literature, allusion cannot be isolated as easily as can various elements in the experiments assigned to beginning chemistry students of qualitative analysis; nevertheless, the general lines of the classification I suggest should allow the necessary distinctions.

I am not done with the difficulties confronting my endeavor to come to terms with allusion. Though it may seem unimportant in this age of unfettered freedom for readers, allusion must be indicated by the text and integrated into its significance; thus, it must have been 'created' previously by an author. Clearly, proof that the author knowingly used the elements of his allusion would be desirable. For such support, one would turn to the recollections of his or her friends, to the author's book reviews, essays, letters, early drafts, manuscript notations, prefaces, or auctorial footnotes. Unfortunately, while evidence of this nature does exist, it is by no means universal. And in respect to the authors I have used as examples, I have not for all my efforts succeeded in locating a passage where Proust said, 'I have alluded to the *Arabian Nights*.' Neither Barbey d'Aurevilly, nor Proust, nor Zola was considerate enough to have helped me in this fashion.

In the absence of such a statement, three possible conclusions may be drawn from an allusion found in a text. Either the author consciously formed the allusion and, for one reason or another, left no external record; or the author did indeed make the allusion, though he was unconscious of having done so; or the allusion is the creation of the reader's overheated imagination. Even if the writer was unconscious of the allusion, it takes nothing from the importance of the allusion, nor from our need to sense it. As E.M.W. Tillyard points out, 'Most poets have their memories stored with the works of other poets, and inevitably they will reproduce, even if they modify, the rhythms that most fascinate them.'[35] Frequently, such unconscious allusions add enormously to the richness of the reading experience. In fact, though, without external evidence, we simply do not know whether or not an allusion is conscious, and, indeed, I am not at all certain that it matters. Whether the allusion is consciously or unconsciously created, the text suggests it, and it becomes a part of the reading experience.

In almost all cases, only the text can tell us whether an allusion exists. And that is good reason for entering a caveat. With nothing but internal evidence, how are we to know who created the allusion – the author… or the critic? The example Tillyard uses for unconscious allusion illustrates the point. He sees an allusion to Keats's 'Ode to a Nightingale' ('Thou wast not born for death, immortal Bird! / No hungry generations tread thee down') in Yeats's 'Sailing to Byzantium' ('That is no country for old men. The young / In one another's arms, birds in the trees / – Those dying generations – at their song. . . .').[36] Personally, I do not doubt that sensing the resonance of Keats would add richness to 'Sailing to Byzantium,' but I suspect that no allusion was intended. Yeats mentioned in a note to the poem: 'I have read somewhere that in the Emperor's palace at Byzantium was a tree made of gold and silver, and artificial birds that sang.'[37] Add to this the fact that birds have long symbolized the souls of human beings, and you probably have the explanation for Yeats's (and Keats's) birds. Internal evidence is subject to error, especially when only one element proves suggestive.

It is rather like the various visions that astronomers have had of Mars. As *Mariner 9* conclusively proved, there is no system of canals on Mars. Still, our astronomers have long seen canals on the planet and have suggested the possibility of intelligent life. As Carl Sagan has remarked, there is no question that the vision was due to intelligence. 'The only question concerns which side of the telescope the intelligence is on.'

When there are a number of references that suggest the same text, a strong case for the existence of allusion exists. The examples I have employed are of this variety. In addition, where it seems appropriate, one could cite material that shows that the authors have at least read the works alluded to and that they had the knowledge necessary to have created the allusions. When accompanied by detailed analyses of the texts in question, such indications should substantiate the existence of a latent allusion that awaits a reader.

It also seems important to know whether or not the author's readers would have been capable of perceiving the allusion. And so I am brought to another problem. I describe it at the risk of appearing a city-bound Berkeley who knows nothing of falling trees: allusion *must* be perceived; its metaphorical terms *must* be united in the mind of a reader. Allusion that is not recognized does not function. If allusion consists of a relationship between two independent referents, the relationship clearly does not abide within the confines of the printed text. Only the reader can establish the connection that allows allusion to take place. For this to happen, the referent text of the allusion must be known to the reader. Because the explicit, alluding textual term does not equal the one (or ones) alluded to, it cannot then transmit the allusive meaning unless the reader helps out. The text would never succeed through its own means in establishing the relationship and communicating the meaning. There is, of course, ample precedent for claiming that whether or not the author's audience could have discovered the allusion – he might after all have misjudged his readers – the fact that it is suggested by the text is quite enough.[38] In the final analysis, this is my argument. It certainly suffices for Proust, who expressly stated that his book was for the knowing reader.[39] It should also serve for recent authors who wrote for our own epoch. In respect to Barbey d'Aurevilly and Emile Zola, I have endeavored to go farther. Occasionally, through much reading and some luck, I have stumbled onto passages that suggest that the material alluded to was available and could have been, or was, known to contemporary readers.

These problems, of course, are only problems to someone who wants to establish in the most convincing way possible that allusion can exist in the reading of a specific text. For those who simply want to enjoy and to profit from the work they have in their hands, only their openness to the possibility of allusion matters. And this, in the end, is what I should like to leave with readers of the present volume. Whether or not my systematization ultimately prevails, I hope it will successfully call attention to allusion, for there can be no question that we must pay more attention to it. The age-old device provides a convincing response to the questions I posed to my professors – very respectfully – in the early 1960s and that my own students put to me in the late 1960s – very aggressively (the mid-1960s seem to be a dividing line in manner, if not in substance): 'Why should we read so much?' 'Why wouldn't it be better to read a few works well than to try to read everything?' Unfortunately, the questions themselves discourage one from replying in the most obvious way: 'Why, for the pleasure of new experiences, new discoveries, new worlds!' We might then turn to other traditional responses that continue to be worthy of consideration – we read widely (1) to form judgment, (2) to gain historical perspective into the evolution of literature, and (3) to acquire essential sociological, psychological, and historical information concerning man and his world. But there is another answer that seems equally important and perhaps more convincing. We read in order to understand novels, poems, and plays that draw on other material. An enormous number of works do. Writers tend to read, whether we do or not. And it puts us at a severe, often disastrous, disadvantage when, as they frequently do, they make use of what they have read.

If Roger Rosenblatt is correct, some teachers of literature choose their texts on the basis of assumed student ignorance. In respect to Robert Graves's delightful poem 'Ulysses,' Rosenblatt says:

The chances are . . . that today this poem would not be taught to students who were unfamiliar with the *Odyssey* for the very reason of that unfamiliarity. . . . Since the students could never be expected to learn about other and older literature, it is supposed that they would be missing more than they would be getting by studying Graves's poem. In fact, this is so. If one cannot refer to the depiction of Odysseus in Homer, much of the meaning of this modern poem is lost. . . . [And] there is a great deal more missing than Homer. Were students to gain a full understanding of Graves's poem, they would need to know about Dante's Ulysses, particularly why Dante located Ulysses so deep in hell. It would be useful to read Daniel's 'Ulysses and the Siren' and Shakespeare's *Troilus and Cressida*. It would be absolutely necessary to study Tennyson's poem on the subject, and to note the development of Ulysses as an introspective and reflective hero. Joyce, too, wrote about Ulysses. Students of modern literature ought to consider why and how this hero has been carried forward as a representative of men from age to age. All of these things ought to be known in reading Graves. Yet should that fact suggest an argument for not reading Graves? . . . . The answer, obviously, is that the poem is worth looking at by anybody, and that the fact that it is apprehensible on both immediate and historical levels only confirms its general merit. If such a poem were actually capable of leading students from modern psychology back to the *Odyssey*, that would be all to the good. Like the *Odyssey*, itself, Graves's 'Ulysses' is literature for people, all people.[40]

Wide acquaintance with literature increases our understanding and enjoyment of a considerable body of literary works. Should readers remain insensitive to the allusions in whatever they happen to be reading, they will fail to achieve complete understanding. The shortcoming may be either affective or semantic in nature, and I suppose, some might not consider it serious. In the case of many of the allusions in *A la recherche du temps perdu*, the reader will simply not have a satisfactory affective response to the main character and his trials. Elsewhere, however, not being aware of the allusion has graver consequences. In many, many works, allusions serve as the primary device for communicating the central meaning.

The following chapters follow a straightforward logic from the uncomplicated to the complicated, from the simple to the complex. What I call parallel allusions are used initially to contrast with other devices and to clarify the way allusion functions. In chapter two, the controversy over 'Un Cœur simple' draws attention to the essential difference between allusion and irony and to the way an a priori commitment to irony radically changes an understanding of Flaubert's tale. In chapter three, after a discussion of how translation, imitation, and plagiarism differ from allusion, Anouilh's use of Sophocles in *Antigone* provides the means to begin considering how the modern author highlights and, indeed, renders inescapable his central theme of fate. Chapter four considers allegory and sources while looking at the way

Barbey d'Aurevilly exploits an allusion to *Le Rouge et le noir* to create an intangible sense of evil in 'Le Rideau cramoisi.' Of course, in 'real' fiction, allusions are seldom so uncomplicated, and I turn in chapter five to Proust's 'allusive complex,' a set of parallel allusions that bring his major character, Albertine, to life. The device appears even more complicated when authors call on it to set up oppositions. In chapter six, I look at the way Giraudoux allusively implies that his *Electre* might not end traditionally, how Gide exposed his pastor's creation of a 'new' Gospel, and how Balzac illuminated Eugénie Grandet's *via dolorosa*. Zola's *La Faute de l'abbé Mouret* provides in chapter seven an example of two opposing allusive complexes that join in an allusive oxymoron to suggest the creation of a new Adam and Eve who once again have the opportunity to begin life and avoid primordial mistakes. Perhaps unfortunately, authors seldom stay within the neat categories I have laid out in these chapters, and in the conclusion, I consider several variations: how Sartre's parody slides into allusion in *La Nausée*, and how Robbe-Grillet constructs three allusive systems that resist integration. The potential of allusion remains as unlimited as the creative minds of authors, but the pattern, I believe, remains quite simple and straightforward. The text I am reading reminds me of another text, and the two texts come together to create an image (or text) quite different from either of the constituent texts.

2

Ironic Interference and Allusion: 'Un Cœur simple'

The real adventures of reading take place in the mind, a fact that can cause numerous, significant problems. Irony, for example, is a conflict between the ordinary significance of the expression and the thought in the author's (and, when successful, the reader's) mind. In its simplest terms, irony is an expression whose literal meaning is the opposite of that intended. It says one thing and means its contrary. A problem comes, however, when readers invent an irony that is not there. Particular confusion can result when someone perceives an irony unintended by the author that then masks an allusion crucial to the creation. The matter does seem worth attention, since careful readers can often discover textual markers that help to distinguish irony from allusion proper and from 'oppositional allusion,' which will be discussed in a later chapter.

The difficulty of establishing irony's presence or absence has been compounded by recent shifts in the emphasis of criticism. It is no longer true that less attention and interest have been accorded to the author, who was for some time not just the absent creator, but the forgotten god. Particularly in psychological studies, the author has been revived. Recent theoreticians, however, have developed a disdain for textual analysis devoted to what Jonathan Culler has called the desire 'to serve literature by elucidating its masterpieces.'[1] The text itself, having fallen increasingly into a vague limbo, a never-never land, perpetually awaits not just its completion but its very reality. It has become little more, perhaps even less, than a pretext – a pretext for misprision. Mere misreading of the text is of course not irony. When the signified is either absent or unstable, irony becomes impossible. Furthermore, there can be no irony where neither the ironic expression nor the meaning, neither the ironic text nor its reading, neither the word nor its sense are fixed. Irony requires two parts: both the ironic expression and the meaning, the ironic text and its reading. At some point, for irony to exist, there must be someone or, if one might anthropomorphize texts and posit a textual consciousness, something that had an intention, a meaning ironically belied by the expression. And while recent theory has increasingly negated the text in favor of the reader, on the one hand, and the author, on the other, irony reimposes all three, a reverse history that progressively weights first the text of the ironic expression, then the intention of author or text, and finally the reader.

I have insisted on a 'textual consciousness,' by which I mean simply that, for irony to exist, the ironic implication must be textually operative. It is not enough to know, for example, that Flaubert did not share Félicité's religious beliefs in 'Un Cœur simple' ('A Simple Heart' [1877]). This knowledge has led some to contend that the novelist's representation of the maid's beliefs is consequently and, indeed, ipso facto ironic. I am aware that, for some, self-consciousness constitutes irony, whether self/other or what De Man has called the 'disjunction of the subject.'[2] Although I shall hold out for the traditional view of irony as an opposition between literal and implied meaning, since it seems a useful means of discrimination, there is, of course, nothing wrong with redefining terms. The trouble comes when the reversion to nineteenth-century *ad hominem* criticism, by highlighting a biographical opposition between author and character, is assumed to function textually and is imposed upon a story's signified. Given that no student of Flaubert's letters, manuscripts, and works can deny that he went to enormous trouble to efface his personal perceptions from his creations, any suggestion that he failed should be supported by evidence. It is not enough to notice a difference between man and creation and assume that 'Un Cœur simple' poses Félicité's faith 'ironically' or negatively and that one should then read her experiences as an indication of auctorial judgment. Flaubert's supposed lack of faith or, conversely, his undoubted anticlericalism might give wise readers pause, but such conceptions are no more authoritative than Flaubert's unequivocal position against an ironic reading: 'When the parrot died, she has him stuffed, and, dying in her own turn, she confuses the parrot with the Holy Spirit. That is not at all ironic, as you suppose, but on the contrary very serious and very sad. I want to move to pity, to bring tears from sensitive souls, being one myself.'[3] The days are past when we would wish to accept an author's pronouncements as a definitive guide to our understanding. Not only are writers occasionally guilty of post-partum wishful thinking, but they not infrequently delight in leading readers astray. Nonetheless, while we all know that artists are notoriously unreliable in respect to their own work, their opinion should not be dismissed out of hand. Their interpretations are at least as worthy of consideration as those of other educated readers. The absence of irony or, indeed, its presence must be textually imperative. If the text does not suggest an opposite meaning, that meaning does not exist, however much a reader might like to invent it. Usually, ironic texts will insist on the irony repeatedly, that is, with aesthetic redundancy.

It is of course true, as Grahame C. Jones has argued, that '[i]rony presupposes the existence of two types of readers: the astute reader who penetrates it and the less perspicacious reader who will not grasp the deep meaning and will consequently be its dupe and, in a certain sense, its victim. Consequently, the ironist destines his work for clever readers: the latter constitute a refined public to whom he addresses winks that the others do not notice.'[4] Irony often depends on the value a person or society places on an object, an event, or a particular turn of phrase. If personal or ideological exigencies cause one to weight Christmas negatively, for example, Faulkner's *Light in August* or Aldous Huxley's *The Genius and the Goddess* become extremely problematic. Likewise, if for traditional or religious reasons certain connotations are imposed on the parrot of Flaubert's 'Un Cœur simple,' readers may see irony where none exists. One can of course argue that it does not matter – the reader is free to ironize or not as he wishes – though to do so is to deny the possibility of communication. For the moment, I would like to posit the reality of human interchange. I then also assume the existence of an author and an objectively verifiable text, though I shall allow the author's incarnation only insofar as he or his intention or his significance are given shape and form by that text. I do so in the attempt to discover whether or not there are means of identifying irony. If communication is possible, the matter is important. As E.D. Hirsch, Jr, says with wonderful understatement, irony's 'presence or absence changes nothing in the text except its fundamental meaning.'[5] My touchstone will be consistency. If irony sets up cacophonies, nonsense, an unseemly break in the warp or woof of the tapestry, then one must suspect that it is not an integral part of the text, rather an element introduced by the reader. The controversy centering on Loulou highlights the problematics of irony.

'Un Cœur simple,' while widely praised for its uncomplicated beauty, has elicited absolutely divergent interpretations. For one critic the story is 'pessimistic,' for others it reveals Flaubert's tenderness, for another the continuation of love.[6] Still, in terms of numbers, even this disagreement is minor when compared to the wildly differing views of Félicité's terminal vision of a parrot *qua* Holy Spirit come to bear the pious servant off to heaven. Almost everyone who has written on the tale has taken a stand on that issue. Scholars like Victor Brombert state flatly, '[T]he satirical function of the parrot extends beyond human speech to the very level of belief and dogma.'[7] Nonetheless, English Showalter, Jr, is not alone in believing that 'It is a mistake to take the final identification of Loulou and the Holy Spirit as an attack on the church.'[8] When readers of such stature take unequivocal but opposing positions, it is perhaps prudent to avoid the problem. Benjamin Bart, for example, says that incarnating God as a 'stuffed parrot is silly or grandiose, depending on your point of view.'[9] It does appear that one should hesitate to accept Bardèche's belief that 'Un Cœur simple' is 'less difficult' than the two other stories in *Trois Contes* (345).

The problematic incarnation of Félicité's confusion of the parrot with the Holy Spirit was carefully prepared. Although Benjamin Bart has called it 'unfortunate,' especially in regard to Flaubert's decision to leave in the passage where Félicité decides that the Father could not have chosen a dove to descend on His Son,[10] the maid reasons explicitly: a dove does not talk, therefore God must have chosen a parrot (618). Flaubert's friends advised him against the development because the thought processes appeared too sophisticated for a simple servant girl. Even without this passage, however, Félicité is clearly rather bright. One should surely not ignore her ability to see through Mme Aubain's tenant farmers' tricks, or the fact that those wily peasants 'left full of respect for her.'[11] Indeed, her reasoning that the parrot is more suitable than a dove for the Holy Spirit is, *pace* Flaubert's friends, good evidence for her intelligence. In the end, however, I am not certain that it matters. The significant question remains the parrot and how its identification with the third Person of the Trinity, the Holy Spirit, should be interpreted. It has been this factor that is cited by most of those critics who view the story as ironic.

Flaubert was at great pains to make the parrot an acceptable analogue of the Holy Spirit. Within the story itself, he worked deftly to show how Félicité could make the confusion. Old age affects her hearing, her vision, perhaps even her mind. 'At church she always thought about the Holy Spirit and observed that He was something like the parrot. His resemblance seemed even more noticeable in the Epinal print of our

Lord's baptism, with his wings of purple He was truly the portrait of Loulou' (617). In the little shrine she has placed in her room, she places Loulou near the color print – 'so that she saw them both together in the same glance. They were associated in her thought, the parrot being sanctified by this connection with the Holy Spirit, who became more alive and understandable in her eyes' (618). What could be more natural than for her to decide that it probably was not a dove descending on Jesus' head, but rather a parrot? After all, the Holy Spirit talks, and doves 'don't have a voice' (ibid.). Little by little she turns away from the print and toward the taxidermal Loulou as she says her prayers.

There are other biblical passages that back up the possibility that God might make use of Loulou. In the book of John, it says clearly that those who believe in Jesus will receive the Holy Spirit (7:39) and, elsewhere, that this Spirit will be a Comforter, the Paraklete (John 14:16), 'whom the world cannot receive because it seeth Him not, neither knoweth Him: but ye know Him; for He dwelleth with you and shall be in you' (John 14:17). We know that Félicité obtained Loulou only because no one else wanted him, but it would take very little for someone like Flaubert's heroine to go another step and assume that they could not receive Him, because they really did not know Him. Certainly, Loulou was a comfort to Félicité. Furthermore, the Holy Spirit will not say just anything. His words are limited to 'whatsoever I [that is, Jesus] have said unto you' (John 14.26). 'He shall not speak of Himself; but whatsoever He shall hear, that shall He speak' (John 16.13). Parrots, of course, are not known for their inventiveness. Their speech is limited to imitation. I even wonder whether Félicité might have heard her priest mention le Paraclet, the French version of the Greek Parakletos (Advocate, Comforter), and confused it with le perroquet (the parrot). The story does not tell us, though it does seem the sort of confusion that an untutored person like Félicité might make.

On carefully rereading the arguments for an ironic parrot, one is struck by the particular slant they place on the irony. While there is no doubt that this text like the rest of Flaubert's work is in a certain sense 'ironic,' a satisfactory grasp of this irony comes only after having conceived the story as a whole and thus as an observation of a society that enables such a reality as this. The tale in its entirety does not ridicule Félicité, however. She should not be viewed as either a parodic or a burlesque figure (whether or not the story impugns Christianity requires further consideration). Still, those readers who take the story as a negative reflection of Flaubert's view of the society around him are not brought to their conclusion by the level of the maid's intelligence. It is rather the thought of presenting God in the guise of a bird that is by nature both filthy and stupid, capable of nothing more than parroting what it hears. The characterization might well appear malicious if not blasphemous. Of course, whether Flaubert understood it as particularly impious is open to question. He had already written 'La Légende de saint Julien l'Hospitalier,' in which several animals speak; he was well acquainted with the *Golden Legend*, where such supernatural events are commonplace; his long preparation for *Salammbô* (1862) and *La Tentation de saint Antoine* (1874) had left him well acquainted with the Bible, in which God uses an ass to speak to Balaam (Num. 22:28–30), in which the promised Holy Spirit 'shall not speak of himself; but whatsoever he shall hear, that shall he speak' (John 16:13), and in which, as Félicité recognizes, the Holy Spirit 'was not just a bird, but also a fire and other times a breath or a rushing wind. It is perhaps His light which flits along the edges of the swamps, His breath which makes the harmonious bells sing' (601).

Félicité's confusion recalls one of the tests for irony developed by Wayne C. Booth: the proclamation of known error.[12] Félicité, we remember, asked Bourais 'to show her the house where Victor lived' (606). The lawyer's mockery leaves no doubt that her perceptions are imperfect – 'Her intelligence was so limited that she perhaps expected to see an actual portrait of her nephew!' (ibid.) – but as numerous critics have pointed out, the episode only increases our sympathy for Félicité and our subsequent delight when Bourais attempts unsuccessfully to sneak by Loulou, amid the parrot's uproarious laughter. There is something approaching pleasure on later realizing that the parrot was right. Beneath the lawyer's façade of learning and respectability lies the heart of a thief. Bourais's scorn turns on the scorner, and Félicité escapes unscathed. As Bardèche has argued, her ridiculous traits do not make her ridiculous, simply more touching (347). Culler goes farther, to suggest that the failure of Bourais's irony attempted against Félicité discourages other attempts. In fact, he says, she makes an unsatisfactory object for irony, since 'her lack of pretension prevents there being anything to deflate.'[13]

Booth's other indications of the presence of irony – conflicts of facts within the work, clashes of style, and conflicts of belief – return us to the importance of consistency. If 'Un Cœur simple' be ironic, other indications of irony directed against the vehicle should occur, either against Félicité or against the supernatural. While the stylistic simplicity through most of the narration contrasts strongly with the lush richness of the concluding few paragraphs, it can be explained as the sudden introduction of the supernatural into a very banal life. And the conflicting beliefs never undermine Félicité.

The claims for Flaubertian irony in this story are not so subtle as Booth's touchstones. As said before, when critics take the trouble to support their belief that 'Un Cœur simple' is ironic, the parrot takes the blame. The problem of interpretation arises from what D.C. Muecke terms conflicting contexts.[14] Those who view the parrot as ironically marked either do not know or are unable to accept the traditional belief that God uses unworthy vessels to communicate with human beings. I suspect there are other factors at play. As Muecke points out, 'since the failure to detect irony is regarded as reflecting upon one's intelligence, those of us who have a horror of being thought unintelligent tend to overcompensate and claim to perceive ironies in what was not meant to be ironical at all.'[15] Most readers come to this story not only wanting to be intelligent but with an awareness of Flaubert as a 'realist,' an anticleric, and, if a believer, a most unorthodox one. Add to this the base, unintelligent nature of birds, and many find it impossible to accept the work at face value. For them, the satirical nature of Loulou is axiomatic, 'Un Cœur simple' is an attack on ignorance and stupidity, on superstition and bigotry, and the case for an ironic reading is clear. The parrot is the key. How one interprets the parrot is the problem. Inconsistencies within the reading should signal misinterpretations.

The difficulties with an ironic interpretation are nonetheless serious and, on consideration, no less clear – so much so, one might even argue, that such an understanding raises more problems than it resolves. There are, for example, no '[s]traightforward warnings in the author's own voice.'[16] Moreover, critics agree with Flaubert that the tale presents Félicité with great sympathy, a persistently positive vision that creates much difficulty for those who believe the story ironic. In fact, barring the treatment of Bourais, where the irony denigrates him, the story has no easily discernible instances of irony. If the parrot is indeed ironic, it is the only clearly ironic element turned against a main character or against the Christian tradition in 'Un Cœur simple,' on the one hand, and *Trois Contes*, on the other – a state of affairs that casts doubt on the existence of irony. I should perhaps qualify this statement. There are numerous elements that have been read as ironic. Paul A. Mankin has, for example, pointed to the names: 'Félicité leads a far from happy life, Mme Aubain brings good luck to nobody and Théodore is hardly to be considered a gift of God' (411). If one follows the narrator's lead and remains centered on Félicité (whose name I shall discuss later), the names reflect what was undoubtedly the maid's first impression. How else would an impoverished rural girl view Mme Aubain but as an *aubaine* (stroke of luck), and the children but as fairytale creatures. As the story's narrator puts it, 'At first, she lived in fear and trembling, caused by the "style of the house" . . . . Paul and Virginie . . . seemed to her formed of some precious substance' (594). The reader indeed understands that Félicité is wrong, but it is important to recognize that the maid never perceives the error. Irony depends upon one's point of view. For Félicité, none of these names would be read as contrary to fact – at least, not at first. If, then, there is irony, it is what might be called 'imposed irony,' conceived by the reader with no textual encouragement. It differs from the 'first stage' or textual or immanent irony as we recognize the justice of the parrot's mockery of Bourais.[17]

As a contrast, one might consider Mérimée's 'Tamango' (1829), where the statements of fact are immediately contradicted – for example, 'The inspectors who scrupulously examined the brig did not discover the six big cases'[18] – and the reasoning is revealed as specious – as in, 'The governor, being a humane man, became interested in Tamango, finding his case justifiable since, after all, he had only used his legitimate right of self-defense; and besides, those he had killed were only Frenchmen' (ibid. 307). Even in such examples as these from Mérimée's tale, one may be certain of irony's presence only after considering whether individual, potentially ironic passages construe with the remainder of the work. If the parrot is the only clearly ironic element in 'Un Cœur simple' and in the incorporating *Trois Contes*, one has to doubt the existence of irony as a significant component of the work, since the irony does not construe with a coherent image of the whole.

There can be no reasonable question that a consistently gentle compassion for the maid permeates 'Un Cœur simple.' This commiseration has much importance, for it raises conflicts with an ironic reading of Loulou. Should not one ask what an ironic parrot means? Is it that the object of Félicité's faith is silly, empty, or heartless? If this be the point, one would not be amazed, given Flaubert's oft-expressed anticlericalism. But just as it is unacceptable to justify the author's compassion by going outside the text, so it should be with an antifaith or anti-Holy Spirit or anti-Christianity reading. It is worth noting that Flaubert's final version of 'Un Cœur simple' no longer contains several passages that might have been understood as an attack on the church. The priest who tranquilly read his breviary in early, discarded versions while Mme Aubain suffered over Virginie's death has disappeared, and the nun who, '[s]mug and absolutely insensitive,'[19] previously announced the girl's death, does so in the final version 'with an air of compunction' (609). Even the parrot has been rendered less objectionable, for while early notes indicate that *'parrots are winged monkeys,'*[20] the published edition suggests nothing of the sort. Flaubert consistently mitigated or deleted negative traits and implications as he revised the story, so that neither Félicité, nor the church, nor Christianity make credible victims.

C.H. Wake remembers the widow's mite of Mark 12:41–4 when he considers the deaf and almost blind old woman's offering of her worm-eaten, stuffed parrot, her 'only wealth' (620), to be placed on the street altar during the Corpus Christi procession. He goes on to point out that the parish priest accepts her offer over the neighbor's objections. Not only does this cast the priest in a favorable light as a kind, understanding person, but the 'gesture gives the parrot an absolute value, in spite of its decay; it gives it, in fact, the full value that it has for Félicité, as the essence of her whole life and love.' The priest of 'Un Cœur simple' is definitely not Emma's Bournisien.[21] In short, there is no clear evidence of an attack against the church or Christianity in the whole of the tale. If we persist in reading it as a parody of the Holy Spirit, we do so on the basis of external evidence – Flaubert's frequently reiterated anticlericalism and a personal conviction that parrots are intrinsically unworthy of such exalted identification.[22] In addition, an interpretation incorporating an ironic parrot confuses the issues of the story, so much so that we must wonder whether 'Un Cœur simple' is truly a masterpiece, as many claim. Finally, ironic understanding of the story's biblical and traditional topoi conflicts strangely with the straightforward presentation of similar material, and critics' non-judgmental understanding, of the following two tales in *Trois Contes*, a work generally held to be unified.[23] For me, this is the most telling argument against an ironic parrot.

I am not arguing against an ironic understanding of *Trois Contes*, only against a prematurely ironic reading. The whole of the work incorporating the three tales may be seen as a commentary on a civilization and a religion that, while promising much, have been reduced to so little. From this point of view, *Trois Contes* seems to me a devastating critique of contemporary society. Félicité's adoration of Loulou is doubtless excessive. Nonetheless, the story consistently attempts to explain and justify this excess. As a comparison, one might remember Molière's *Le*

Misanthrope (1666), in which the playwright's Alceste is nowhere rendered acceptable. Despite the claims of his atrabilious apologist, Rousseau, Molière's character is left with no excuse for his extravagances. Not only is Célimène patently unworthy of such jealousy, much less a comparable love, Alceste has the experience and training to have known better. The same cannot be said for Félicité. Her passion is consistently prepared and extensively exonerated. In short, manuscript and textual evidence seems overwhelmingly in favor of refusing to view the parrot as ironic commentary.

Nor do I argue that there should be any change in the perception of Flaubert's attitude toward the Catholic church or Christianity. I do believe that there is sufficient internal evidence to remember Flaubert's frequently reiterated position concerning the impersonality of art. In effect, as he said many times, 'Art must rise above personal affections.'[24] The rewards are great, it seems to me, if we reject the parodic view of the parrot and allow it to enter into the widespread network of parallel allusions to the New Testament. Should we do so, it appears at least possible that Flaubert recognized the usefulness of this fixed body of literature, not as an object of belief, but as a literary resource. 'Un Cœur simple,' I suggest, alludes to the life of St Felicity and to the biblical Beatitudes.

Characters and events from the Bible and from ecclesiastical tradition were well known in Flaubert's day. Numerous practicing Catholics heard the Scriptures read from the pulpit weekly, if not daily. In addition, Flaubert's period was intensely interested in the new field of comparative religions. Anthropologists were making frequent discoveries that not only cast light on the Bible as a historical text but also provided the meat for amateur and professional students of religions. Ernest Renan, whom Flaubert mentioned repeatedly in his letters, had made biblical material the subject of popular reading and controversy. Even for those separated from the church, his *Histoire des origines du christianisme* (1863–81) and *Histoire du peuple d'Israèl* (1887–93) had considerable impact. His *Vie de Jésus*, the first volume of the *Origines du christianisme*, was particularly successful and made the New Testament a matter of frequent conversation. Renan was by no means the only author drawn to such subjects, though his skill as a writer made his learning more accessible to the general public. Nor was this interest limited to France. Stein is unexceptionable when he calls the Bible the 'principle subtext of Western culture as a whole.'[25]

The Bible was but a part of the nineteenth-century's cultural baggage. Any average *lycée* graduate of the time had in addition a good knowledge of the classics. This was the period when scholars all over Europe were becoming passionately involved in the mythology, legends, and religions of many cultures. Serious scholars like Jacob Grimm, Friedrich Creuzer, Max Müller, William Jones, and the Burnoufs had been churning out book after book on the subject. The Burnoufs were French, and some of the other work was translated into the French language. Men like L.-F. Alfred Maury, François Lenormant, Jules Michelet, Edgar Quinet, and Ferdinand Loise were busy synthesizing, speculating, and often reaching a wide audience within France, while the well-publicized work of anthropologists kept the matter before the public's eyes. Of course, because the Bible was an integral part of the Frenchman's roots and because it was comparatively unvarying, it had certain advantages for the creative writer who wished to make use of allusion within his own works. Although researchers frequently discovered variations in standard versions of myths – a new Aphrodite, a corrupt Zeus – Scripture was relatively stable. Abraham, Moses, Jesus, Paul were fixed; one need not wonder which version an audience might know. While the nineteenth-century French person might or might not believe in Jesus as the Son of God, there was widespread awareness of the events of His life and the traits of His character. All of which makes the Bible a marvelous resource for such a writer as Flaubert, a resource he exploited in *La Tentation de saint Antoine*, in *Salammbô*, and, perhaps especially, in each of the *Trois Contes*.

'Un Cœur simple' shows that Flaubert was at pains to make Félicité a saint.[26] The theme of sainthood is one of the dominant elements that bring the three tales of the volume into a unified whole. While Julien was an easily recognized figure from the *Golden Legend* and Iaokanann (John the Baptist) from the Gospels, the theme is introduced and developed in 'Un Cœur simple.' Any possible doubt of Félicité's saintliness dissipates on remembering the Carthaginian slave girl, St Felicity, who in 202 was martyred by a wild bull in the city's Roman forum. William J. Beck is surely correct to insist on the parallels between the early saint's martyrdom and Félicité's adventure when her courage and quick thinking save Mme Aubain and the two children from an enraged bull.[27] The episode awakens resonances in readers of saints' lives and sets the scene for what is to follow.

Ideally, at least according to certain linguists, proper names are discrete denotative referents, that is, they refer to only one subject or person.[28] The theory runs into trouble in regard to popes, kings, and families with onomastic traditions. Likewise in literature, though a name is undoubtedly important as a reappearing constituent for the creation of a character, authors frequently use it as well to bear meaning, in precisely the same way as any other word. Félicité's name becomes, not just the marker indicating a character, but a reference that points to a person canonized by tradition and existing primarily outside the pages of Flaubert's work. The name brings the life of the third-century saint into the story and creates an allusion that highlights Félicité's saintliness or, perhaps more accurately, prepares the reader to see her in the guise of a saint. There are elements of the ecclesiastical legend that Flaubert does not exploit: St Felicity had just given birth to a child when she was martyred, while Félicité was never that directly involved with motherhood. Nonetheless, as with a word that may have dozens of possible meanings only a few of which are activated by a text, so an allusion may establish viable relationships with but some of the potentially relevant elements within the complex. The rest remain unilluminated in our mental background, like any possible but unexploited lexical significance. Just as we do not think of communism when discussing a red dress, so we do not think of St Felicity's offspring if nothing brings that element of the saint's life to mind.

The name bears another meaning that draws attention to an even more important allusive parallel. 'Un Cœur simple' alludes to the Beatitudes. A considerable number of critics have observed that Félicité's name must be ironic, for she is not particularly happy, her life being nothing but drudgery. Here again William Beck points out pertinently, '[A]ll derivatives from the root *felicit* have as their initial meaning, "beatitude." . . . In strictly objective terms, Félicité is scarcely "happy"'; she is 'felicitous,' in the sense of 'blessed.'[29]

Beck has persuasively argued that 'Un Cœur simple' alludes to the Beatitudes.[30] Commentators like to suggest that the first Beatitude, 'Blessed are the poor in spirit: for theirs is the kingdom of heaven' (Matt. 5:3), constitutes the essence of the Sermon on the Mount. It is frequently read as a companion to Luke 6:20, 24 – 'Blessed are ye poor: for yours is the kingdom of God. . . . But woe unto you that are rich! for ye have received your consolation.'[31] The point is simply that the kind of humility that Félicité demonstrates is difficult to achieve when one has great wealth. Félicité is indeed poor. Her accumulations at the end of a life of hard work and dedication are pathetic: a few castoffs in a tumbledown house belonging to others. Perhaps more important is her humility, epitomized by the scene where she and Mme Aubain share their sorrow in an embrace. 'Their eyes fixed on each other, filled with tears; finally the mistress opened her arms, the servant threw herself into them; and they embraced, satisfying their pain in a kiss which equalized them. It was the first time they had ever done anything like that, Mme Aubain not being of an expansive nature. Félicité was as grateful as if it had been a favor, and from then on she cherished her with animal-like devotion and religious veneration' (611). Félicité's humility is so pervasive that she seemingly cannot grasp the extent of Mme Aubain's debt to her, and she remains to the end a committed, self-sacrificing servant. Even when she has done something outstanding, as when she saved the family from the bull, 'Félicité drew no pride from it, not even suspecting that she had done anything heroic' (597). Félicité, virtually devoid of pride, is the perfect exemplar of the first Beatitude.

The second Beatitude, 'Blessed are they that mourn: for they shall be comforted' (Matt. 5:4), touches on an important and repeated part of Félicité's life that the story stresses in several ways. With depressing regularity, either through betrayal or death, Félicité loses everyone she has loved: Théodore, Victor, Virginie, Mme Aubain. Through it all, she carries on her duties and devotes herself to others: to Victor, to the Polish refugees, to the Père Colmiche. Indeed, 'The goodness of her heart developed' (612). She comforts others; for example, in response to Mme Aubain's grief, she 'preached to her gently; she must take care of herself for her son, and for the other, in memory "of her"' (610). In the process, of course, she fulfills the fifth Beatitude: 'Blessed are the merciful, for they shall obtain mercy' (Matt. 5:7). Her selfless control in moments of grief contrasts with Mme Aubain's debilitating incapacity, and her willingness to give up Loulou represents but another step in the process of sainthood.

The word 'meek,' in 'Blessed are the meek: for they shall inherit the earth' (Matt. 5:5), does not suggest weakness. As Sherman E. Johnson says, 'If "poor in spirit" is the opposite of proud in spirit, "meek" is the opposite . . . of aggressive. They are not harsh, not self-assertive, not covetous, not trampling in brute force: they are humble in the strength of reverence. Others claim their rights, but the meek are concerned about their duties.'[32] The appropriateness of the explanation might make one believe the exegete was describing Félicité. Despite her insight into the tenant farmers, her tact in handling the drunken Marquis de Gremanville, her courage with the bull, her constant and continuing skill in everything she does, she never makes an issue of what the family owes her. She surely knew that 'the housewives of Pont-l'Evèque envied Mme Aubain her servant' (591), but she does not use the information to extract any sort of concessions from her mistress. She is meek.

Beck sees Félicité's 'hunger and thirst after righteousness' and the purity of her heart – the third and fifth Beatitudes – in her daily attendance at Mass and in the rosary beads that join her before the fire in the evenings. He may be right. I suspect, however, that Flaubert had these Beatitudes more in mind when, he had her resist Théodore's brutal advances, despite her love. 'She was not innocent in the same way as young ladies – animals had taught her – but reason and instinctive honor kept her from weakening' (594). She is a 'good' girl. Her sense of honesty obliges her to show the Polish refugee who had asked her hand in marriage to the door when she discovers him helping himself to Mme Aubain's food. For all her selflessness she nonetheless has it in her to be offended, at least for a moment and for the sake of another. When Mme Aubain maligns her nephew, Victor, for example, 'although brought up with rough treatment, she was indignant at Madame, then forgot' (606). The passage masterfully situates Félicité's strong though humble character, for it underlines her sense of what is right, indicates that her anger is not for herself but for someone else, and ends with forgiveness so total that the incident itself is forgotten. After her outrage when Théodore abandoned her for the wealthy Mme Lehoussais, Félicité was offended on several occasions, but never on her own account. It is because Mme Aubain slanders Victor, because the refugee makes free with Mme Aubain's food, or because people insult Loulou. 'They compared Loulou to a goose, a hunk of wood: they might just as well have stabbed Félicité!' (613).

It is perfectly in character that her most profound religious experience comes not when she herself takes her first communion, but when her young charge, Virginie, does. Especially after coming to work for Mme Aubain, she seems the epitome of a selfless person. 'Her mistress often told her, "My God, are you dumb!" "Yes, Madame," she would reply, while looking around her for something' (615). When she suffers, it is for someone or something else. Of course, suffering in itself will not qualify for the blessedness of the last two Beatitudes; for that one must be persecuted for righteousness' sake; one must be reviled for the sake of God.

The possibility that Félicité has indeed been reviled and persecuted 'for My sake' may be formulated only after the fact, only after we have completed the story, accepted the identification of Loulou and the Holy

Spirit, and remembered what happened as Félicité was on her way with Loulou's body to Honfleur and the twice-mentioned roadside Calvary (604, 605). The mail-coach driver, enraged that she did not move out of the way, 'raised his arm and, without slowing down, lashed her with his big whip so hard from stomach to chignon that she fell over backwards' (616). When she regains consciousness, her first thought is for Loulou. Somewhat farther on, at Ecquemauville, 'she felt faint and stopped, and the destitution of her childhood, the disappointment of her first love, her nephew's departure, Virginie's death came back all at once like the waves of the tide and, rising in her throat, choked her' (616). But she finds the strength to stand and continue. In her humble way she has repeated certain elements of the passion and suffered for Loulou, if not for God.[33]

Even at the end of her life, the pattern of saintliness continues. She knows that the only way to remain 'pure in heart' is to forgive and to ask forgiveness. Shortly before her death, 'she declared that she needed to talk to Fabu. . . . "Forgive me," she said, trying to reach out her arms. "I thought you were the one who killed him!"' (620). The ladies caring for her put it down to mental weakness brought on by old age and sickness, but it is the pattern of her life. Consciously or unconsciously, knowingly or unknowingly, her behavior is that of a simple but kindly, caring person, incapable of resentment, wanting only for everyone to be happy. She is a peacemaker, devoted to the well-being of others. In short, Flaubert saw to it that she satisfies all the requirements for blessedness. As promised by the Beatitudes, we may fully expect her to have the rewards: she will be called a child of God; indeed, hers 'is the kingdom of heaven' (Matt. 5:10); she will 'see God' (Matt. 5:8).

And so she does. 'An azure haze rose in Félicité's room. She spread her nostrils, breathing it in with mystical sensuality, then closed her eyes. Her lips smiled. Her heartbeats slowed one by one, each fainter, softer than the last one, the way a fountain dries up, the way an echo disappears; and when she exhaled for the last time, she thought she saw a gigantic parrot hovering above her head in the half-opened heavens' (622). Through the years, critics who have wished to suggest that Flaubert wanted his reader to recognize the absurdity of Félicité's vision have made much of the phrase, 'elle crut voir . . . un perroquet [she thought she saw a . . . parrot].' Mankin has a brief but, I think, convincing response: 'I believe that Flaubert injected "crut [thought]" because the exclusive use of the past definite form of "voir [to see]" would have been too dramatic and too abrupt a vision for the agonizing old servant. The very sound of "elle vit, dans les cieux entr'ouverts, un perroquet gigantesque [she saw, in the partially opened heavens, a gigantic parrot]" is too brutal for the desired effect. Whether Félicité saw or only thought she saw seems to me entirely beside the point.'[34] Willenbrink mentions that Flaubert actually wrote 'voyait [was seeing]' in an early version (Willenbrink 229). One might also suggest that *vit* (saw) or *voyait* would have indicated a remarkably direct experience for Félicité, indeed out of character. The 'crut voir' maintains the maid's hesitant, secondhand, almost apologetic relationship with the divine. It may also be that Flaubert's desire to have readers 'suspend their disbelief' required the distancing brought by 'crut.' Supernatural tales in nineteenth-century France were most often removed from the present in either time or space, perhaps because writers felt that the middle-class reader would reject suggestions of the preternatural in their own reality but might accept it in alien times and climes. This 'crut' separates Félicité's vision from the reader, as the epoch separates those of 'La Légende de saint Julien' and 'Hérodias.'[35]

I would hesitate to use 'Un Cœur simple' as ammunition in an argument concerned with Flaubert's views on anything at all. *Trois Contes* comes as close as anything the master did to achieving autonomy, if by that quality we mean a refusal either to comment on or attempt to influence an aspect of the world outside itself. While it brings other systems into its functioning – the nature of language requires that we apply meanings that are per se external to the linguistic signs – the tale draws no conclusions about the middle or working classes, or about the class system, or about Christianity, or about the church and clerics. It simply is. The biblical allusion establishing an allusive backdrop, which reminds readers of the Beatitudes, works from start to finish. It provides a context of sanctity and reminds us that Félicité is not merely a nice woman. As she gradually becomes a living illustration of the Blessed, the biblical allusion encourages readers to see her as an exceptionally good person, an unsophisticated but saintly peasant who bears some resemblance to her patronym. Loulou's identification with the Holy Spirit merely extends the allusion. It warns readers well in advance that Félicité's reward will be great: not only will she enter the Kingdom of Heaven, she will see God (Matt. 5:8, 10, 12).

Without the allusion, 'Un Cœur simple' would be a well-written but otherwise undistinguished story of an ignorant servant who bore her lot without complaint. With the allusion, Flaubert has written a story of the supernatural situated neither in the Middle Ages, like the following story of St Julien, nor at the time of Christ, like 'Herodias.' Félicité rises in Flaubert's day above her social position. And the story itself resonates with supernatural overtones. Unbelievers can appreciate it much as they would any story of the supernatural; believers can accept it more or less at face value. But however one perceives it, no one can doubt that Félicité is 'un cœur simple' and that a simple heart is blessed.

When the parrot is allowed to integrate itself into the story, it does so completely. There is no break in the narrative fabric of 'Un Cœur simple' or, perhaps more important, of the cycle Trois Contes. Should we bring our prejudices from outside the work and take the parrot as ironic commentary, however, suddenly the warp breaks, leaving an unsightly thread to unravel in the smooth expanse of the whole, since both 'La Légende de saint Julien l'Hospitalier' and 'Hérodias' construe brilliantly with the hagiographic tradition. One might even argue that a negative interpretation of the bird creates more difficulties than it solves. If so, the story should be viewed, not as an attack on ignorance and stupidity, but as a sympathetic view of an innocent person's confrontation with what she, at least, thought of as divine. Of course, one can refuse to pay attention to those textual elements that encourage integration, and the story will fail. Communication is a fragile thing, none too successful in the best of situations. It occurs only on our accepting the conventions governing the message.

The elements of irony and allusion – whether names, objects, images, quotations[36] – are interpreted like any word or sequence – that is, according to context, on the one hand, and conventions on the other. The cry that floats up from the streets above Nana's putrefying body at the end of Nana: 'To Berlin! to Berlin! to Berlin!' cannot be interpreted as though it were a nineteenth-century variation on 'Go west, young man, go west!' To the contrary, it must be understood in the light of the courtesan as a symbol of France, of what will happen in La Débâcle, and of the insurrections and defeat of 1870 and 1871. It would be as inappropriate to deny that Antipas's executioner saw ('had seen') the Great Angel of the Samaritans guarding John the Baptist (2.617), or to doubt that the leper became Jesus who bore Julien off to heaven (2.648), as to question the literary sincerity of Félicité's deathbed belief that she saw a parrot hovering above her. Each supernatural event has a carefully prepared context that insists upon the allusion and renders an ironic interpretation difficult to support.

3

From Translation, Imitation, and Plagiarism to Parallel Allusion: *Antigone*

Translation theory, especially as described in Glyn Norton's fine exposition,[1] may provide a means of pursuing an explanation of how allusion works. Whether translators are interested in giving a precise rendering of the original text, or are willing to settle for a partial transferral of the actual material, or the concepts, leaving the devices aside, translation cannot exist without the co-existing authority of what Norton calls the 'source text' (32). It is not the difficulties of translation that interest me here, though no one would deny them, but rather the coexistence of two supposedly equal texts. In the best of all worlds, the meaning of the translation would equal that of the original. The translator claims no originality, except in his ability to transfer the one into the other, and we consider the creator of the source text to be the author of the translation.

To look at the two texts is, of course, to see enormous differences. The physical appearance of the print in *La Guerre et la paix* has little resemblance to that in *War and Peace* and still less to the original. Even if it were possible to find and read a perfect translation of Racine's *Phèdre*, it is not certain, given the readers' differing conditions in time and place, that those who know French and English well would have the same image. If perfection were possible, one could perhaps posit identical contexts for reader, writer, and texts (same background, experience, weather conditions, health, degree of attention, etc.), in which case the image created in the reader's mind on reading the translation would theoretically equal the one he formed on reading the original. In fact, such ideal conditions never occur. As Quintilian understood, the image resulting from a precise copy, even in the same language, will not equal the original, for the context will have changed (*De Institutione Oratoria*

10.ii.26). Two identical, independently conceived and executed creations separated by several hundred years would differ radically in meaning. This is the idea at the heart of Borges's 'Pierre Ménard, Author of the Quixote.'

Sixteenth-century theorists were well aware of the many facets that existed in an original and that would ideally be transferred into its translation. There was general agreement that one could translate the *res*, variously understood as plot and character, subject matter, or themes. Du Bellay advised ignoring the problems of *elocutio*.[2] Others were more demanding. Jacques Peletier du Mans considered translation the truest kind of imitation (Cave 57), and, indeed, one can understand both the challenge and the benefit of rendering Latin and Greek models into French. The impossibility of doing so in depth raised other issues. Should one insist on exact restitution in all its detail? Should one concentrate on the intellectual subject matter and produce what might be called a paraphrase, filling in, expanding, explaining – in short, glossing? As Pierre Gaultier saw, the linguistic activity of translating could succeed only through a process of taking apart by analysis and of regeneration (Norton 76). Words, seen as the unitary constituents of discourse, could be arranged differently. If that in fact happens, as Leonardo Bruni and others understood, it would inevitably affect the *res* or content. When Bruni demanded the correct transferral of a text from the original language into another, he wanted to maintain the 'corporal and pictural integrity' of the original (Norton 39–43, 72). Inevitably, translators began to wonder whether one might not do better by producing more or less radical regenerations.

Translation's problems, and indeed the solutions to those problems, continue to haunt translators. When Scott-Moncrieff, in his justifiably famous translation of Proust's *A la recherche du temps perdu*, decided that the connotations of French *rose* (pink) were often more closely communicated by the English 'red,' he immediately lost many of the associations tying French *rose*, for example, to flowers in general and to roses in particular. If Scott-Moncrieff was aware of the associations, which I have argued are important,[3] he clearly decided that other considerations outweighed them. Nonetheless, the impoverishment that occurs in the English version, whether one settles for 'red' or, indeed, for 'pink' (which is by no means the same as the French *rose*, though it is probably the best we can do in English), illustrates the distance of real translations from the ideal. For our purposes, however, the idea of transferrals from one language to another establishes the concept of two physically separate and differing texts despite (it is to be hoped) identical content. The translation is then different in appearance from but theoretically identical in content and effect to the original. Despite the physical differences in the text, the image produced by one should be the same as that produced by the other, thus permitting the experience of one to equal the experience of the other.

Imitatio raises other issues. For the ancients, and for many later writers who proclaimed the importance of imitation and models, it was only the first step, the beginning, which should lead gradually to an increase in invention. Erasmus, while he asserted that one would never be wrong to imitate Cicero, points out explicitly that imitation alone is insufficient, for no one can equal the model he follows.[4] As Matthew of Vendôme put it around AD 1175, 'It is not enough to render word for word, in order to achieve a faithful imitation' (Murphy 166), not enough to pay close attention to all the numerous elements Quintilian listed under the rubrics of *dispositio* and *elocutio* – for example, lexicon, figures, characters, and so on. In fact, rhetoricians from at least Quintilian on seem to have understood that imitation could never truly rival the original model. Quintilian said flatly,

[W]hatever is like another object, must necessarily be inferior to the object of its imitation, just as the shadow is inferior to the substance, the portrait to the features which it portrays, and the acting of the player to the feelings which he endeavours to reproduce. . . . For the models which we select for imitation have a genuine and natural force, whereas all imitation is artificial and moulded to a purpose which was not that of the original orator. . . . Consequently, there are many who, after excerpting certain words from published speeches or borrowing certain particular rhythms, think that they have produced a perfect copy of the works which they have read, despite the fact that words become obsolete or current with the lapse of years, the one standard being contemporary usage; and they are not good or bad in virtue of their inherent nature . . . but solely in virtue of the aptitude and propriety. (10.ii.10–13)

The ideal of imitation, as Du Bellay saw, required digesting the Greek and Latin models (Cave 64) and then regenerating what might on the physical surface seem absolutely distinct. The practice and results of imitation were more complicated. Benedetto Grasso (1566) is only more explicit than most of his contemporaries when he points out that imitation may take several forms. It may be nothing but a simple translation. It may go farther, however, and make use of different words. Or it may produce an entirely new treatment, different in subject matter, words, and other devices.[5] In many instances, 'literary imitation is a supplement which seeks to complete and supplant the original.'[6] It wishes to equal or improve on the model.

The point is that imitation produces two individual texts that are different in reality, since to produce a similar image in the minds of the audience (to remain in Quintilian's conceptual framework), it might be necessary to use very different words, devices, or even subject matter. The ideal imitation had two physically different texts that elicited a similar image but that could rightly claim to be the products of two different authors. Unlike successful translations, which have one author, two texts, and similar if not identical images, imitations have two authors, two texts, and one image. To enjoy a perfectly translated work, one need only know the translation, though, as Aristotle pointed out in the fourth chapter of *On the Art of Poetry*, appreciation of an imitation requires knowledge of both the imitation and the work imitated. The matter is further complicated when only one aspect of the model is imitated, when the relationship between the model, or 'source text,' is hidden in the attempt to give oneself the virtue of originality where none exists (as with plagiarism), or when the relationship between the model and the imitation is exploited in the attempt to add significance to the latter (as with the various devices of intertextuality).

From the standpoint of allusion, imitation's complexities become most interesting when the modeled text exploits the model itself. In such an event, the model becomes a semiotic/semantic unit, an element like any other, integrated into the later of the two creations. It operates in a manner similar to but less complicated than a word with multiple denotations and connotations, not all of which will be activated by the context. Take Montherlant's *Les Célibataires* (*The Celibates* [1934]), the title of which will encourage readers to think of Balzac's collection of three novels gathered together. Montherlant's and Balzac's creations share the same general subject matter in that they both treat unmarried people who, furthermore, display the same unabashed selfishness and cruelty. Both novels exploit every opportunity to generalize and to moralize, though Montherlant indulges in apothegms somewhat more often than his predecessor. The possibility that the relationship I suggest might have been accidental dissipates immediately on opening Montherlant's work. There one makes the acquaintance of an old man excessively concerned with keeping his feet warm and dry, and one is surely authorized to remember the similarly obsessed Abbé Birotteau of the second 'scene' of Balzac's *Célibataires, Le Curé de Tours* (*The Priest of Tours* [1832]). Not too many years ago, a critic might have been satisfied to suggest that Montherlant was overtly acknowledging a source, and I suppose that would not be entirely wrong. On reconsidering what happens during the actual reading of Montherlant's *Les Célibataires*, however, it seems to me that more is involved. Balzac's trilogy is deeply involved in the experience of Montherlant's novel, and not just as a means of evaluating originality. Previous knowledge heightens and deepens our perception and understanding of Montherlant's ego-driven creations. The two works are aesthetically related.

To some degree this is true of any imitation. The imitator establishes a metonymic filiation, bringing some of the luster (*cum* afterglow) of the antecedent model into the subsequent creation. Renaissance writers gained by writing in the tradition of Horace or Petrarch, for example. Like works that purport to belong to a genre, they put the readers on notice to expect certain devices, certain subject matter, certain forms. Readers who recognize the tradition will be prepared to have a richer experience, though the basic understanding of the work in hand may depend little on foreknowledge. When the previous work or works have been more actively, intimately incorporated into the later text, the relationship becomes metaphoric, and its recognition more essential to comprehension. On seeing Montherlant's title, for example, one thinks of the preceding literary experience, and one has certain expectations, but one also reads the work with the burden of this background in mind. On confronting once again the petty, egocentric self-indulgence of unmarried people, readers' expectations are justified. They know that someone will be hurt, and their previous literary experience increases the suspense. One knows the result of celibate self-centeredness; the question is who will be destroyed by whom and how? Because of what we discovered on reading Balzac, our experience becomes a meaning that is metaphorically added to Montherlant's novel.

Allusion differs from translation and imitation in that there is no attempt to replicate the previous text. The alluding author takes a preexistent text and exploits it in his own creation. His use neither suppresses nor denies the preceding text or author, it merely takes what exists outside and makes it a 'reference' or a 'meaning' of his own work. To the degree that knowledge of the earlier model(s) is desirable in some texts, the distinction between modeling and allusion is not always sharp, no more than the distinction between the colors red and orange or between a book as something to be read and a book-object that serves primarily as an artifact. The conceptual material within a case of modeling lacks the precision of an allusion, which is relatively precise, focused, and directed.

Plagiarism is perhaps more troublesome, since it has long been confused with allusion. The results of this lack of distinction have not infrequently been disastrous. I think of Zola's critics who knowingly or unknowingly misinterpreted his many allusions to Balzac as plagiarisms. As a result, the frequency of Zola's attempts to bring Balzac's work into his own decreased precipitously after *Nana* (1880), to the considerable impoverishment of *Les Rougon-Macquart*.

To add to the confusion, numerous writers have enjoyed the age-old game of shocking the staid and stuffy (*épater le bourgeois*) by loudly proclaiming themselves guilty of plagiarism. Giraudoux, for example, had his character Robineau say in *Siegfried*: 'Plagiarism is at the base of all literatures, except the first, which, however, is unknown.'[7] The actual existence of such theft turns on whether the sources are truly *used* in an artistic fashion, which is to say, on *how* they are used. As Zola put it when accused of this sin: 'I take my documents where I find them, and I believe I make them my own.'[8] The statement by Giraudoux's Robineau may provide an illustration. When, in 1959, Anouilh quoted him without acknowledgment, though with a few transpositions – 'All literature is basically plagiarism except for the first which is unknown'[9] – he might have plagiarized. Such, at least, was John Harvey's conclusion.[10] Valéry, as is so often the case, has a word of wisdom in the midst of much obfuscation: 'A plagiarist is someone who has poorly digested the substance of others: he renders recognizable pieces. Originality, a matter of cheek. There are no *original* writers, for those who merit the name are unknown, and even unknowable. But there are those who act like they are.'[11] Elsewhere, Valéry discusses the impossibility of absolute originality: '[A] work is made by a multitude of 'spirits' and events – (ancestors, states, chance, anterior writers, etc.) – under the direction of the Author' (2.566). Flaubert puts the issue in terms of the aesthetic milieu all writers need and the continuing education they must seek in other writers: 'Talent, like life, is transmitted by infusion. You have to live in noble surroundings, in the company of masters, and take in its spirit. There is nothing wrong with in depth study of a genius completely different from your own, because you cannot copy it.'[12] The question of originality or plagiarism is not decided by the existence of a source, for everything we know has a source, someplace, somehow. As Zola said, 'What I take and use becomes mine.'[13] Material regurgitated without creative changes is a pale, uninteresting copy. When one hides the fact that one has copied in part or in whole, without making use of the source in some new way, one has plagiarized.

These writers struggle with the fact that nothing is created from nothing. While it may be true as Henry James suggested that authors can imagine a reality from nothing more than a glance into it,[14] in fact, the materials they use are all to be found elsewhere. Genius is revealed in choice, in combinations, in arrangement, in timing, in context. In short, plagiarism consists of two authors and one text, whereas two of each are purported. When the relationship of identity between the two is revealed, the value of the copy is impugned. As Herman Meyer suggests, the acknowledged use of previous work is not plagiarism, which must, by definition, be unacknowledged.[15] Unfortunately, it is not always so easy to decide whether plagiarism has occurred. The key rests in whether the subsequent text has gained more from a source through unacknowledged repetition or whether it has used the source as an element in a new creation that would be enhanced by the reader's recognition of the previous creation. As Meyer points out, discovery of a hidden theft (plagiarism) 'may result in a certain philological satisfaction, but no aesthetic delight' (*Poetics of Quotation* 7). Conversely, apprehension of a preexistent text functioning in the passage or work in hand may reveal imitation, allusion, parody, or any number of other possibilities. The test is in whether or not the two texts work together within the reading experience, and if so how.

There are other ways of dealing with the interrelations of present and past texts. There is a certain ponderous enjoyment in following Roland Barthes's lead and allowing Proust's apple trees in bloom to arise from a text by Flaubert.[16] Or one can delight in Michel Tournier's dispute with the priority of precedence when he considers his 'feeling of bitter frustration' on noting certain passages in other writers he was 'from the beginning of time predestined to write.'[17] He gives an example from his *Roi des aulnes*, a scene that resembles one in Alain-Fournier's *Le Grand Meaulnes*: 'People have not failed to point it out to me. I answer that that episode belongs to me more justifiably than to Alain-Fournier, because it only has an episodic, almost anecdotal, character in *Le Grand Meaulnes*, while in *Le Roi des aulnes*, it prefigures everything that follows, growing from that "phoria" that constitutes the only subject for the novel. It seems to me that Alain-Fournier's temporal priority will not hold out in the face of such a strongly founded thematic priority, and that if one of the two, Fournier or Tournier, must be taxed with plagiarism, if there is any justice it is Fournier who must be condemned' (ibid. 53).

The intertextual or, more precisely, the allusive relationship may result from more or less parallel texts, or, in a much more complicated way, from a progression. Just as Octavian Augustus succeeded Julius Caesar, so Zola's Octave Mouret succeeds Balzac's César Birotteau. The firm links joining the two are all the more clear on comparing 'Chez Guillaume' with 'Au Vieil Elbeuf,' and then with Zola's modern department store, 'Au Bonheur des Dames.' Zola is, of course, stressing the changes that have taken place in the days since Balzac considered merchandising. The progression from one novel to the next was emphasized by the reference to the parallels between the Roman Empire and the Second Empire. Zola, who was very aware of the rotten undergirding of Napoléon III's regime, called himself the 'Suetonius of the Second Empire.'[18] The moral decline that Zola emphasized repeatedly is also apparent here, for the moral probity at the base of César's failure is in no sense shared by the owner of Au Bonheur des Dames. In short, Zola used what I shall later call an 'oppositional allusion' in order to establish a parallel with the historical decline of Rome.

The literary tradition exploited by Montherlant in Les Célibataires, La Reine Morte, and other works is directly pertinent to Anouilh's Antigone, which was first performed on 4 February 1944. Anouilh, like many others, announces his allusion in the title, an allusion to a mythological figure represented most notably by Sophocles in the fifth century BC.[19] Both plays exploit the Theban saga of Oedipus and his family. For those who might not know the story, Anouilh told it in the program for the first season at the Théâtre de l'Atelier:

The story begins when Eteocles and Polynices, Oedipus's two sons who were to take turns reigning for one year each over Thebes, fought and killed each other beneath the walls of the city. Eteocles, the elder, had refused to give the position to his brother at the end of the first year in power.

Seven powerful, foreign princes that Polynices had won to his cause, were defeated before the seven gates of Thebes. Now the city is saved, the two brothers are dead, and Creon, the king, has ordered an imposing funeral for Eteocles, the good brother, but Polynices, the scoundrel, the rebel, the lout would be left without tears and without sepulture, the prey of crows and jackals. Whoever dared administer burial rites to him would be mercilessly put to death.

But Antigone, sister of both the rebel and the faithful prince, thinks that there are other laws than the laws of men, other laws that make no distinctions between the two brothers. In spite of the terrible threat, she tries to bury Polynices.

Surprised by the soldiers who are guarding the body, she is brought before Creon who is going to try to have her accept the laws of men and to save her from death.

In vain. When all her good reasons for dying have been killed, one by one by Creon, Antigone finds another reason, more secret and more true, in her own heart.

And it is perhaps not for Polynices, but rather it is so she can forever say 'No' to everything that is not as pure as she is – 'No' to men and to life itself – that Antigone will die this evening – once again as she has for three thousand years – dangerous, absurd, and limpid – but as necessary for the world as its laws.[20]

Those who come rushing into the theater at the last minute, just before the curtain rises, and who may not then have read the program notes, are greeted by the Chorus. He repeats the first two paragraphs from the program's account almost word for word. For the rest of what he says, though there are variations, the essence of the program remains. The actors on the stage 'are going to act out the story of Antigone.'[21] The Chorus points to the skinny girl who is deep in thought. 'She is thinking that she is going to be Antigone in a little while. . . . She is thinking that she is going to die. . . . She is named Antigone, and she is going to have to play her role to the end' (ibid.). The Chorus goes on to introduce the others: Haemon, who will shortly die; Creon, the king; Eurydice, who will continue knitting until 'her turn comes to get up and die' (10); the messenger, the Nurse, and the soldiers.

If anyone were adding up Anouilh's debt, it would seem substantial, for the plot is very similar, the list of characters virtually identical, and, most obviously, as though there were no innocents to protect, the names have not been changed. Several of the funniest lines given to Anouilh's hapless guard, to whose lot it falls to report the terrible event, come straight from Sophocles. Some might even wish to add Anouilh's name to Henri Peyre's list of writers (among them Giraudoux, Cocteau, Pierre Mille, Jules Lemaître, and the Gide of *Œdipe* and *Perséphone*) who 'perhaps betray, in taking up again subjects which have been treated hundreds of times, the secret weakness of so many modern authors: the lack of imaginative fire, the fear of drawing from the well-spring of life itself, which is often vulgar and brutal, and the preference for material which has already been purified, sublimated and filtrated by many a predecessor.'[22]

On closer examination, however, major differences between the *Antigone* of Sophocles and that of Anouilh become apparent, so much so that one indeed wonders why the modern playwright bothered to preserve the classic names and basic plot structure. Antigone, for example, has a very different character in the two plays. Gabriel Marcel feels she has been so drastically changed that she is truly unrecognizable.[23] Despite the fact that Sophocles' Antigone is physically overcome by the guards, who are sufficiently strong to prevent her from completing the second burial, one cannot fail to be impressed by her moral strength. As the Leader of the Chorus puts it, 'The maid shows herself the passionate child of passionate sire, and knows not how to bend before troubles.'[24] At no point does she doubt the justice of her act or the righteousness of her cause. She insists, '[T]here is nothing shameful in piety to a brother' (204). Yes, Polynices was a traitor; he may well have been a scoundrel. Nonetheless, 'Hades desires these rites' (205). As Creon's attendants conduct Antigone to her 'tomb, bridal-chamber' (218), an image Anouilh will subsequently exploit, she mentions both the tragedy of her birth into 'the famed house of Labdacus' (218) and her maiden status – 'no bridal bed, no bridal song hath been mine, no joy of marriage, no portion in the nurture of children' (219) – but little time is spent on such plaints, and Sophocles' play leaves no doubt that her desire to uphold the laws of the gods has far more weight. It is helpful to compare her to Anouilh's 'little Antigone,' whose youth is essential, especially since her death early on seems to have as much to do with juvenile stubbornness and a temper tantrum as with a clear sense of what is right. In Sophocles, Antigone's age has no importance. She seems ageless, rather than childish; a woman of awesome force rather than a child of uncertain temper. Indeed, for all Aristotle has taught us about the importance of pity to tragedy, Sophocles' Antigone is more tragic than piteous.

Creon too seems cut from other cloth. Whereas Anouilh puts before his public an experienced and knowing bureaucrat, Sophocles calls forth a petty tyrant to strut before the people his decision to leave Polynices unburied. The latter's desperately stubborn weakness is brilliantly illuminated. He dares not back down for fear of damaging his image. 'For since I have taken her, alone of all the city, in open disobedience, I will not make myself a liar to my people – I will slay her. . . . [W]homsoever the city may appoint, that man must be obeyed, in little things and great, in just things and unjust' (210). Despite the many warnings that he has made a mistake, Creon rejects youth and blood when he refuses the counsel of his son; and when the city's leaders echo Haemon, Creon rejects the counsel of age. He suspects enemy bribes are responsible for the murmurs of the city. In Sophocles' hands, Creon is limited, incapable, without the insight required by his position, surpassed by events, rigid with fear, blinded by pride. 'Am I to rule this land by other judgment than mine own?' he asks (213). When Tiresias offers the sure wisdom of a trustworthy prophet whose physical blindness has only increased his spiritual insight, Creon accuses him of having been suborned. It is clear that even then the pathetic king could have accepted the rebuke and changed his ways, but after the prophet angrily condemns him and leaves, his repentance arrives too tardily. The gods will punish his 'stiff-necked' (212) pride: 'Great words of prideful men are ever punished with great blows' (234), the Leader of the Chorus summarizes. The differences between the modern and classical versions are stressed by the disappearance of Tiresias from Anouilh's version, where Creon's lucidity renders the blind seer unnecessary.[25] As William Calin points out, Anouilh has ennobled Creon.[26]

Sophocles differs most significantly, however, in the central theme of his play, summarized by the Chorus: 'Reverent action claims a certain praise for reverence; but an offence against power cannot be brooked by him who hath power in his keeping' (218). The laws of man conflict with the laws of the gods, and while there is no denying the importance of humanity's legal systems, Creon does not understand the priorities. Whatever the consequences may be, wise men bow to the wishes of the gods. Although the classical *Antigone* mentions hubris (234), the ship of state (193, 212), fate (218), and the differing roles of men, women, and children (189, 210), it does so only in passing and the elements are of little significance. Everything is subordinated to the central issue of Creon's blind insistence on his own will even in the face of clear warnings that the gods do not approve of his decision.

Anouilh's play is very different. Although many of the same images reappear, they are built into something very powerful but of a different sort, and their thrust changes. The Sophoclean 'vessel of our State. . . . our country . . . the ship that bears us safe' (193) is transformed from a passing reference into Creon's memorable monologue: 'Someone has to take over and guide the boat. It's leaking everywhere, full of crimes, of stupidity, of misery… And the tiller swings wildly. The crew doesn't want to do anything anymore; they only want to pillage…' (57). For

Anouilh's Creon, the monologue focuses attention on his sole justifica-
tion for his role: he governs because it is his job. Someone has to do it.
For Sophocles, however, the 'ship of state' merely provides a context for
the laws of man that retain their importance up to the point where they
come into conflict with the laws of the gods and are thus revealed as
vanity.

Legions of critics have shown the way Anouilh's *Antigone* highlights
the opposition between the ideal and the real, idealism and pragmatism,
purity and compromise, youth and age, beauty and ugliness, ephemeral
life and reified death. Spingler goes farther in an impressive reading
and shows how the play puts Romantic sentimentalism in conflict with
tragic action. As Creon erodes the ethical positions – or '"Greek" reasoning' – that undergird Antigone's act, the cause of her death is
revealed as nothing but her character, considered both as 'role-playing
and [as] theatricalism.'[27] Sophocles touches on several of these antago-
nisms, and passes on without pause, while in the modern version they
blaze with significance. Still, Anouilh's play subordinates them all to the
overriding theme of death. Announced in the program, highlighted by
the prologue, mentioned in virtually every speech, death reigns. Sophocles' material is presented as though the outcome of Antigone's ritualis-
tically burying her brother were open, subject to variance, thus capable
of arousing suspense in the audience. However much the Greek audience may have known the outcome or the Chorus may remind us of the
'mysterious power of fate' (220), Tiresias talks as though Creon has a
choice: '[T]hou standest on fate's fine edge' (222), he says. The subdued
significance of destiny to Sophocles constitutes the greatest difference
between the two plays. Anouilh's Antigone is caught in the grip of
destiny, however – what Cocteau would call the infernal machine. 'She
has to die,' the king says. 'Antigone was made for being dead' (69).

Anouilh wrote at a time when the classical portion of the curriculum
had long been subordinate or absent, and he was forced to educate his
audience. Otherwise the spectators might not know that Antigone is
destined for death. While on the one hand this may seem a serious
disadvantage, on the other it gives Anouilh some freedom, for it allows
him to revise the story, as he does: by recreating the characters, by
adding and subtracting from them, and by changing the thematic content. He can, in short, define the myth, shade it as he pleases. Those
who know the Sophoclean version will allow certain adjustments, since
myths change. Those who bring their blank slates for the modern playwright to write large upon have no choice but to accept the image pre-

sented. If emphasis and frequency are any indication, the most important concept for Anouilh centers on and, I suggest, is focused by Antigone's death. The program insists: 'Antigone will die this evening – once again as she has for three thousand years – dangerous, absurd, and limpid – but as necessary for the world as its laws.' The Prologue reiterates: 'She thinks that she is going to die' (9), and he invites us, 'who don't have to die this evening,' to relax and watch (9). As Hubert Gignoux says, 'Her destiny was attributed to her with her given name.'[28] And death spreads. The brothers are dead. Haemon's princely title gives him only 'the right to die' (10). Eurydice will soon 'rise and die' (10). The messenger will come to announce Haemon's death. The lexicon of 'death' – 'body,' 'cadaver,' 'burial,' and various ways of bringing it about ('assassinate,' 'cut-throat,' 'spit') – mark the play with a staccato rhythm.

Critics have made much of Antigone's reasons for dying. On considering Anouilh's play carefully, however, one cannot fail to note that every one of her explanations crumbles. She really has no duty to bury her brother; she does not believe that priestly mummery serves any function; she finally admits that her brothers were in actuality nothing but vile, self-serving, petty criminals. The *endsieg* or 'all or nothing' mentality that leads her to uphold an absolute ideal and to revolt against life's inevitable compromises, against aging, against the less-than-perfect 'happiness [*bonheur*]' of day-to-day existence, eventually forces Creon to send her to her death. Even her ultimate justifications and the purity of her final motives dissipate in the pathetic scene where she dictates the letter: 'My darling, I wanted to die. . . . I no longer know why I am dying. I'm afraid...' (79). Anouilh uses the dictation ploy to echo the words and emphasize Antigone's sense of loss (79–80). In Anouilh's version, she dies for one reason alone: destiny. She is destined to die. Just as she has died for the last three thousand years, she will inevitably, certainly, and of necessity die this evening. From first to last, Anouilh's *Antigone* is ruled by what Borgal calls an 'absurd logic.' '[N]o mortal is spared; and the condemnation confers not the least grandeur. . . . Calamity oppresses all human destinies without distinction' (78).

It is as though Anouilh had looked in his dictionary of literature and, on finding 'Sophocles, *Antigone*,' discovered the following 'meanings': (1) laws of man and laws of gods; (2) wise counsel ignored; (3) frustrated youth; (4) death and marriage; (5) fate, and so on. While Anouilh did not ignore the primary 'meanings,' what really drew his attention were fate – a minor element in the Sophoclean text – and death. He then recast the image of the original and used his new version as the focus of his allusion. Whether the individuals in his audience were previously aware or not, he turned to the image of the ancient text to insist on Antigone's fated death. The fact of her dying brought with it the assurance of a three-thousand-year-old tradition, and we understand only with difficulty how anyone could possibly doubt what the play's insistent, clear repetition and the tradition assure: Antigone will die again.[29] Fate becomes essential in Anouilh. Antigone is predestined to die. The concept of tragedy, which had generic importance for Sophocles, shifts as well to assume thematic importance and becomes another means of focusing on death for Anouilh.

Now the spring is wound tight. Nothing remains but for it to unwind. That's the handy thing about tragedy. You give it a little nudge so that it will start. . . . That's all. Afterwards, you just have to let it alone. You are at peace. It unrolls all by itself. . . . Tragedy is clean, restful, certain. . . . It is not because someone kills and someone else is killed. It's a question of casting. And then, especially, tragedy is restful, because you know that there is no more hope, no more dirty hope, because you are caught, you are finally caught like a rat. . . . In melodrama, you struggle because you hope to get out of it. It is ignoble, utilitarian. But tragedy is gratuitous, the stuff of kings. And there's nothing else to try. Finally. (38–9)

The Chorus is there to explain to the audience. The situation has been established, and because this is tragedy, there is no question about the outcome. Antigone has to die.

One of the more effective devices of the absurdists was to confront the audience with an unrealistic, highly stylized, sometimes comic situation, and then suddenly emphasize the horrible truth of reality by making the audience realize that Brecht's stylization or Ionesco's guffaws cover the anguishing truth of thoughtless men and women trailing off to slaughter, as, for example, in *The Repressible Rise of Arturo Ui*, or of helpless individuals unable to communicate or to love, as in *La Leçon*.[30] It requires a *prise de conscience*, a sudden realization that all is not as it seemed. Anouilh's *Antigone* works this same magic.

I do not know when the spectators suddenly realize that Antigone is in fact their surrogate. Perhaps it is when the guards, 'lacking imagination' (11), joyfully discuss the way they'll spend their reward while, unknowingly, under threat of death. We have just heard Creon promise that Antigone can change her mind and no one will know what she has done: 'I will have these three men disappear' (46). Perhaps it is when Creon and Antigone's debate makes it clear that there is no satisfactory reason either to live or die. Perhaps it is when the Chorus 'enters suddenly' to announce: 'That's it for Antigone. Now, Creon's turn is coming. Everyone has to go through it' (81). Perhaps it is not until the end: 'All those who had to die are dead. Those who believed one thing and then those who believed the opposite – even those who believed nothing and were caught up in the story without understanding any of it. All of them dead, very stiff, very useless, very rotten. . . . Now Creon will begin to wait for death' (84–5). Perhaps then the audience will recall that though it is possible that they 'do not have to die this evening' (9), inexorable death does await them, inevitably, certainly, and of necessity.

Anouilh's frequently mentioned success in universalizing the play, by having his characters wear modern dress and sprinkle their speech with fast cars, bars, and spicy colloquialisms, also serves the function of joining past and present and insisting that nothing has changed. Human beings die.

This version of *Antigone* has been severely criticized for depending on Sophocles and for failing to understand that the Sophoclean universe is alien to modern consciences.[31] There is neither any doubt that Anouilh did depend on Sophocles for his most powerful effect, nor that few similarities exist in the respective visions of the ancient and modern playwrights. Unfortunately, such criticism ignores the degree to which Anouilh controlled his Sophoclean text. The many, detailed similarities between the plays show how closely Anouilh had studied his Greek predecessor. Still, the changes were not accidental. Differences point to differences of intent between Anouilh and Sophocles. They thus have a function. As Sachs writes, for example, the nurse, who does not exist in Sophocles, appears in the modern version to highlight the childlike nature of Anouilh's heroine (7).

It is difficult to discover what constitutes the genesis of *Antigone*, whether it was a rhythm, or a rhyme, or an image, or a concept, or a feeling, but at some point Anouilh knew where he wanted to go, and at some point he decided to join the traditional Antigone to the work he was creating. This constitutes a parallel allusion. There are two images that are related to each other and that include elements that are virtually identical, thus revealing a common heritage, and there are elements that are more or less distinct. The differing factors of a parallel

allusion, like Anouilh's insistence on purity or integrity, remain operative in the text (or play) before our eyes, since elements having nothing
to do with the allusion continue to function, while differences like
Tiresias in the classical text are not activated and simply do not function
in the new environment. They continue to exist in the classical work
outside the alluding text. Should one turn away from Anouilh to antiquity, Sophocles' version has been neither destroyed, nor negated, nor
even impugned by what the modern playwright has done. The image
that Anouilh uses, however, is under his sway. In allusion there are two
authors of two different texts. The author of the later text takes an
image of the former and integrates it into his own work. Although the
resultant creation retains recognizable elements that allude to and thus
recall the past text, the resultant combination or outgrowth is something
quite different.

Anouilh exploits the image of Antigone much as writers exploit the
denotations and connotations of words. Should an author exploit the
word 'red' to refer to pigment and light, for example, the usage has not
negated other meanings like that of 'communist'; the latter merely
remain in the background, inactivated for the moment, but ready to be
brought in when needed. Anouilh builds an image of the traditional
Antigone that stresses death and dying, youth and fate. His Sophocles
joins tightly with the modern text. The metaphoric bond takes, the
creation grows into something that is both different from what the
classical writer did and from what Anouilh could have done without
the tradition. Because of the parallel allusion, the spectators are emphatically confronted with the inevitability of Antigone's death. It shades
every speech, every word, every movement. The allusion incites spectators to universalize the lesson of death and then to realize that they live
an absurdity similar to Antigone's. In their life, they race toward a
certain death.

Of the different varieties of allusion, those whose constituent terms
are parallel seem the simplest and are the most common. The most
famous example is doubtless Virgil's allusion to *The Odyssey* in *The
Aeneid*. One might also mention Faulkner's and Stendhal's similar allusions to the Christ story in *Light in August* and *Le Rouge et le noir*, or
Balzac's to *King Lear* in *Le Père Goriot*.[32] Extended parallel allusion is, of
course, only one manifestation of this kind of allusion. I have already
mentioned synoptic allusions like that in Du Bellay's 'Heureux qui
comme Ulysse.' Parallel allusions are often keyed by names. Zola, for
example, gave one of the protagonists of *Thérèse Raquin* the name of

Laurent. By alluding thus to St Laurent, who, according to Jacobus de Voragine's *The Golden Legend*, is considered the most excellent example of martyrdom because of the number and cruelty of the tortures he suffered, Zola stressed the physical effects of Laurent's torments.[33] But whether allusion is limited to a word, a phrase, or a part or is extended to serve as the primary device for unifying the whole of a work, as in Anouilh's *Antigone*,[34] its result is always the same: it creates an outgrowth or image that means something other than its constituent terms. Anouilh's *Antigone* is not only different from Sophocles', it is different – much different – from what it would have been if the Greek tragedy had not been available for exploitation. Still, because of the great predecessor, Anouilh was able to use allusion to invest his own play with exceptional power, as he insists upon what some consider the ultimate absurdity: vital human beings must inescapably die.

4

From Allegory to Parallel Allusion and Sources: 'Le Rideau cramoisi'

The strategy of contrasting allusion with related devices brings with it significant problems, especially when there is disagreement over the term's meaning and function, since it forces me to step into the quagmire of definition. All the intertextual terms I shall use are consecrated by tradition, this means that they have all been used and abused and become more than a little fuzzy around the edges.[1] The definitions that I advance in this study are colored, on the one hand, by my desire to avoid lexical adventurism and remain faithful to the general understanding, and, on the other, by the need to gain fuller understanding of allusion.

Once upon a time, everyone knew what an allegory was. Pierre Fontanier's definition was typical: allegory is 'a proposition which has a double meaning – one literal and the other spiritual – taken together, and which presents a thought through the image of another thought.'[2] For educated people the term was accompanied by legions of examples: Bunyan's *Pilgrim's Progress*, Ibsen's *Peer Gynt*, Goethe's *Faust*, Spenser's *The Faerie Queene*. Probably the best known example was Paul's explanation of the story of Moses as an example or type that should be understood as a spiritual quest leading to Christ (1 Cor. 10:1-11). Later writers complicated the issue somewhat. Dante, for example, thought that the interpretation could be divided into several categories: literal, mystical (which others called typological), tropologic, and anagogic.[3] Despite such refinements, the basic understanding of allegory remained pretty much the same. For Coleridge as for Aristotle, as indeed for Dante, allegory was a narrative mode of composition and interpretation that must be conceived as a binary system.[4] It occurred in many if not all the literary forms, and it used a story that gains its full meaning only when it appears in the full light of its second, abstract level. The spiritual significance of Christian's progress beyond the Giant Despair, Mr BigEnds, Ignorance, the Slough of Despond, and so on, must be conceived as John Bunyan's understanding of all pilgrims' spiritual battles as they make their way to salvation.

Recently, allegory has become considerably more troublesome. For the purposes of my attempt to illuminate the processes of allusion, neither the fact that allegory may use both personification and symbolism nor the fact that it generally exploits a context of community values (or, more recently, attitudes like Kafka's alienation) is terribly important. Identifying readers' grasp of its abstract narration with 'interpretation' has, however, enormous importance, since it has led to the suggestion that all texts and all interpretations are allegorical.[5] If interpretation and allegory are identical, then readers always construct allegories without distinction, whether reading *Le Roman de la rose* or Baudelaire's 'Correspondances' or Balzac's *Le Père Goriot*. The classical view would not readily allow the identification of allegorizing and interpretive activities, for while all texts require interpretation – whether of lyric poetry or of allegory, whether of allegory's literal or of its abstract sequences – not all texts are allegories, and imposing an allegorical interpretation on a tragedy does not an allegory make. The perimeters of interpretation and allegory are limited, distinctive, and quite clear within traditional conventions.[6] In reading allegory, the literal understanding, while reasonably coherent in and for itself, refers most importantly to another abstract understanding, which may be divided into several categories, the sum total of which constitutes an interpretation. I suppose one could compare allegory's literal and figural sequences to a living bone, where the literal plot gives support for the figural marrow. Both bone and marrow are internally coherent; they are in addition interdependent, though one might reasonably argue that the (spiritual) marrow has more importance than the (literal) bone. Readers of allegory are expected either to oscillate between literal and abstract sequences or to conceive both simultaneously and independently. As Coleridge insisted, allegory 'presumes . . . disjunction of faculties' (Coleridge 99). It is *a* binary mode of composition and interpretation.

Northrop Frye's *Anatomy of Criticism* perhaps brought the confusion of allegory and interpretation. His understanding of allegory is quite conservative: 'We have actual allegory when a poet explicitly indicates the relationship of his images to examples and precepts, and so tries to indicate how a commentary on him should proceed. A writer is being allegorical whenever it is clear that he is saying "by this I also (*allos*) mean that." If this seems to be done continuously, we may say, cautiously, that what he is writing "is" an allegory. . . . Allegory, then, is a contrapuntal technique, like canonical imitation in music' (90). Where Frye's analysis has caused trouble is in the statement that 'all commentary is allegorical interpretation, an attaching of ideas to the structure of poetic imagery' (89). It is worth insisting, however, that Frye did not indulge in the vague application of the term 'allegory' to all works of literature. His statement should be read in the light of his previous distinction: 'All formal allegories have, *ipso facto*, a strong thematic interest, though it does not follow, as is often said, that any thematic criticism of a work of fiction will turn it into an allegory. . . . Genuine allegory is a structural element in literature: it has to be there, and cannot be added by critical interpretation alone' (53–4). The crux of Frye's distinctions resides in his view of a continuum encompassing literature. At one extreme,

we meet the continuous allegories, like *The Pilgrim's Progress* and *The Faerie Queene*, and then the free-style allegories [like the work of Ariosto, Goethe, Ibsen, Hawthorne 'in which allegory may be picked up and dropped again at pleasure']. . . . Next come the poetic structures with a large and insistent doctrinal interest, in which the internal fictions are exempla, like the epics of Milton. Then we have, in the exact center, works in which the structure of imagery, however suggestive, has an implicit relation only to events and ideas, and which includes the bulk of Shakespeare. Below this, poetic imagery begins to recede from example and precept and become increasingly ironic and paradoxical. Here the modern critic begins to feel more at home, the reason being that this type is more consistent with the modern literal view of art, the sense of the poem as withdrawn from explicit statement.   (91)

If I reserve the term 'allegory' for Frye's first and second categories, I accept the classical view, and I prepare a useful distinction with allusion. 'Interpretation' remains troublesome, however, at least if it is without exception allegorical. It seems more useful to term 'interpretation' that naive or sophisticated mental process taking place when texts are read. Although in reality we do not understand exactly what happens in a reader's mind, there seems no doubt that readers make certain distinctions. While the interpretation may rightly or obtusely refuse to include anything but the story of a character acting, it may recognize another parallel sequence that adds some sort of figural meaning to the first. Allegory's second, abstract sequence is suggested and controlled by the first. If the abstract sequence is, however, integrated into the first in a way that distinguishes it from allegory, the metaphorical union simply broadens the significance of the complex of meaning occurring in the reader's mind, as is, of course, the case with most 'mimetic' litera- ture of the last several centuries. Such an integration is not allegorical. When Proust's *A la recherche* intimates that the hero constitutes a Parsi- fal on a sacred quest, he is by no means suggesting that the reader establish an independent tropological sequence. Rather, the allusion falls or folds back onto the 'literal' sequence, adding such concepts as inno- cence, quest, holiness, and so on to the increasingly polysemous pro- gression of complexes. The second 'chain' of images may resist integra- tion into the first, maintaining its independence. If the first, literal sequence is subordinate to the second, we may have allegory (subject to such things as personification, symbols, community values, and coherence). If the reader's other mental sequence involves a preexisting text and combines metaphorically with the first, we have allusion. In allusion, all the sequences in the reader's mind, whether literal or figural, maintain their identity, though they go on to create something additional, thus knighting Proust's hero, for example, or crowning Anouilh's Antigone with fatal destiny, or adding the satanic to Barbey's 'Le Rideau cramoisi' ('The Crimson Curtain').

In 1874 Barbey d'Aurevilly published a collection of six stories that he called *Les Diaboliques* (*The She-Devils*). Barbey had pinned his hopes on the collection. For years he had been working steadily as a novelist and short-story writer, but few people knew of him as anything but a critic. He expected this collection to make his reputation once and for all. That it did, and it remains his crowning achievement. Unfortunately, the notoriety that quickly surrounded the tales aroused the interest of the public prosecutor. Barbey was accused of a crime against public morality, and all the unsold copies were seized. The case never actually went to trial, but it was a close thing. To quash the charges, Barbey had to agree to the destruction of the 480 copies in the prosecutor's hands. Still, *Les Diaboliques* did bring him a certain amount of money and fame, and from then on he was able to place his creative work more easily.

Les Diaboliques has been frequently acclaimed a masterpiece. Remy de Gourmont even went so far as to say that if Balzac had written the collection, it would have been Balzac's masterpiece.[7] When one thinks that Balzac wrote *Le Père Goriot*, *Le Cousin Pons*, and *La Cousine Bette*, to name but three, it is hard not to believe that Gourmont was somewhat carried away by his enthusiasm. Unquestionably, however, the stories in *Les Diaboliques* are excellent. All of them turn around a diabolical woman, all are peopled by extraordinary characters filled with a seemingly inexhaustible supply of passion, and most include at least one horrifying, indeed monstrous, event. Barbey, whose love for the Gothic novel is evident, was clearly a descendant of the Romantics. Violence, vengeance, cruelty, sex, blood, murder, blasphemy – these are his subjects. And like so many of the Romantics he constantly aimed at causing an effect in the reader.[8] His subject matter and his treatment imply a Barbey who wanted his reader to shiver with dread and horror. Although the stories take place in realistic settings, the narrators recount extraordinary rather than commonplace happenings, and they tell of them as though their truth cannot be doubted.

Several important features make *Les Diaboliques* distinctive, however. In reading writers like Pétrus Borel, Monk Lewis, or Hoffmann, whatever their intent, one is struck not by their characters' souls, but rather by what they do. With Barbey's tales, one is always drawn to wonder *why* they do as they do, to divine the deepest corners of their hearts, to penetrate the mysterious reality hidden behind the deeds and persons of the stories. Barbey was, I suppose, interested in evil deeds, but he was far more interested in evil, a quality that cannot be described. It can only be suggested. As Marcel Proust pointed out in a remarkably perceptive passage, Barbey Aurevilly's stories and novels always have at their center a 'hidden reality revealed by a material trace.'[9] That reality remains a tormenting mystery. When Barbey succeeded in creating the conviction that it existed, he had done what he set out to do.

'Le Rideau cramoisi' appears among the examples Proust cites. The story sets up a series of veils: the curtain, the table, the hand, the girl herself. Though we penetrate several layers, the mysterious reality beneath continues intact, and the girl remains forever an enigma. What is her power? What drives her? What is she? The title revolves around the moral being of the girl – if, indeed, she has one. The story shows, I think, Barbey d'Aurevilly at his best, and, what is more important for our purposes, it provides an excellent example of extended parallel allusion in a context of considerable complexity and one that can also help us to distinguish allusion from allegory and source.

Like so many of Barbey's tales, 'Le Rideau cramoisi' is a story within a story. The first speaker, whom I shall call the narrator, remembers a trip he once made in a coach shared with the Viscount de Brassard. Because of an accident, the coach stopped for repairs beneath a window from which shone 'light . . . softened by a double crimson curtain.'[10] After Brassard mentioned the curtain, the narrator saw the viscount's deathly pallor and sensed his trembling – both reactions that were highly uncharacteristic of this brave dandy. At the narrator's prompting, Brassard began his revelation. Some thirty-five years before, as a young officer, he had lived in that very room behind such a curtain and had taken his meals with his undistinguished bourgeois hosts. One day, without having received any prior warning, he was confronted by their astonishingly beautiful daughter, Mlle Albertine (or Alberte, as she was also called). The impassive Albertine paid him no attention, and he soon became indifferent to her. Then, one evening, while maintaining her 'air of a princess during a ceremony' (RC 2.35) she reached beneath the table and squeezed his hand. Brassard immediately fell in love, and the girl's parents did not suspect the 'mysterious and terrible drama which was taking place beneath the table' (RC 2.34). References to her graceful hands and her queenly manner begin to reappear insistently. The next night he slipped her a letter, but a month passed without further communication. Though the young man's love for the impassive girl slowly turned to hate, he could do nothing to combat his obsession for the girl. One night his door opened, and she fell into his arms half nude. They consummated their passion while listening fearfully for the sound of her parents. In her eyes he saw madness, and neither of them was able to forget, 'in the most passionate of our transports, the horrible situation she was creating for both of us' (RC 2.45). But their virtually wordless affair continued for more than six months. Alberte/Albertine came every other night, unless she accidentally awakened her parents while passing through their room. When that happened, she found a satisfactory excuse and returned to her bed.

At this point the narrator interrupts Brassard once again 'so as not to seem too caught up in his story, though I really was, for with dandies scarcely anything but a joke will get you a little respect' (RC 2.48). He knows of a similar story: every night Mlle de Guise's lover used to come in through the window and join her in the bedroom she shared with her grandmother. Once, the young lady's enjoyment was a bit too noisy, and she awakened the grandmother, asleep behind the bed-curtains. Though the elderly lady was reassured with an excuse, the girl never again dared open the window for her lover.

Brassard brushes off the implied comparison. Despite all dangers, Alberte/Albertine continued to frequent his room until she finally died during a voluptuous spasm. With a touch typical of Barbey, the viscount, thinking she had only fainted, continued his love-making. Then he became aware of her lifelessness, and he made frantic attempts to resuscitate her. All efforts failed, even blood-letting which only resulted in mutilating her arm. The young man was terrified for himself and ashamed of the fear that dishonored him. Furthermore, 'The thought of this mother whose daughter I had perhaps killed in dishonoring her, weighed on my heart even more than Alberte's corpse' (RC 2.52–3), but he was far too frightened to return the girl's body through her parents' bedroom to her bed. Instead, he fled the room, the house, and the town, leaving the dead body on his couch and his problem in the hands of his colonel. No one ever told him what happened, and, prevented by 'something which resembled this fear that I didn't want to experience again' (RC 2.56), he never asked. Throughout the rest of his life the Viscount de Brassard bore a 'black stain' that 'diminished the pleasure of his dissipations' (RC 2.57). Because of his cowardice and what the story specifically terms his crime against hospitality and justice (RC 2.46), the girl and her family were undoubtedly dishonored.

Then, the story told, the interlocutors fall into a moody silence. Suddenly the viscount grasps the narrator.

'Look!' he said. 'Look at the curtain!'
The slender shadow of a woman's figure had just crossed it.
'Albertine's shade!' said the [viscount]. 'Fortune is mocking us tonight,' he added bitterly.   (RC 2.57)

But the coach starts on its way, and the narrator concludes, 'We soon left behind the mysterious window that I still see in my dreams with its crimson curtain' (ibid).

So the story ends. Although the melodramatic elements have little to recommend them to modern tastes, the tale is surprisingly powerful. Le Corbeillier even considers it a 'masterpiece of composition and style.'[11] I would not go so far. It seems to me that there are flaws, particularly in Barbey's command of his characters' idiom. I think particularly of Brassard's description of his feelings while holding Alberte/Albertine's hand, which runs to exclamations and clichés.

No, I'll never be able to make you understand this sensation and my astonishment! I felt a hand which daringly took mine beneath the table. I thought I was dreaming... or rather I didn't think anything at all... I just had the unbelievable sensation of that audacious hand which sought mine under my napkin! And it was as extraordinary as it was unexpected. All my blood, fired by this touch, rushed from my heart to this hand, as though drawn by it, and then, as though forced by a pump, it rushed furiously back up to my heart! I was dazed... my ears rang. I must have become terribly pale. I thought I was going to faint.   (RC 2.33)

The rather imprecise words of an impressionable and inarticulate young man continue for another page, despite the fact that, at the moment of telling the story, Brassard has become a dandy par excellence, the master of any situation, and certainly articulate. These qualities are essential to the tale, making Brassard's unevocative clichés seem out of character. Elsewhere, for example in the death scene, Barbey more skillfully preserves the mature Brassard's speech while nonetheless communicating the emotions felt long ago as a youth.[12]

I do not wish to continue picking at 'Le Rideau cramoisi.' Fault-finding is an easy game and can be done with the best of works. Far better, though considerably more difficult, to wonder why it seems so powerful. The very fact that it has passed the test of time, that critics continue to study it and readers to read it, is suggestive. The effect of the story does not seem limited to any one element; the tale is rather so much of a piece that even its minor flaws fail to damage seriously the experience it provides. Nonetheless, it does seem to me that a prior reading of *Le Rouge et le noir* (*The Red and the Black*) is of considerable importance to the power of the entire tale. Because Stendhal had successfully used his novel to create a certain type of emotional response, Barbey was able to play on this affective preparation with parallel plot, themes, and images.

I would even suggest that the success of 'Le Rideau cramoisi' results to a great degree from Barbey's skillful use of the sentiments Stendhal had aroused with another story. Barbey's creation was not a copy of Stendhal; nonetheless, it is very close. Regardless of the fact that Mathilde initiated their affair by squeezing Julien's arm rather than his hand, in both cases the women are the instigators. Like Brassard, Julien violated the codes of honor, hospitality, and justice in seducing Mathilde. Stendhal's protagonist also dishonored the women he loved and their families. And *Le Rouge et le noir* likewise terminates with a mutilated body. The love-war analogies that Kelly highlights in Barbey's seduction are at least as important in Stendhal's seminal account.[13] It makes little difference that Alberte/Albertine went to Brassard's room and Julien to Mme de Rênal's and Mathilde's, or that Barbey's female and Stendhal's male are disfigured in death. The parallels are too clear to be missed, though the differences doubtless point to the respective characters who bear the burden of guilt. Julien and Brassard both make love to their mistresses despite the danger of parental discovery; their egotism leads them to commit crimes that result in intense feelings of guilt and dishonor; and the two stories end with the damaged body of one of the principals. Brassard, because of what he calls 'the cowardly state of my demoralized soul (one of the Emperor's phrases that I later understood!)' (RC 2.54), considers suicide, as does Julien. Brassard rejects the idea because of his dedication to the career of arms. Julien, because, as he puts it, 'Napolean lived.'[14] Stendhal makes it clear that society represents the most important culprit in Julien's adventure, while Barbey's descriptions of the little provincial town, which is devoid of interest and activity, serve to suggest a similar, though not identical, cause. Moreover, the 'large couch of blue morocco,' on which Brassard takes Alberte/Albertine, appears repeatedly,[15] as does the 'large blue couch' on which Stendhal's Mathilde habitually sits.[16] The English word 'Really' that served Barbey as an epigraph parallels that of Le Rouge et le noir: 'Truth, the bitter truth' a quotation Barbey used as the epigraph for another novel with the Stendhalian title L'Amour impossible. The title of 'Le Rideau cramoisi' also comes from a passage in Le Rouge et le noir that Barbey, obsessed with themes of blasphemy, could scarcely have missed, for Julien attempts to murder Mme de Rênal inside a church whose windows are hung with crimson curtains: 'Julien went into Verrières' new church. All the high windows of the church were hung with crimson curtains. Julien found himself a few steps behind Mme de Rênal's bench. . . . At that instant, the young cleric who was serving the mass rang for the elevation. Mme de Rênal bowed her head . . . Julien fired at her.'[17] But the clearest reminder of Le Rouge et le noir occurs in the seemingly digressive story about Mlle de Guise and her lover, with which the narrator interrupts Brassard. We remember that on Julien's second visit up the ladder and through Mathilde's window, the latter's laughter awakened her mother (RN 360).

Within Barbey's text, the allusion works metaphorically, with one term Le Rouge et le noir and the other the story told by Brassard. As we pass from the title, the epigraph, and the descriptive detail to the events recounted and the characters involved within 'Le Rideau cramoisi,' the Stendhalian term gradually becomes more consistent and more powerful. Were we to consider Le Rouge et le noir isolated from Barbey, as is normally the case, it clearly has polyvalent significance – much of which has little if anything to do with 'Le Rideau cramoisi.' Brassard's story certainly does not represent an attack on the values of a corrupt society, for example. Neither is the viscount a hypocrite; nor is he unable to establish viable relationships with other men. Irrelevant Stendhalian associations remain, however, in the background, unilluminated. Other devices highlight the significant elements in Brassard's tale that are not pertinent to the allusion.

On considering *Le Rouge et le noir*, one should note that Stendhal's Julien represents a tragic figure possessing a tragic flaw (that is, his class, his genius, and his egotism, which thrust him into a Hobbesian world of warfare where, at least until his imprisonment, he is able neither to communicate effectively with his equals nor to form viable human relationships or conventions based on honor, respect, and reason). As Borgerhoff and, to a lesser degree, De Sacy and Hemmings have seen, Julien is fated to fall and die.[18] Stendhal also insists that Julien is not really responsible for his actions – for example, in the epigraph to chapter twenty-one of book one: 'Alas, our frailty is the cause, not we: / For such as we are made of, such we be.' Consequently, although I think some efforts to whitewash Julien go too far, I agree with the basic conclusions of those modern critics, starting as nearly as I have been able to determine with Léon Blum,[19] who would absolve him and shift the blame to his youth, his insensitive father, the perverse Mme de Rênal, who seduced him (such, at least, is Blum's opinion), his hypocritical fellow seminarians, the intractable Mathilde, who forced herself on him, the repressive unfeeling society of the day, and his courage and sense of honor, which would not allow him to bypass a challenge. Indeed, Julien appears incapable of controlling his destiny in any but a superficial way. Still, he trespasses against his fellows, and his seemingly predestined fate is clearly foreshadowed by the blood and decapitation imagery. He thereby resembles the traditional conception of a tragic hero. In another epoch he might well have succeeded, but like many other Romantic heroes, he was born as a functional exile at a time and place where understanding and success were impossible.

Barbey's Brassard, likewise an exceptional man, 'differed . . . so much from the men of our day' (RC 2.17). True, he did not suffer from a tragic destiny, but he confronted an equally inexplicable series of events against which he seems powerless. At no time was he in command. On the sole occasion when he attempted to assume the masculine role by writing a 'beseeching, imperious, intoxicated letter from a man who had already had his first taste of happiness and who demanded a second' (RC 2.36), he found himself denied even a repetition of what he had already experienced.[20] Alberte/Albertine resembled an 'Infanta' (RC 2.31, 33, 37, 48) or a 'Princess' (RC 2.35, 45); she took his hand and with 'the same sovereignty' (RC 2.34) pressed his foot; and 'it was far more she who took me in her arms than I who took her in mine' (RC 2.45). In short, she initiated their affair; she caused him to make love to her; she chose the parental home for their meetings; and when she died at such an inauspicious moment, who could blame an ordinary young man for his indecisiveness and cowardly flight? But is that enough to absolve Brassard? We know that his courage was later thoroughly tested and proven (even his youth would seem insufficient to explain the radical deviation from the pattern apparent in the rest of his life). The additional fact of his self-sufficiency and vanity (he loved to don his dress uniform for his solitary pleasure) makes it even more surprising that he would so forget himself as to act the poltroon. 'Le Rideau cramoisi' emphasizes that Brassard was no ordinary man. His uncharacteristic cowardice is understandable only if we accept another movement worked into the fabric of the story: diabolism and diabolical she-devils.

No one can doubt that Alberte/Albertine is a diabolical woman. Prepared by the collection's title, *Les Diaboliques*, the identification of Alberte/Albertine and the devil finds support in a number of passages. Her black, cold eyes and general coldness are frequently noted. When she takes Brassard's hand and later presses her foot against his, he feels as though he has been immersed in 'one of those baths which are at first insufferably hot, but to which you become accustomed and in which you are finally so comfortable that you would willingly believe that one day the damned might become cool and comfortable in the blazing coals of their hell' (RC 2.34). She has 'such a frightening precocity in depravity' (RC 2.35) and is both 'devilishly provocative' (RC 2.36) and 'infernally calm' (RC 2.41). In addition, Brassard talks of 'the face of that devilish woman who possessed me as pious people say the devil does' (RC 2.43). Finally, when she actually appears in his room, she is compared to a 'supernatural . . . vision' (RC 2.44).

Barbey seems to have been so sure of his ability to make Alberte/Albertine appear diabolical that he weakened the significance of vocabulary related to 'devil.' For Brassard, 'devil' and its cognates are mere expletives. He speaks, for example, of his own 'devil of a face' (RC 2.23). By attenuating the force of such words, Barbey avoided 'almost too great an insistence' on the theme of diabolism.[21] Nevertheless, the suggestion of the infernal provided by this vocabulary offers sufficient indication of the only possible explanation for Brassard's helplessness and cowardice. For those not deaf to the reverberations of Stendhal's masterpiece, where the theme of tragic fate is so strong, the many allusions to *Le Rouge et le noir* compel a conscious or unconscious search for an analogous movement in 'The Crimson Curtain.' In Stendhal's novel, internal and external forces destine Julien for destruction. In Barbey's tale, only an external power seems at work, but its strength is no less potent. While ambition, personality flaws, and an unjust society cause Julien's damnation, only one force dominates Brassard: Albertine. The devil works through her. By the devil, I do not necessarily imply that character of whom the Romantics were so enamored, though I would not follow Colla and rule him out definitively;[22] I mean simply an overpowering force of evil. But whether or not the red-suited villain is at work, Albertine leads Brassard into torment. Because of her diabolical power, Brassard was no more responsible than Julien, though he nevertheless committed crimes for which he suffered throughout the rest of his life.

Of course, *Le Rouge et le noir* is not the only element that creates the sensation of Albertine's diabolical nature. Constant awareness of the themes of the accompanying tales and of the group title *Les Diaboliques* would doubtless reveal the satanism so important to this story. Nor is the story devoid of other allusions – as might have been desirable for this example of uncomplicated parallel allusion. The well-established theme of the devil incarnate as woman[23] may also encourage the reader to see Albertine as a *diabolique*. It is similarly possible, as Mark Suino suggested to me, that the crimson of the curtains acts in the manner of what a Russian formalist critic would term a 'minus device.' If so, the color, which normally represents life, blood, passion, or the fires of hell, automatically suggests its opposite – black. Death and the dark forces would then be conjured up, and *Le Rouge et le noir* as well. Consideration should be given to this suggestion, for the story turns around 'a hidden reality,' whether it be the banal silhouette that makes Brassard shiver, the acceptable front Albertine and Brassard display above the table while beneath there is hand-play, or, finally, Albertine herself, the reality whose opposite is suggested but not explained. It may even be that Barbey expected his heroine's name to suggest the operation of diabolical forces. In Hoffmann's 'Le Choix d'une fiancée' (1819), two of the three suitors of an Albertine are fiendishly afflicted through the intervention of a sorcerer. Hoffmann was enormously popular in France and well known to Barbey.[24] Still, there are only two corresponding elements: the name, Albertine, and the background thaumaturgy.

There are, then, other means by which Barbey suggests Albertine's fatal power. The most important and the most pervasive is, however, the allusion to *Le Rouge et le noir*. If 'Le Rideau cramoisi' were separated from the other stories in the collection and from the group-title, I suspect the diabolical influence on Brassard would be sensed strongly only by someone familiar with Stendhal's masterpiece. This, I think, is the essential function of the allusion. As suggested before, it highlights the egotism, the crime, the punishment, and the dishonor. Because it encompasses the whole story, the death of Albertine also gives the feeling of completion – of closure. It appears more important, however, that the repeated, even insistent, allusions to Stendhal's work cause the two terms of this enlarged metaphor to be seen in conjunction and, thus, elicit the latent but principal theme. One term of Barbey's allusion, *Le Rouge et le noir*, has tragic destiny among its associations. When metaphorically related to the other term, the story told by Brassard, the latter's inability to control his adventure is emphasized. Immediately, the descriptions Brassard gives of his condition after the girl's death become even more striking: 'this hideous fear,' 'the horrible situation,' 'my mind cruelly spinning like a top,' 'Dreadful hallucination! there were moments when Albertine's corpse seemed to fill the whole room,' 'the collapse which was taking place within me,' 'the horrible abyss in which I was struggling' – in short, phrases destined to depict a fear so great that even the much older and far more cynical dandy would still feel the effects. The allusion prepares and elicits the belief that an evil force was at work.

Though the potential of allusion was not unknown to Barbey in other efforts,[25] perhaps nowhere else did he show such a mastery of this artistic device. He apparently recognized that by alluding through image, plot, and theme parallels to another well-known work of literature, he could stimulate affective patterns of a previous response, and this by extremely subtle means. The allusion highlights and supports Brassard's story and, as well, elicits powerfully the theme of diabolism, which is nowhere referred to explicitly. Only after 'Le Rideau cramoisi' receives a careful critical reading does the allusion become clear, though it doubtless worked below the surface of understanding before. When one becomes conscious of the allusion, one might assume that Barbey's use of *Le Rouge et le noir* as a vigorous tool to further his own artistic ends and affect his reader constitutes one of the major reasons for the success of 'Le Rideau cramoisi.'

And readers do think of Stendhal while reading the story. Jacques-Henry Bornecque said for example in his edition of *Les Diaboliques*: 'Barbey was not unaware that Stendhal (who is the first example which comes naturally to one's mind) wrote . . . of two women who subordinated everything to love, then – after having created Mathilde de la Mole, of whom Albertine is occasionally worthy – that he...'[26] Nonetheless, to the best of my knowledge, no one has noted the allusion that interests me here. In the case of modern critics, there is perhaps a good reason why they would resist or repress resonances of *Le Rouge et le noir*, why, even if fully conscious of Stendhalian overtones, they would hesitate to write about it. The fact is that Barbey's allusion depends upon a dated understanding of *Le Rouge et le noir*. Today Stendhal no longer means what he did to his nineteenth-century audience.

These former readers watched Julien while his obsessive ambition and vanity drove him to grasp and hold Mme de Rênal's hand, to seduce and in the process dishonor her, to defy the wishes of his friend and benefactor, the Abbé Chélan, by troubling the uncertain peace the poor woman found after Julien's departure. They followed Julien as he capriciously misused his power (e.g., *RN* 278–9), as his undoubted courage was proved, and as he betrayed the confidence of his friend, the Abbé Picard, and of his patron, M. de la Mole, by accepting the spoiled willful Mathilde's invitation to possess her. And they were filled with anguished fascination, well aware of the attractions of this charming, genial, valorous protagonist and of his infernal misdeeds. Despite Julien's genius, his occasionally sincere love for both Mme de Rênal and Mathilde, and the courage revealed in his attack on the oppressive forces of society, he committed heinous crimes: not only did he attempt to murder Mme de Rênal, but he betrayed his friends and benefactors and dishonored his women. Though the nineteenth-century reader might, like Taine, try to understand the motivations of this protagonist, such an attempt never implied an effort to excuse him. 'I do not wish to excuse him; I wish only to show that he is basically capable of being very generous, very grateful, good, disposed to tenderness and all the niceties of disinterested action, and yet act like an egotist, exploit men, and seek his pleasure and greatness by means of others' misery.'[27] As Babou put it in 1846, Julien was a 'sublime knave' filled with 'repugnant grandeur.'[28] Even Julien knew, and repeatedly said, that he deserved death (*RN* 452, 454, 456, 482). Both his guilt and the fatal fascination he inspired are essential to 'Le Rideau cramoisi.'

In 1854, Sainte-Beuve, a decidedly unenthusiastic critic of Stendhal, announced 'a new generation which is beginning to become infatuated with his works, to inquire into him, to study all aspects of him almost as though he were an ancient, almost as though he were a classical writer' ('Stendhal' 301). Judging from Chapron, the admiration of some readers later approached religious veneration:

It was during an intermission of an opening night at the Cluny theater. The critics, strangely drawn by two acts worthy of a loony bin, had taken refuge in the nearest cabaret. . . . Barbey, accompanied by a young man with an agreeable face, came in. . . .

'Ouf!' said the young man as he collapsed in a chair, 'I'm in a state of inverted imagination!'²⁹ Instinctively, I raised my head and let out a sort of whinny, like a warhorse at the familiar sound of a bugle.

Negligently, affecting a disinterested air, I murmured . . . in respect to the author of the play: 'Ah! if lettres de cachet still existed he wouldn't have dared!' In his turn, the young man shivered. These two quotations from Stendhal placed this stranger and me on friendly ground. The admiration, I would even call it the mad love for *Le Rouge et le noir* forms a sort of freemasonry.

Jean Richepin who happened by . . . introduced us. Richepin is also a Stendhalian or, more exactly, an admirer of *Le Rouge et le noir*. Between us, he isn't up to par. Starting with the two hundredth page, he can't remember some of the text.

My new comrade, Paul Bourget, the delicate critic and the charming poet, passed the rest of the evening with me. We recited *Le Rouge et le noir* until the wee hours.³⁰

Perhaps Zola had good reason to go after this group of Stendhalians (who gathered, I might add, well before the oft-cited 1880 date Stendhal picked as the point at which he would come into his own) who glorified the Romantic elements, that is the 'phantasmagoric parts, the pigheaded exaggerations, the temperamental bombast.' Indeed, Zola felt that Barbey's understanding of Stendhal and Balzac was 'the attack of Romantic insanity which spoiled his talent.'³¹

Barbey's admiration for Stendhal was to prove long-lived. As early as 1853, in 'Stendhal et Balzac,' he had equated Stendhal with Balzac: both were masters, he insisted, but of different sorts. Other reports make it clear that his veneration for 'Stendhal, who published . . . things that were as new as they were profound, Stendhal, the inventive author of *Le Rouge et le noir*' ('Doudan' 300), was not restricted to his published criticism.[32] He must have known aesthetes like the later Chapron and Bourget who shivered on hearing phrases from the novel worked into conversations. He could doubtless watch the phenomenon described by Bourget: 'the effect of incurable intoxication. When this novel doesn't revolt the reader, it bewitches him' ('Stendhal' 309). And he surely knew, as did Bourget, that *Le Rouge et le noir* continued 'to have better than admirers, it had fanatics, and thus justified the statement of one of his contemporaries: "Those that Beyle has bitten remain bitten"' ('L'Art du roman' 43). Barbey must have known all this, for in 1853 he said, 'As for us, we do not know whether someone as superfine as Stendhal-Beyle, with this flavor and rarified taste, will ever be popular, but we do know that he has resolved the most difficult problem of literature ... which consists in exercising great power without having great popularity' ('Stendhal et Balzac' 13).

As Harry Levin has suggested, Bourget attempted to retell *Le Rouge et le noir* in *Le Disciple* (*Gates of Horn* 128). By comparison, his version seems clumsy and overt, while Barbey understood more fully the potential of the enchantment that remains long after reading Stendhal's masterpiece. Subtly, he alluded to it. The most ardent Stendhalian might not be consciously aware of the allusions, but the bewitchment Barbey sought does not result from an appeal to the conscious mind alone. He suggested as much in the dedication of a copy of *Les Diaboliques* that he sent to Marthe Brandès: 'If you bewitch all of them, / Sorceress be cruel to them... / But you, Mademoiselle, you! / Let none of them bewitch you!' (2.1599–1600). With the title, numerous details, and plot parallels, Barbey attempted, and, I suggest, succeeded in reactivating the pattern of fascination and horror etched deep in the minds of *Le Rouge et le noir*'s admirers by Stendhal, whom Barbey termed, 'this strange spirit who resembles a serpent, who has its coils, its windings, its tortuosity, its flicking tongue, its venom, its prudence, its passionate calm, and for whom everyone's imagination will be Eve' ('De Stendhal' 37). Even as early as the 1850s, Barbey could be sure of a public that, at the very least, would sense the resonance of his allusion to Stendhal's novel, and by 1874, when 'Le Rideau cramoisi' appeared, this audience was quite large. This fact should not be overlooked, for as suggested before, allusion must be perceived by someone – perhaps just the author when he becomes his own reader, though Valéry would have us believe that 'no one writes for himself alone.'

And so we have an author and an audience that knew *Le Rouge et le noir*, and 'Le Rideau cramoisi,' which alludes to it with title, epigraph, image, detail, character, and plot parallels. Stendhal's novel serves as one term of the metaphorical allusion, and the tale told by the Viscount de Brassard the other. The conjunction of the two terms emphasizes the common elements: egotistical protagonists who, seemingly without volition, confront a force greater than themselves, and in the process offend against the social codes of honor and hospitality. Moreover, the metaphorical functioning of the allusion serves as the principal device for eliciting the essential theme of satanism. The two earlier terms are not equal, and one term alone cannot communicate allusive meaning. That comes only when the sensitive reader synthesizes both, thus bringing *Le Rouge et le noir* into a reading of 'Le Rideau cramoisi.'

The external orientation of much Barbey scholarship seems directly relevant to the fact that, while the allusion of 'Le Rideau cramoisi' to *Le Rouge et le noir* has been ignored (surely, at one point or another, it was sensed though not acted upon), scholars have in vain devoted much effort to discovering the source of the story. With no proof other than the titillating love stories he and other biographers have constructed from scanty facts, Canu claims, for example, that: 'The adventure of 'Le Rideau cramoisi' happened in his youth to him [i.e., Barbey] and not to the Viscount de Brassard.'[33] According to A. Le Corbeillier, Pierre Louÿs suggested as a source a story in the *Mémoires du Père de la Joye* where the narrator carried two drugged sisters back to their bed located next to their mother's, after having ravished them (83). Had the roles simply been reversed from 'Le Rideau cramoisi' or *Léa* (as is the case when Mirbeau's concupiscent Célestine causes the death of Monsieur Georges in the *Journal d'une femme de chambre* [1900]), without the addition of the narcotic, one might be more convinced. As Jacques Petit clearly understood, stories with such superficial similarities are legion. To prove his point, Petit cites Balzac's story of a doctor who delivers an illegitimate child after having crossed the room of the woman's unknowing and sleeping husband (2.1280). Philippe Berthier suggests an anecdote in Stendhal's *Rome, Naples et Florence*: Don Niccola S*** nightly risks his life by going through the terrible Prince C***'s bedroom to visit his daughter, Lauretta.[34] One could also recall Valmont's adventure with Cécile Volanges in *Les Liaisons dangereuses*, or Brantôme's 'very honest and beautiful lady' who leaves her sleeping husband to guard 'the cuckold's nest' while she communes with a visiting lover,[35] or Nerval's story of Angélique de Longueval, whose lover used to visit her by using the window as a door (he too ran the risk of death),[36] or, of course, Julien Sorel's trips to Mme de Rênal's and Mathilde's rooms. These examples relate to only one aspect of Barbey's story: illicit love coupled with a dangerous passage and the peril of discovery. I know of no story prior to 'Le Rideau cramoisi' that has as well the themes both of the devil incarnate as woman and of necrophily, though *Le Rouge et le noir*, if we remember the vision of Mathilde kissing Julien's decapitated head, might present a possible exception (*RN* 507). But should we not insist on a prior combination of all the themes and events found in Barbey and settle for sources of isolated elements, as is the custom of scholars interested in such matters,[37] the possible sources increase enormously. Théophile Gautier's 'La Morte amoureuse' includes necrophily and a 'fatal woman,' but so do many others, as Mario Praz has established in *The Romantic Agony*. I have already mentioned Hoffmann's 'Le Choix d'une fiancée.' Such themes were commonplace throughout the nineteenth century and before. How many writers have been inspired by the Hero-Leander or Pyramus-Thisbe myths? Barbey knew the work of Brantôme, of Gautier, of Hoffmann, of Nerval, of Balzac, of Stendhal. He may have known the *Mémoires du Père de la Joye* or any number of other similar stories. Confronted with such a multitude of potential sources, we should not be surprised that this search has thus far ended with a question mark. The source may have been in a story Barbey heard or read; or it might even have been one of his own adventures. He may have had no source other than his imagination. We do not know. It is interesting to note, however, that the quest for sources has not provided the slightest comprehension of why 'Le Rideau cramoisi' is, although not a masterpiece, 'one of Barbey's most successful tales' (Rogers 109). Further – on leaving aside Hoffmann's 'Le Choix d'une fiancée,' which, as already mentioned, functions minimally – only one of the suggested 'sources' has any importance, if we consider Barbey's story as a completed work, subject to a reader. That one, *Le Rouge et le noir*, works within 'Le Rideau cramoisi' and, though perhaps not required for its understanding, is essential to its effect. The other 'sources' remain external to the tale and contribute nothing, which is not to say that they had no impact on the composition. At the moment of writing, they may well have influenced Barbey enormously. We have no way of knowing. And if Stendhal's novel not only functions as an allusive element, but constitutes a source as well, there are surely others. We still cannot be certain of Barbey's source. We do know the work to which he alluded.

I do not wish to question the validity of source studies. The more-or-less-tenuous conclusions about influences on an author or his sources frequently give insights into the creative processes. Robert J. Niess's finely nuanced, solid study, *Zola, Cézanne, and Manet: A Study of L'Oeuvre*,[38] is a case in point. Niess dispels the beliefs that Zola either plagiarized or wrote a biography of the young Cézanne, and he goes on to make us more conscious of the authors' invention and art. Likewise, though for different reasons, Mario Praz's monumental *The Romantic Agony* is valuable, for it helps us to understand a major aspect of the nineteenth century. Perhaps it is worth remembering, however, that contrary to the impression with which one is left after having read Fernand Letessier's edition of Chateaubriand's *Atala, René, Les Aventures du dernier Abencérage*,[39] we do not discover an artist's artistry by subtracting all his sources. Moreover, in a somewhat different vein, although it may well be important, as Plattard has suggested, 'in order to analyze [the] artistic invention [of Rabelais], to know what image his memory retained of contemporary society,'[40] it is more important to study the way the 'sources' finally function in the completed text.

In the end, whether other works actually become a part of the text being read determines whether a possible 'source' deserves a reader's attention. Take, for example, the already mentioned episode in *Le Journal d'une femme de chambre* and a similar adventure in a popular espionage novel by Jean Bruce, *Les Espions de Pirée* (*OSS 117*).[41] Barbey's 'Le Rideau cramoisi' may have been the source for both. In Bruce's novel, Enrique tells that he once rendered nightly visits to the daughter of a deaf mother by passing through a bedroom window. One night, after he had 'started to do this and that to her,' he discovered that she was dead, and 'I ran as though the devil were after me.' Neither Mirbeau nor Bruce makes significant use of Barbey's creation; only the elements of plot are borrowed; the resonance of Barbey's tale is not exploited. Perhaps the story of sex and death has value for itself alone, in that it may excite a reader's interest; it may also help to build an understanding of Bruce's Enrique and, in Mirbeau, of Célestine. In these two cases, the recognition, however tentative, of the source in no way helps us to understand the novels; it does not lead to a deeper appreciation; nor, for that matter, does it help us to evaluate the two works, if indeed there is any qualitative difference between them. Consequently, it seems of little critical interest. It may, of course, be useful to those concerned with the creative processes of writers.

Still, despite the fact that not all influences, reminiscences, or sources are equally interesting, it would be absurd to agree with Béraud that 'the search for influences and sources ... is a pedant's delight.'[42] Béraud is worth citing because he actually says what many believe and because he goes on to advocate the investigation of affinities over sources. Such studies proliferated as doubts arose about the validity of source hunting. Here again, however, serious problems occur, for all too often the statement of affinities fails to take into consideration whether and how authors have employed preceding or contemporary literature. Redfern's conclusion after a careful comparison of Stendhal's *Le Rouge et le noir* and Camus's *L'Etranger*, provides a good example: 'Both writers are linked by their Romantic premise that the good die young; that, if they lived longer, they might deteriorate. Both stories tell of a young man's error. But Julien's passions drive him to choose his own mistake. Meursault's mistake is almost made for him. Perhaps this is the main difference, in nature and quality, between the unashamed and the unembarrassed Romanticism of these two prisoner-heroes.'[43] Certainly, one would not censure comparison for the sake of evaluation. On the other hand, one cannot but wonder at the validity of this judgment that does not take into consideration *L'Etranger*'s allusion to *Le Rouge et le noir*, Camus's use of Stendhal's novel. One might also wonder why more attention has not been paid to Julien Sorel and Meursault as Christ figures who die to bring a new 'Gospel.'[44] Why do we miss so many allusions? Perhaps because too little attention has been paid to the device. Perhaps because we do not expect to find it in periods where the past is not revered.[45] Perhaps because an interest in sources leads to a concern with either identity (which would be proclaimed either plagiarism or a debt) or distinction (which receives an accolade for originality). The thought that virtual identity can be original – that subtle distortions and outright differences can prove an intimate relationship – seems antithetical to the underlying orientation of such analyses.[46] Furthermore, because a convincing demonstration of either depends on unequivocal resemblances, the subtler examples of allusion may be overlooked. Perhaps the most skillful instances of allusion remain undiscovered because their importance does not reside externally in some other work and because their integration into the story is so complete that they become apparent only when we subject the story itself to a thorough analysis.

In Barbey's case, I suspect he feared that a clear reference to *Le Rouge et le noir* might have made it difficult for the reader to give his story undivided attention. As Barbey well knew, 'Unfortunately, I am neither Montesquieu nor Beyle [Stendhal], neither an eagle nor a lynx' (2.1429). Had a comparison of *Le Rouge et le noir* and 'Le Rideau cramoisi' been

encouraged, Barbey's little work might well have come off a poor second, for it does not equal Stendhal's masterpiece in complexity,
breadth, or depth. Nor did he wish us to read *Le Rouge et le noir*
through 'Le Rideau cramoisi,' as though it were an allegory, with Stendhal's *Rouge* representing the abstract dimension. Barbey was, however,
able to exploit Stendhal's work by stimulating the sympathetic vibra-
tions of those affective chords so powerfully played upon by Stendhal.
Barbey's allusion becomes an artistic device that turns his good but not
excellent tale into a powerful short story. Apparently, he took Stendhal's
masterpiece in the same way he would take a rhetorical device, a traditional symbol, or a word from the common language and used it in his
own way for his own artistic purposes. *Le Rouge et le noir* is nothing but
a building block for Barbey, and Barbey owes Stendhal the same debt
that he owes to the French language for the words and connotations he
uses.[47] Consequently, although Barbey's allusion may indicate a source,
as far as 'Le Rideau cramoisi' is concerned, its importance lies in its
allusion. Doubtless some will not agree. Robbe-Grillet for example,
makes a curious distinction, which I do not accept. In an interview
conducted by J.J. Brochier, he said, 'When I photograph an object which
exists, I am also taking something from someone. When I write a book,
I am truly the creator of everything in it. But when, in a film, I photograph a monument, this monument already belongs to an author: the
sculptor who conceived it.'[48] I should think that the debt would be the
same whether he alludes to the Oedipus myth in *Les Gommes* or the
Orpheus myth in *L'Immortelle* or employs the statue as a leitmotif in
L'Année dernière à Marienbad. In both cases, although he has taken something from someone else, his use is entirely his own. Similarly, although
Stendhal's *Le Rouge et le noir* belongs to Stendhal, Barbey's allusive use
of the novel belongs to Barbey, for it was his own invention. And, if we
were to use Eliot's yardstick for a measure, it would appear a very good
allusion indeed.

One of the surest of tests is the way in which a poet borrows. Immature poets
imitate; mature poets steal; bad poets deface what they take, and good poets
make it into something better, or at least something different. The good poet
welds his theft into a whole of feeling which is unique, utterly different from
that from which it was torn; the bad poet throws it into something which has
no cohesion.[49]

5

Allusive Complex: *A la recherche du temps perdu*

Marcel Proust's *A la recherche du temps perdu* (1913–27) persists in giving critics trouble. Still, the fact that we continue to turn its pages, to think about it, to find long after arriving at the end that it shapes our thoughts as we look at our world, the fact that we have not stopped writing about it – these mark its success. The drafts included in the most recent Pléiade edition, stretching the earlier somewhat manageable three volumes to four ungainly tomes, make it even more difficult to understand, however, that Proust dominated his art. Unlike the image presented in studies by Albert Feuillerat or Robert Vigneron, he was not out of control, unable to stop writing, and encouraged by the lengthy war years, which interrupted book publication, to spill random recollections from society, history, and literature onto page after page of manuscript, even after his book was really complete.[1] It is worth remembering that the public on which he supposedly dumped the disorderly meanderings of a retentive mind was by no means helpless. To the contrary, rather than turning away from his masterwork, Proust's audience has grown through the years in both quantity and fervor both within and beyond France.

The novel is long, and had Proust lived, it would have been longer. It is unconventional, and its nuclear construction would not have changed had he lived a normal life span. There is no neat plot to tie the various episodes together, no completely developed character to give the ungainly mass the semblance of shape – none, that is, except the 'I.' Still, despite his novel's length and unconventionality, Proust was very conscious of his future readers, and he maintained control over *A la recherche*.[2] Indeed, the novelist's masterful ability to orchestrate his novel in order to bring about certain responses in readers is the reason we cannot resist his masterpiece. It has not stopped working its insidious magic on its public. The madeleine, the three steeples of Martinville, the three trees of Hudimesnil, the septet continue to call. Perhaps more of us need to stop and wonder what those images are saying.

Proust's novel seemingly justifies poststructuralist criticism, since he fully recognized the power of the reader to shape literature. Far from being dismayed by the degree to which literature is dependent on those who read its pages, the novelist gloried in literature's ability to incite, to encourage, and to form artists who will go out and create their own works of art. As he put it in an early passage, 'And there, in fact, is one of the great and marvelous characteristics of beautiful books (which will cause us to understand the role, both essential and limited, that reading can play in our spiritual life) that for the author could be called "Conclusions" and for the reader "Incitations." We sense very clearly that our wisdom begins where the author's ends, and we would like him to respond to us, when all he can do is give us desires. And he cannot awaken these desires in us except by making us contemplate the supreme beauty that the utmost effort of his artistry has permitted him to attain. . . . What is the end of their wisdom appears to us nothing but the beginning of ours.'[3] Proust was convinced that the success of *A la recherche* depended on the ability of readers to bring numerous strands and images together into meaningful wholes.

Contrary to the more radical representatives of poststructuralism, however, Proust went beyond empowering his reader. He gave equal authority to the reality of his text. While delighting in literature's dependence on readers, he was also aware that art exists only after those smudges on paper, or canvas, or celluloid are translated according to convention into images. Then, moreover, they must be combined meaningfully in the reader's mind. Proust was sure that while readers may pick and choose among the objects, characters, episodes, and plots that novelists present for their delectation, in the end those readers will be formed and will be brought to have an experience of great importance that will give shape to their understanding. He expected his signs to be mentally converted according to the conventions of language, and he had no patience with careless readers.

Beneath the surface of Proust's novel there exists an interwoven pattern of imagery that suggests experiences outside the text and that simultaneously highlights the various thematic movements of the book. Proust the writer was in the business of creating images. The most striking discovery gained from studying his manuscripts comes from his apparent efforts to set off and illuminate essential images. These passages then become nuclei of a particular nature. Their component elements take on the meaning of the environment and carry it with them when they reappear later in other nuclear passages. In my *Color-Keys* I tried to show that Proust's choice of colors can be explained by large-scale semantic systems functioning both symbolically and structurally. As just one example, there is the orangeade that became a sign of the Guermantes's gatherings. 'No one had ever known the Guermantes to serve anything in these after dinner gatherings in the garden but orangeade'.[4] When it reappears at a party given by Mme Verdurin in her new guise as the Princess de Guermantes (R 4.447), it highlights both her arrival in the ethereal realms of Parisian society and the degradation of the aristocracy. One is reminded of Genette's passing insight: 'Verdurin (*via duras*),'[5] which seems especially appropriate in light of the difficulty involved in the Verdurins' aggressive *arrivisme* and as a prefiguration of Mme Verdurin's odyssey – after the death of M. Verdurin, she spends some time as the Duchess de Duras before becoming the Princess de Guermantes. Moving from the micro to the macro level, the gatherings themselves, whether organized by the protagonist's family at Aunt Léonie's or those dominated by the Duchess de Guermantes, bring the reader's attention to many of the novel's major themes and images.[6]

Proust understood that readers turn words into images as they read and that these images then combine with other images to make complexes of meaning. We call this process interpretation, but it is nothing but good reading. Normally novels depend on plot and character as the central filaments tying various episodes together, but Proust's plot of a hero who seeks a subject for his work, only finding it in the last pages, is very weak and shows minimal textual commitment. The configuration of the main character takes shape only when the reader perceives that the narrational 'I' is the sum of everything he lives, whether as observer or participant. In *Novel Configurations* I called this 'negative structure,' which rather resembles an intaglio, 'a negative surface which must be filled and cast off in order to reveal the true figure at the center of the narration. I am reminded of those strange hollows archaeologists found in and around Pompeii. Only when some clever person thought to fill the empty spaces with plaster of Paris and chip off the shell of hardened lava, did they discover the forms of dogs and men writhing in the agony of death by burns' (*Novel* 149). Suddenly everything that was 'out there' reverses its field of being and becomes 'in here,' and one conceives the novel's main character, the protagonist/narrator identified as 'I.'

It is rather the images that give unity to Proust's novel as they are brought into being by the text and as one recognizes constituent elements when they subsequently re-form in other patterns. Among the many image systems in *A la recherche du temps perdu*, allusions make up some of the most important. I call this interwoven pattern of allusion an allusive complex. I chose the word 'complex' in the hope of insisting that the numerous allusions and systems of allusive images included in Proust's book work together to help produce the final aesthetic experience.[7]

Names are one point of departure in approaching an understanding of the essential substructure of literary allusion. I would not go so far as Roland Barthes who suggests that 'the (poetic) event that "lanced" the *Recherche* was Names. Without question, as early as the *Sainte-Beuve*, Proust had already disposed of certain names (*Combray, Guermantes*), but it was only between 1907 and 1909, it seems, that he put together the main elements of the *Recherche*'s onomastic system: once the system was found, the work was immediately written.'[8] Still, the importance of names cannot be denied. Not only is their significance apparent in both the projected and actual subtitles of *A la recherche*,[9] but many pages are devoted to discussions of their evocativeness. The names are appropriate because they are an integral part of the development of the images and because they are firmly embedded in the allusive complex. While Proust clearly sensed that a name offers one of the simplest means of marking a character and of giving him or her the breath of life, he sought names that additionally have paronomastic, etymological, and eponymic reverberations. One could even point out that in attempting to know Albertine, to imprison her, and to capture her essence, the protagonist is repeating the error of Lohengrin's wife, and not surprisingly, when Albertine departs, like Lohengrin who left behind his ring, she left behind her rings.[10] Lohengrin's boat was pulled by a swan; Albertine's was to be named *Le Cygne* (*The Swan* [R 4.38]). Names offer efficient means of introducing history, the Bible, legend, or myth to a text. Proust's names do all of these things, though I believe one of their most important functions is to encourage the reader to join the protagonist in the formation of images from names and thus to provide a shimmering backdrop that illuminates the joys, dangers, and despairs of the hero's search for self-definition, determination, and meaning on the road to artistic expression.

We know that Proust particularly admired an ability to suggest the unseen and unseeable. As he pointed out in a remarkably perceptive passage, Barbey's stories and novels always have at their center 'a hidden reality revealed by a material trace' (*R* 3.877). The narrator notes as an example 'the hand of "Le Rideau cramoisi"' (ibid.). That reality, usually the active presence of evil, remains a tormenting mystery, but when Barbey managed to make his readers believe that it actually existed, he had accomplished his goals. As was discussed in the last chapter, 'Le Rideau cramoisi' sets up a series of layers that must be peeled away, whether the curtain, the hand, or the girl herself. Though we penetrate several levels, the mysterious reality beneath continues intact, and the girl remains forever an enigma. Barbey's Albertine is repeatedly compared to the devil, and when Brassard feels the sensuous touch of Albertine's hand, he feels that he is thrust into the fires of hell itself. Why is she so powerful? Is she the agent of some other force? Does she incarnate evil itself? The title revolves around the girl's moral being – if, indeed, she has one.

At one point, Proust's Albertine recalls previous literary experience in Barbey's 'Le Rideau cramoisi.'[11] The much older narrator tells of his younger counterpart's emotions when he dreamed of holding Albertine's hand during a game of 'button, button, who's got the button.' For Proust's protagonist, as for Brassard, Albertine's hand represents a spectacular, though hidden, reality. But whatever sensuality, voluptuousness, and mystery there may have been exists only in the Proustian hero's mind. Albertine is merely trying to pass him the 'button,' and he misinterprets the signs, as he discovers to his embarrassment. Brassard is right, since his Albertine is a *diabolique*. By using the allusion, Proust makes us smile at the adolescent's bumbling while simultaneously continuing beneath the surface to build a sense of Albertine's uncanny power that will eventually enslave the hero. In what is billed as the last version reviewed by the author of *Albertine disparue*, the hero searches a building hoping to find his departed mistress. The key to one locked room is missing, however, and he leaves 'convinced that Albertine was behind this curtain.'[12] Whether Proust knew other eponyms in Hoffmann's 'Le Choix d'une fiancée' (1819), Amédée Achard's *Les Fourches caudines* (1866), or Goethe's *Les Années de voyage de Wilhelm Meister* (1821–9) is an open question, though none of the associations would detract from Proust's creation.

Balbec, perhaps a deformation of the French town of Bolbec, is a case in point. Proust's 'Balbec' comprises several of the interlocking patterns of allusive support. The homonymous Persian city, now in Lebanon, was named after the false god Baal, mentioned in the Bible, and thus joins the two biblical cities, Sodom and Gomorrah, found along the protagonist's way. Brichot, the author's pedantic professor who corrects many of the Curé de Combray's false etymologies, points out that -*bec* means stream in the Norman dialect (*R* 3.328). Victor E. Graham has insisted on the importance of this information, for it fits Balbec into the water imagery of *A la recherche*.[13] Brichot is not sure about *Bal-*. He suggests it is a corruption of 'Dalbec' (*R* 3.327). There are other possibilities, of course, especially if we take the narrator's comment about the etymologies of Oriental languages (*R* 4.560) as an indication of the author's interests: Proust may have chosen the first syllable of Balbec because of a belief that the Baal of the Persian city Baalbek meant 'sun.'[14] He may have known that Baalbek was renamed Heliopolis (city of the sun) by the Greeks and that the famous temple of the sun was erected there.[15] It is also possible that he was aware that *Bal-* in many French place names derives from the Celtic sun god Belenus.[16]

For Proust's protagonist, despite his early expectations of fog and storms, Balbec came to represent the place of the sun. Even when forced to leave the resort because of the humidity and cold, he rapidly forgets the intemperate weather and remembers only the intense light (*R* 2.305). Because of the 'excessive light' (ibid.), the curtains of his hotel room are drawn, but outside his window there is the summer day, compared to a mummy 'embalmed in its golden robe of gold' (*R* 2.306), casting 'a golden cylinder' like a 'luminous column' (*R* 2.305) on a wall. That Albertine derives from an etymon meaning splendor and brightness assumes a particular importance, for the narrator frequently remembers her next to the sea on the 'luminous and sounding beach' (*R* 3.679). When the protagonist feels that she escapes him, she is associated with the 'dizzying power of the sun' (ibid.). The metaphorical description of his relationship with Albertine also includes solar imagery. In one instance he compares his experience of Albertine with Saint-Loup's vision of her by saying, 'When [love] has reached a point where it causes such pain, the construction of sensations interposed between the woman's face and the eyes of the lover . . . has already gone so far that the point where the lover's eyes stop, the point where he meets his pleasure and his suffering, is as far from the point where others see it as the true sun is distant from the place where its condensed light appears to us in the sky' (*R* 4.22)

Such frequent comparisons serve to relate Albertine to the sun as intimately as to the sea and to flowers (frequently roses). It is fitting that the announcement of Albertine's death be followed by the setting of the sun:

> Tomorrow, day after tomorrow, a future with a common life perhaps forever was beginning. My heart soared towards it, but it was no longer there. Albertine was dead.
>
> I asked Françoise for the time. Six o'clock. Finally, thank God, the heavy heat that I used to complain about with Albertine, and that we loved so, was going to disappear. The day was coming to an end.   (*R* 4.61-62)

The above passage concludes the sequence that begins on the Balbec train where the boy sees a magnificent sunrise and a milkmaid who strangely resembles the sun: 'I could not take my eyes from her face which grew larger and larger similar to a sun that you can fasten on and that approaches until it is right next to you, allowing you to look at it close up, dazzling you with gold and red' (*R* 2.18). Selecting these two points is of course arbitrary. Proust was far too masterful a poet to begin abruptly either the primary thematic movement or the supporting imagery of these pages. The sequence is prepared by the hero's satisfying love play with Gilberte and by his social aspirations centered on Odette, for example. Yet, although fully integrated into the novel and subordinate to the total organism, it has a unity of its own. Between the sunrise on the protagonist's train trip to Balbec and the sunset at Albertine's death, the major theme is the protagonist's domination by the present. After his moment of revolt on realizing that his room in the hotel at Balbec signifies the death of his past selves, he placidly allows life to act on him. 'The exhilaration of the present moment' (*R* 2.172) dominates him. 'I was enclosed in the present, like heroes, like drunks. Momentarily eclipsed, my past was no longer projected before me like this shadow of myself that we call our future, placing my life's goal not in the accomplishment of my dreams of this past but in the joy of the present minute. I saw no further than this' (ibid.). Almost without exception, the protagonist's interests in this period are oriented toward immediate gratification: sensualism in all its forms, friendship, society. By the time he imprisons Albertine, he is frantically and futilely attempting to maintain the present, to avoid change, to prevent a future different from his current existence, to deny the death of his past. But Albertine is 'like a great goddess of Time' (*R* 3.888). She propels him 'in search of the past' (ibid.). With Albertine's death, he must recognize that the moment cannot be petrified. Until he accepts the fact of passing time, he continues to be incapable of resurrecting the past. The solar imagery supports this movement, just as it prepares for the dark night of Paris in the pits of Sodom and war.

Although not wasted (e.g., R 4.497–8), the years spent with Albertine were filled with dangers. Swann, the collector, provides an example of the result of an inability to break with a constant orientation toward the present (cf R 1.221). He is only a collector, and the role of an artist remains beyond his capabilities. The implicit conclusion is clear: the hero too could have become a Swann. This hazard receives allusive support through a parallel with the Icarus myth. We remember Brichot's announcement that Incarville[17] means 'village of Wiscar' (R 3.485). The narrator repeatedly stresses how such information affects the boy: 'So it was not just place names in this region that had lost their initial mystery but the places themselves. The names, already half emptied of a mystery that etymology had replaced with reasoning, had descended another rung' (R 2.22).

Both Incarville and Parville (*Paterni villa*, according to Brichot [R 3.484]) exist in France. In *A la recherche* they are situated along the little railway line. It was at Incarville that Cottard aroused the young man's jealousy on seeing Albertine dancing with Andrée (R 3.190–4). For a time Albertine lived there with Rosemonde (e.g., R 3.177), and the hero often met his sweetheart there (e.g., R 3.180). In Proust's mind, the names of the two towns were inseparably coupled. We know this since on several occasions he confused Parville and Incarville.[18] This confusion is not surprising. As suggestive names they are inter-changeable. Both allude to the same myth; for in Ovid's *Metamorphoses*, Icarus had passed over the isle of Paros when he flew into the sun. Daedalus said,

'I warn you, Icarus, to fly in a middle course, lest, if you go too low, the water may weight your wings; if you go too high, the fire may burn them' [. . . They take wing.] And now Juno's sacred Samos had been passed on the left, and Delos and Paros; . . . the boy began to rejoice in his bold flight and . . . directed his course to a greater height. The scorching rays of the nearer sun softened the fragrant wax which held his wings. The wax melted; his arms were bare as he beat them up and down, but, lacking wings, they took no hold on the air. His lips, calling to the last upon his father's name, were drowned in the dark blue sea, which took its name from him.[19]

After the train has left Incarville, the last station before Parville (*R* 3:498), which like Paros was near the sea (*R* 3.393), Albertine tells the young man that she knows Mlle Vinteuil and her friend very well. 'With these words spoken as we entered the Parville station' the vision of what he had seen at Montjouvain is projected suddenly in his mind (*R* 3.499). Back at the hotel the memory is still present as he watches the sun rise, but 'To Miss Vinteuil, while her friend tickled her before falling on her, I now gave the enflamed face of Albertine' (*R* 3.504). With full realization that he is forced to tie himself to Albertine, he sits in front of the window like a sacrificial victim offered to the sun god:

I could not hold back a sob when, in an offertory gesture accomplished mechanically and which seemed to symbolize the bloody sacrifice that I was going to have to make of all joy every morning until the end of my life, a solemn renewal of my daily chagrin and of the blood from my wound celebrated at every dawn, the sun's golden egg, as though propulsed by the rupture in the equilibrium that a change in density would bring at the moment of coagulation, barbed with flames as in paintings, bounded through the curtain behind which for the last few moments I had sensed it quivering and ready to appear on stage and spring forward, and whose mysterious, congealed crimson it wiped out in floods of light. I heard myself crying.   (*R* 3.512–13)

The protagonist does not fly too near the sun, but the text suggests the very real hazards of his affair. His liaison with Albertine is perhaps essential to his personal development; nonetheless, to say that he is playing with fire becomes more than a cliché. The similes relating Albertine to the sun and the allusions linking the protagonist to Icarus help to produce a feeling of intense danger and imminent tragedy in the reader. Without this portion of the allusive complex, the long, image-filled passage I have just quoted would have seemed malapropos, if not nonsense. The allusion to myth intensifies and supports this portion of the young man's progression toward those moments at the Princess de Guermantes's when his vocation is revealed to him.

In addition to supporting the solar imagery in this portion of the hero's experience, the very name of the area where he first sees Albertine may call up visions of mystery, magic, and the enjoyment of sensual pleasures, for 'Baâlbeck' appears in the *Arabian Nights*.[20] Scheherazade's tales are cited throughout *A la recherche*, from the overture (*R* 1.18) to the conclusion (*R* 4.620). There are more examples of explicit references to this collection than there are to the works of

Baudelaire, Mallarmé, Leconte de Lisle, Zola, Anatole France, Vigny, Voltaire, Pascal, or Virgil. Of course, this does not prove the literary importance of the *Arabian Nights* to *A la recherche*, but it indicates that possibility.[21] The narrator apparently supports such an inference when he tells us that he 'used to reread them ceaselessly' (R 3.753). At one point (R 3.230), the merits of the Galland translation are compared to that of Mardrus (1898–1902). Later the protagonist substitutes outings with Albertine for 'the charming reading of the *Arabian Nights*' (R 3.234), and Albertine's captivity is compared to the imprisonment of the Princess of China in a bottle (R 3.888). Indeed, these stories have left a more indelible mark on *A la recherche* than mere mentions of the title or the names of some of its characters. Echoes of the *Arabian Nights* most notably form a portion of the allusive backdrop supporting the Balbec-Albertine sequence of *A la recherche du temps perdu*.[22] They add a shimmer of the mysterious and of the sensuous Orient to Albertine.

The protagonist's relationship with Albertine includes pervasive, though inexplicit, allusions to the account of the romance of Hassân and the jinni, Splendeur ('The Adventures of Hassân Al-Bassri').[23] In this tale, Hassân finds lodging in a magnificent palace with the seven daughters of a king of the jinn. From a terrace, Hassân sees the arrival of ten enormous birds that land beside a large lake in a countryside beautiful 'as a garden' (*AN* 10.49). Hassân watches as they remove their feathers and bathe in the lake. Struck with love for the most beautiful, a girl with black hair and eyes who appears to be the leader of the group, he recites the following verses:

The girl came to me, dressed in her beauty as a rose bush with its roses, and her breasts thrust forward, o pomegranates! . . .

I was mistaken! To compare your cheeks to roses, o maid . . . what an error!

For roses can be inhaled and pomegranates can be gathered but you o virginal maid, who can flatter himself that he has smelled or touched you? (*AN* 10.50–1 and 67)

The girls don their plumage and fly away.

Bouton-de-Rose (Rosebud), Hassân's protectress at the palace, reveals that his beloved is Splendeur, the youngest daughter of the king of all the jinn kings. She advises him of a way to capture this marvelous creature. Following her instructions, at the next new moon Hassân waits beside the lake for the girls to return. He steals the magical cloak of the 'beautiful bird from the air' (*AN* 10.65), thus putting her in his power. Splendeur passively becomes his wife. Soon afterward, he assures Bouton-de-Rose and her sisters that he will visit them annually and takes his bride home to his mother.

Hassân leaves wife and home to make the promised visit a year later. While he is away, Splendeur's feathers are returned to her through the insistence of the caliph's wife. Immediately, Splendeur takes wing. Before flying from the room, she pauses and says to Hassân's mother,

O mother of Hassân, certainly, leaving like this grieves me greatly, and I am distressed because of you and your son, Hassân my husband, for the days of separation will break his heart and darken your life. But, alas, I can do nothing. I feel the intoxication of the air invading my soul, and I must fly off into space. But if your son ever wishes to find me, he has only to seek me in the Wak-Wak islands. Goodby then, o mother of my husband! (*AN* 10.94)

With that declaration she flies away. Hassân, after many trials and marvelous adventures, finds her again. Full of remorse, she helps him as they escape new dangers to return home. There, they live out their days in happiness.

One of the more salient aspects of the tale is that Splendeur has plumage that makes her look like a bird and endows her with the power of flight. To deprive her of this ability, one need only seize her feathers. This done, she is overpowered and becomes the willing captive of Hassân. In *A la recherche*, bird imagery is frequently related to Albertine and the little band. When the protagonist first sees them, although not on a terrace as in the Hassân story, he is standing in front of the hotel where the guests arrive and where the hotel's inhabitants sit to watch the passing spectacle. At the far end of the sea-wall, he sees a group of girls that he compares to 'a band of gulls that executed with measured steps . . . a stroll whose goal seemed as obscure to the bathers whom they did not appear to see as it seemed clearly determined in their ornithological spirits' (*R* 2.146). There, 'above the sea' (*R* 2.150), instead of a lake, they walk. When they pause they resemble 'a confab of birds that gather when they are on the point of taking off' (ibid.). The vision of Albertine and the little band in front of the sea recurs insistently in the young man's mind,[24] as do the bird comparisons. Albertine, like her friends, chirps (*R* 2.261; 3.622), and Albertine's laugh resembles cooing (*R* 2.272). The little band is analogous to a group of migratory birds (*R* 3.510).

As Hassân selected Splendeur, so the protagonist concentrates on Albertine. He succeeds in capturing her and she becomes a captive bird, encaged in his home (R 3.521, 576, 678). As Albertine's escape approaches in the narrative sequence, the bird imagery increases to notable proportions. In the final sequence of La Prisonnière, which begins on page 889 and ends on page 915, there are fourteen references to birds and four to airplanes. Albertine is wearing a Fortuny gown and seems 'invaded with Arab ornamentation like Venice, like Venetian palaces hidden like sultanas behind a veil of stone openwork . . . like columns whose oriental birds . . . are repeated' (R 3.895). And after she leaves the protagonist's room he hears her throw up her window as though she were saying, 'This life suffocates me. Too bad! I need air!' (R 3.903). The young man immediately recognizes that she thereby proclaims her freedom (ibid.). Soon, Albertine leaves. As the narrator points out, no single cause suffices to explain her departure (R 4.194). Years later, he accepts the simplistic explanation that she left him for Octave (R 4.309). Nevertheless, the most insistent of the proposed reasons for her flight is that she wanted to be free (R 3.903; 4.6, 7–8). When Splendeur felt the liberating force of her wings, she seems not to have been able to prevent herself from flying away. Apparently, Albertine realized that there were other possibilities for her than remaining with the protagonist, and she wanted liberty. After her departure her letters reveal a desire to return, although she dies before doing so. The two stories are not identical, but the similarities are undeniable and reverberate strongly throughout this portion of Proust's masterpiece.

To the bird imagery correlating the bird-jinni, Splendeur, and the 'marvelous bird' (R 4.55), Albertine, should be added that of flowers. The importance of floral comparisons is evident in 'The Adventures of Hassân' from the fact that the poem 'The girl came to me, dressed in her beauty as a rosebush with its roses...' is repeated twice in relation to Splendeur. In A la recherche, the protagonist finds that making Albertine's acquaintance is as exciting as 'cultivating rosebushes' (R 2.236). Albertine is frequently compared to a 'rosebush' (e.g., R 3.884) and to roses (e.g., R 2.242). She is 'like a rose at the edge of the sea' (R 2.647). She is 'the most beautiful rose' (R 3.577) surrounded by other 'rose stems whose principal charm was to stand out against the sea' (R 2.296), and 'the ties of flowers were twined . . . around her' (R 3.185). But Splendeur is more than a rose, 'For roses can be inhaled . . . but you o virginal maid, who can flatter himself that he has smelled or touched you?' (AN, 10.51, 67). Nevertheless, Hassân succeeds in possessing her.

Likewise, Proust's hero has the opportunity to 'know the taste of the rose' (R 2.659).

The parallels between the story in the *Arabian Nights* and the Albertine sequence of *A la recherche* also include the similarity of the names 'Bouton-de-Rose' and 'Rosemonde' as well as the moon-like qualities the girls have in common (e.g., R 2.278; AN 10.90). And there are further similarities between Albertine and Splendeur. The latter's hair is black, as is Albertine's, at least on occasion.[25] Hassân notices the brilliance of Splendeur's black eyes (*AN* 10.5), and the protagonist attempts to decipher 'the black ray' emanating from those of Albertine (R 2.152). Although the text does not say so, one would expect a brunette in an Arab tale to have dark skin. Albertine's 'brown skin' contrasts with her companions' like that of 'a Magi of the Arab variety' in a Renaissance painting (R 2.148). The most telling indication of the relationship is found, however, in the names of these two characters. Albertine derives from Æthelbryht which means 'Noble Splendor.'[26]

Although I am convinced that Albertine's name would never have appeared in *A la recherche* had the name not been an integral part of the book,[27] I do not wish to dispute the suggestion that Proust originally constructed Albertine's name from a verbal play on the names of his friends.[28] The similarity to a combination of one of the Alberts he knew and (Alfred) Agostinelli remains too enticing to be completely discounted. 'Albertine' may well have occurred to Proust before he read the *Arabian Nights* carefully.[29] Because of his interest in etymologies, apparent in *A la recherche* and in his letters,[30] he would undoubtedly have known the derivation of 'Albertine.' Consequently, 'Splendeur' would have fascinated him as he read the *Arabian Nights*. But no matter which came first, similarities in imagery, plot, and name are too clear to be ignored. Taken separately, these parallels might be regarded as accidental. Together they assume significance and importance.

I have dealt at length with these few examples of allusion to literary experiences that are outside Proust's novel in the attempt to demonstrate the existence of consistent patterns of association within *A la recherche*, but my analysis is nonetheless incomplete. For example, I have ignored such things as the archetypal importance of the sun, which is traditionally related to the rational mind rather than the unconscious. One could argue that the solar imagery supports the depoetization of names, places, and people in this portion of the novel.[31] I have also stopped short of mentioning all of the sequence's allusions to myth, legend, and works of literature.

It would be possible to point out that Albertine is but one derived form of the etymon Æthelbryht. Another variant is Alberich, the name of the elf who, in Wagner's *Der Ring des Nibelungen*, forged the ring he was eventually forced to surrender. Albertine left her rings behind when she escaped (*R* 4.45–6), though as I indicated earlier, I suspect that these rings have more to do with the Swan Knight legends. I could mention that the 'flowering girls' (*R* 2.716) are joined by the 'young girls in bloom' to allude to 'die Mädchen ganz wie in Blumengewändern, selbst Blumen erscheinend [maidens so totally festooned with flowers that they seemed themselves to bloom]' in the garden of Klingsor's castle through which Wagner's Parsifal had to pass to secure the spear. This allusion is further supported by the resemblance of the name 'Guermantes' to that of Parsifal's guide, Gurnemanz.[32] This is a part of the richest of Proust's onomastic 'incitations': the Guermantes-Swann imago. I couple these names deliberately, since the textual allusions link the families as firmly in the protagonist's childhood as they are joined many years later in Gilberte's and Saint-Loup's daughter, Mlle de Saint-Loup. For the reader who remembers that Odette was one of the swan maidens in *Swan Lake*, there are no surprises in discovering that Gilberte, the daughter of a Swann and a swan maiden has become a member of the family of Gilbert le Mauvais, Gilbert and Marie-Gilberte de Guermantes. It would be neither the first Gilberte nor the first swan in the family. After all, legends tell that an early duchess de Brabant married the Swan Knight, and, moreover, the Curé of Combray has told us that the Guermantes descend from Geneviève de Brabant (*R* 1.103). That the 'hoarse voice' of the Guermantes women can be attributed to the ancestral swan who gave birth to the family through 'the mythological impregnation of a nymph by a divine Bird' (*R* 2.732) may leave some dubious, but it is suggestive when the narrator compares Oriane's husband to Jupiter (*R* 3.551). And King Oriant was, moreover, the father of the Swan Knight. Nor does Proust neglect the paronomastic potential. The mythic Orion, now a constellation, was killed because he vexed the Greek goddess of the hunt, Artemis. Much later, the author of *A la recherche* exploits the story for several comparisons. On one occasion, the narrator sees Oriane de Guermantes 'deviate from her stellar course' (*R* 2.672), and on another she moves 'like a huntress' (*R* 2.727).

Other imagery related to Oriane becomes clearer in looking at the name 'Guermantes.' It opens onto the Parsifal legend, another rich vein that the novelist exploited extensively. As he wrote in an early, marginal note in one of his notebook manuscripts of *Le Temps retrouvé*, 'I will present the discovery of lost time in the spoon, tea, etc. sensations, like an illumination à la Parsifal.'[33] Proust's source is uncertain. It may well have been Wagner, whose work he knew and loved.[34] There was however considerable interest at the time in other versions of this and related legends. Many potential sources for Proust's information exist. What is, of course, more interesting than where he learned of this material is what he did with his allusions.

The two texts most clearly brought into our reading experience by the name 'Guermantes' are Chrétien de Troyes's unfinished *Conte du Graal* and Wagner's *Parsifal*. They differ considerably, but both seem to have left traces in *A la recherche*. In Chrétien's version, Perceval has been taken to a sylvan retreat in an attempt to turn him from the chivalric profession that had killed his father and two elder brothers. But the call to adventure is too strong, and the boy abandons his weeping mother to the care of his uncle, Gornementz. In the course of the young hero's wanderings, he comes to the castle of the Fisher King, where he sees the Grail. Had he asked the Fisher King his name, had he asked a question designed to elicit an explanation for the strange ceremony he witnesses, the king would have been freed from an enchantment. This would have brought ineffable happiness for him and his hosts. Unfortunately, Perceval remains mute, and the necessary question is not asked. The vision evaporates, and, desperate for another experience of the Grail, Perceval begins his quest.

Proust's treatment of this theme begins with the humorous description of the intense interest Tante Léonie takes in all the details of Combray life. '[A] person "whom we didn't know" was as incredible a being as a mythological god, and in fact we did not remember that each time one of these stupefying apparitions ... had taken place, careful research had finally reduced the fabulous personage to the proportions "whom we did know," either personally, or abstractly in his civil status as having a certain degree of family relationship with people in Combray' (*R* 1.56–7). Even a dog that 'she didn't know' was a major event (*R* 1.57), and after upsetting his aunt by telling her that he has seen a stranger near the Pont-Vieux, the young protagonist is warned by his parents to avoid such impetuousness in the future. A stranger is an important event that interests everyone, though in most cases it takes little or no effort to reduce the wondrous being to a flesh-and-bone person belonging to one or the other of the local families.

This preparation makes it difficult to understand why the boy did not ask the identity of the 'fisherman in the straw hat ... the only person whose identity I never discovered' (R 1.165). He started to quiz his parents: 'I wanted to ask his name then, but they waved me silent so as not to frighten the fish' (ibid.). And the event drops away. We should perhaps wonder ourselves why the question was never asked, but I suspect we forget, as well.[35] The memory of this peculiar behavior may return in later instances, however, when we begin to perceive that the protagonist's failure to ask the necessary questions constitutes a serious flaw in his character. While strolling on the Guermantes Way, for example, he often has a feeling of intense pleasure on observing a roof, sunlight on a rock, an odor. While he has the impression of something hidden behind the scene, he rapidly abandons any attempt to understand.

So arduous was the duty imposed on me by these impressions of form, fragrance, or color – to try to note what was hiding behind them, that I did not delay in finding excuses for myself that would allow me to shirk these efforts and spare myself this fatigue. Luckily my parents would call, I would sense that I did not at present have the tranquility necessary to pursue my research usefully. . . . Then I would no longer pay attention to this unknown thing that enveloped itself with a form or fragrance, at peace when I would bring it back to the house, protected by the sheathing of images under which I found it alive, like the fish that, on the days when they let me go fishing, I would bring back covered by a layer of grass that preserved their freshness. Once back at the house, I thought of other things.   (R 1.177)

Only once is there an exception, after seeing the three steeples of Martinville and Vieuxvicq (R 1.177–81). If he had continued to be as persistent and perspicacious as he is on this occasion, he would have saved himself much torment and many years.

In one way or another, the reader is made privy to frequent cases of the protagonist's avoidance of the mental effort necessary to come to terms with his life and thus find a subject for his art. The most clear-cut and perhaps the most significant experience of this nature, however, occurs during his vacation at Balbec. Mme de Villeparisis has taken them on a ride to Carqueville. The church's shifting, ivy-covered, wind-blown façade makes it difficult to perceive the true outlines of the church and, thus, provides an excellent analogy with the way images are hidden in our minds by the bombardment of new sensations. It then prepares what is to follow. First off, the hero sees and meets a beautiful fisher girl, but he is content merely to make an impression on her. He fails to find out anything. Likewise, when he sees the three trees near Hudimesnil, though the narrator hints at the reason for his joy by referring to the three Martinville-Vieuxvicq steeples, the boy does not persist in his efforts to plumb his pleasure.[36] As he rides off, the trees seem to say, 'What you do not learn from us today, you will never know. If you drop us at the end of this road where we were trying to raise ourselves up to you, a whole part of yourself that we were bringing to you will fall forever into nothingness' (R 2.79). He turns his back, 'sad as though I had just lost a friend, died to myself, denied a dead person or failed to recognize a god' (ibid.). Of course, the reality he should have continued to seek exists not outside but within himself. This discovery only comes long years and much anguish later, when he finally persists in his attempt to understand, to ask the Fisher King the appropriate question.

Wagner's version serves allusively to stress other aspects of the protagonist's quest. There we begin by learning that King Amfortas's condition is worse than ever. Seduced by Kundry, one of the evil Klingsor's temptresses, he allowed the sacred lance to be taken from him. The wound that the magician then inflicted causes him terrible and continuing torment, which will be healed only when 'a pure fool, who has been taught by compassion,' recaptures the lance and touches the wound with it. Parsifal's arrival is heralded when one of the sacred swans falls at the knight's feet, shot by an arrow. Gurnemanz, one of the oldest and most revered of the Grail Knights, reproaches the boy who, overcome with shame, breaks his bow and arrows. He then learns that his forgotten mother has died. Though Parsifal is filled with sorrow at this additional evidence that he is a 'shallow brained fool,' that 'senseless Folly dwells in me' (as Corder puts it in his translation [41]), Gurnemanz is quite content. His hope grows at the sight of this simpleton. He takes the boy under his wing and teaches him everything a knight should know about combat and chivalrous conduct. Parsifal is filled with compassion as he watches the tortured Amfortas, the Fisher King, prepare and bless the sacrificial meal when it is exposed in the Holy Grail before the assembly of knights. After the knights have received their sustenance, the chalice's supernatural glow fades and it is put away. Parsifal determines to wrench the sacred lance from Klingsor's wicked grasp and thus heal the pathetic Amfortas. He sets out for Klingsor's castle and those maidens who had previously caused Amfortas to fall. Parsifal too is tempted – at this point he, like the protagonist, is 'on the wrong track' (R 1.563) – but after sinking to Kundry's couch in Klingsor's enchanted garden and receiving a kiss, he feels as if something has been thrust in his side, and he pushes the flower girl away. Grasping the holy lance, he sets out for the Grail castle. On finally arriving, he of course heals Amfortas and then succeeds him as King of the Knights of the Grail. It is for good reason that 'the unknown quality of her [Guermantes's] name' makes Proust's narrator sense 'a strange sense of a medieval tapestry, of a Gothic stained glass window' (R 2.506).

The previously mentioned allusion to *Swan Lake* illuminates Swann, the socialite and idolatrous art worshiper. Prince Siegfried, we remember, fell in love with the Swan Queen, Odette, but was tricked into marrying Odile, who was disguised by the enchanter, Von Rothbart, to look like his true love. According to legend, as long as swan maidens have the power of transforming themselves into swans or, to phrase it another way, as long as they are free, they retain their youth.[37] Proust's Odette, of course, preserves both her youth and her freedom. Even when the calendar should have forced her into retirement, she seems 'a challenge to the laws of chronology that was more miraculous than the conservation of radium to those of nature' (R 4.526). She has no trouble keeping the duke de Guermantes under her thumb. Though Mme Swann, as Odette/Odile, is surely not responsible for her husband's seeming inability to rise to an acceptable understanding of life and, thus, to the creation of art, the allusion will doubtless emphasize and enliven that failure. Wagner's Amfortas may, as well, intensify our sense of Swann's pain and suffering for 'a woman whom I did not like, who was not my type' (R 1.375).

Wagner's Parsifal adds a warm aura to the Guermantes name. The implication that Mme de Guermantes may take Gurnemanz's role in training Proust's protagonist prepares us for a quest of importance. She will go fishing with him, teach him the names of flowers, and provide him with the subject matter for the poetic Grail he will create (R 1.170). The allusion may also add a shiver of dread when we see the boy following in Swann's path, as though he were indeed Parsifal hazarding himself in Amfortas's footsteps. The danger he runs is clear for the reader to see, especially when the hero says, 'And certainly I would have been less troubled in a magical cavern than in this little waiting room [belonging to Mme Swann] where the fire seemed to proceed toward transmutations as in Klingsor's laboratory' (R 1.518). When he arrives at Balbec, 'A l'ombre des jeunes filles en fleurs,' his seduction is complete. 'And yet,' he decides, 'I was perhaps not wrong to sacrifice the pleasures not only of society but of friendship to the one of passing an entire day in this garden' (*R* 2.260). He is figuratively, if not in fact, 'Parsifal in the middle of the flowering girls' (*R* 2.716) in Klingsor's garden. His later introduction to the Guermantes circle is little improvement. He merely adds 'flowering women' (*R* 2.833) to the 'flowering girls' (ibid.).

Like Elstir, the narrator is not ashamed of having wasted so much time among either the Parisian socialites or his unintellectual girl-friends.[38] Both the protagonist and Elstir learned from the hindrances of sensuality and society, but they prevailed over them in their quest for an aesthetic grail. The Parsifal analogies are but a portion of the quest imagery found throughout the book.

All of these allusions are present in consistent patterns within *A la recherche*. But it would be ill-advised to suggest that Proust has constructed a 'vulgar allegory' (*R* 3.768). Splendeur, Icarus, and Parsifal are too inextricably interwoven to permit total isolation. Should any one of such supporting patterns of association be abstracted, the whole point of the book would be lost. Furthermore, to make an allegory of *A la recherche*, one would have to ignore the multifaceted nature of images and characters. Mme de Guermantes, for example, is indeed a guide for the hero in the Faubourg. Because of the Guermantes family he learns many of the lessons he will need to know as an artist. In addition, she represents one of the basic problems that he must resolve before he is able to believe in his vision and transcribe it into a 'spiritual equivalent' (*R* 4.457) or art. The portions of the allusive complex to which I have referred are too clearly intrareferential to be allegorical. The whole of *A la recherche* leads to an understanding of the primary importance of the subjective vision of the artist. Should the analogy of the Icarus myth, for instance, bring the reader to a meditation on Ovid, he will certainly never gain an understanding of Proust's work. The chances that a reader will mistake *A la recherche* for an allegory are slim, however. These allusions are so subtle, so clearly a part of the total movement, as to discourage anyone from making such a suggestion.

Consideration of the way these allusions appear in the book may make it possible to suggest their function. In every case they illustrate and illuminate the object of the artist's attention. The Icarus myth helps to reinforce the terrible danger of the hero's standing in the heat of the sun, prepared, as he is, to make a sacrifice of himself; Splendeur highlights the mystery, the magic of the marvelous Albertine; Parsifal joins Icarus in emphasizing the hazards of the protagonist's adventures and, further, serves to suggest the final goal: for Parsifal, the Grail, and for the protagonist, art.

Occasionally, the use of such allusions may be an attempt to achieve economy of expression. Because Proust believed the virile homosexual to be unknown to French letters prior to his work,[39] many pages are devoted to describing Charlus and putting him into his familial and social context. Thanks to the existence of *Le Père Goriot*, Proust's comparatively short description of the relations between Berma and her selfish offspring produces a powerful effect (R 4.572–6, 590–2). The clear parallels with Balzac's novel support the episode in *A la recherche* and aid in evoking a suitable response.

The portions of *A la recherche* devoted to Albertine, however reveal no attempt to achieve conciseness. The very length, complexity, and completeness of the various episodes in this sequence indicate a sustained effort to make the reader feel that the band is composed of 'fabulous beings' (R 2.301), that the loved one is accompanied by 'obscure divinities' (R 3.511), and that Albertine is a 'magician' (R 2.646) in a 'magical picture' (R 2.656). Should readers not share the young man's emotion (e.g., R 3.575–6), they can neither sense the terrible deception that comes with a more 'realistic' vision of Albertine nor feel pain from watching 'the whole of the graceful, oceanic mythology that I had composed during the first days' (R 2.301) dissipate. The allusions to the birdlike jinni, Splendeur, as she appeared beside a lake help us to empathize with the protagonist during the oscillations from magic creature to banal adolescent that Albertine undergoes in his mind. Like Parsifal, the young hero must move beyond the sensual, present orientation inherent in the 'flowering girls.' The Parsifal allusions keep the protagonist's quest ever present and make us more aware of his danger as he attempts to capture the solar figure, Albertine.

Whether the reader consciously identifies the references or not, if the imagery stimulates the memory of an experience the reader has had, the response produced by Proust's text will be stronger because the thematic movement has been supported with allusions to a world evocative of the pertinent mood. By taking advantage of a portion of the background he could expect in a cultured reader, Proust enabled the text to strike chords that have resonated before. It may be that he meant such allusions to stimulate the reader's 'involuntary memory.' Certainly, when confronted with the allusions I have mentioned, a reader who has known and loved Wagner's *Parsifal* or the Mardrus translation of the *Arabian Nights* would tend to react in a manner similar to that of the protagonist when tasting the madeleine. The explanation might not come immediately; indeed, like the young man's experience at the sight of the three trees of Hudimesnil, it might never come; but one of the many allusions incorporated in Proust's novel will eventually produce a 'blessed moment,' and the reader will have learned the joy of such truths:

[I]f the memory, thanks to forgetfulness, has been able to establish no tie, to throw no link between it and the present moment, if it has remained in its place, at its date, if it has kept its distance, its isolation in the hollow of a valley or at a summit's peak, it makes us suddenly breathe new air precisely because it is air that we previously breathed, this air that poets have vainly tried to have reign in Paradise and which cannot give this profound sensation of renewal unless it has already been breathed, because the true paradises are the paradises that have been lost. (R 4.449)

Not only does the allusive complex support the thematic development of *A la recherche*, but it provides a lens for the reader to read within himself. The experience that Fiser has called 'the meeting-sensation-memory-by analogy'[40] is explained in detail in relation to the madeleine, the spoon, the towel against the protagonist's lips. If we follow this explanation carefully, we may understand the theory in abstract. But abstractions are not truth, nor are they reality. Before we are able to know the paradise of the poem *A la recherche du temps perdu*, we must have our own revelatory moment. Proust provided many such opportunities with his allusions to other literary experience.

6

Oppositional Allusion: *Electre, La Symphonie pastorale, Eugénie Grandet*

Allusion of opposition has been virtually ignored.[1] Like other forms of allusion, this category requires the formation of a metaphorical relationship where the reference and referent come together to create something different from either. Allusions of opposition present particular difficulties, however, for their ironies and paradoxes usually bring nuances of extraordinary complexity to bear on some aspect of the created world. Differentiating the relationship as *allusive* in opposition to *satirical* constitutes a watershed operation. The controversy raised by Félicité's parrot in 'Un Cœur simple' has served as an example. If satirical, the bird is rejective, for Flaubert then mocks – thus rejects – the possibility that the Holy Spirit would come for his heroine in the guise of a parrot. If, however, Loulou is meant to bring the Holy Spirit into the reading and suggest a whole complex of allusions to sanctity, the parrot is integrative (thus establishing a metaphor as it alludes) and joins the other parallels to the same tradition, which has importance in each one of the *Trois Contes*.

Two recent versions of the mythic Electra story illustrate the difference between satiric and allusive functions. Much can, and has, been made of the significant differences between the classical versions of Orestes' murder of his mother and her lover, Aegisthus, and those of both Jean Giraudoux's *Electre* (1937) and Sartre's *Les Mouches* (1943). Giraudoux has invented his version's Mendiant (Beggar), if not out of whole cloth, at least as a major revision of the Greek choruses. The peripheral crisis between Agathe and her cuckolded husband is not only an addition to the classical model but out of character with the more focused Greek predecessors. And Sartre's cynical but futile Jupiter is inconceivable in the works of Euripides, Sophocles, or Aeschylus, as is the unmitigated declaration of personal liberty and responsibility that ends *Les Mouches*. Indeed, no single, textual source may be cited for either of these recent revisions. As in Aeschylus, although Sartre's Oreste performs a just act in punishing the murder of his father, he will not go unscathed, but rather will be pursued by the avenging Furies. Still, Sartre's jaunty hero leaving with his swarm of flies little resembles the tormented Aeschylean character of *The Choephori*. Though Lise Gauvin is undoubtedly correct to say that Giraudoux's *Electre* 'is noticeably closer' to Sophocles' version than to those of the other Greek playwrights,[2] the celebratory air of the Sophoclean conclusion is by no means obvious in the modern counterpart. *Electre's* much discussed 'sunrise' at the end of Giraudoux's version gives no assurance of its specific promise, and the arrival of the attacking enemy has brought a bloodbath. In addition, neither of the recent writers shows much interest in the vengeance that serves as the focus for Euripides' *Electra*.

The bare story of Electra is quickly told. It begins when the girl's mother, Clytemnestra, and her paramour, Aegisthus, murder Electra's father, Agamemnon, just after his return in victory from Troy. Orestes, the son, is spirited away, while Electra is kept in virtual slavery by the new rulers of Argos. Orestes returns one day and makes contact with his sister, after which they work together to kill their father's murderers. In some versions Electra is already married to a peasant; in others she is about to be. In some, she quickly recognizes Orestes; in others it is a long-drawn-out process. In several, the matricide is punished by the Furies; in others, Orestes has served as the just instrument of just gods. Occasionally, Electra cares for Orestes as he suffers from the afflictions of the Erinyes; in others she distances herself. As with most major myths, there are many variations. Sartre and Giraudoux merely add two more.

It seems safe to conclude that neither Giraudoux nor Sartre has attempted to imitate an earlier version or model. One would better think of what might be termed an archetypal model – that is, a relatively constant image whose emphases may shift and whose constituent elements may be rearranged, added to, and subtracted from, without altering the essential nucleus that continues in successive ages and in the work of diverse authors.[3] Sartre repeats the broad-brushed model rather closely, a strategy that makes the differences between the two images rather striking. Despite the fact that his audience might not know the antecedent well, as his characters, setting, and themes are incarnated on stage, the sense of the model's classical nature cannot be denied, and the more-or-less-vague extratextual image emphasizes the assurance of a conventional conclusion. When Oreste refuses guilt, however, his refusal stands out against a background of well-established parallels between the modern play and the ancient myth. The deviation is then highlighted. Raymond Williams is probably correct to believe that 'one's attention is directed to the philosophical change . . . [T]he legend is not so much a *form* as a *case*.'[4] But when the grotesque Jupiter intones, 'Abraxas, galla, galla, tsé, tsé' (1.1) and explains the expiring flies that result as a parlor trick ('Sometimes I charm flies' [ibid.]), he recalls Offenbach rather than Mount Olympus. He thus prepares a modern Oreste who can say to a god, 'I am my liberty' (3.2) or 'You are a god and I am free' (ibid.). The old woman whose grandson has been steeped in the awareness of his 'original sin' (1.1), a city of people who enjoy their noisy confessions and showcase remorse, all serve for the delight of a derisory, insecure god who has no defense when Oreste simply refuses him allegiance and claims his own freedom. Sartre uses Jupiter to hold theistic religions up to ridicule. He is central to the author's parody.

Although in either Giraudoux's or Sartre's play one might think of burlesques, where trivial or serious subjects are treated respectively in elevated or debased forms or styles, or perhaps of those satirical imitations we call parodies, Sartre's play alone contains the element of ridicule of something else that one expects in parody and burlesque. Sartre's Jupiter, like all satiric figures, 'suggests what kind of behaviour is stupid or despicable, what ideas are contemptible or risible. . . . [Its] effort is directed toward the rejection of what is valueless.'[5] As Duisit explains, though allegorical like satirical modes operate through doubling, the doubling of the satire, burlesque, and parody is subversive;[6] the double's function is to insist on the ridiculous or contemptible nature of the 'other.' While allusion integrates, parody repulses.

Harold Bloom's insights into certain forms of influence can be used to emphasize another point. He argues that strong authors normally react against the influence of preceding texts, traditions, or 'fathers,' in either revisionary or rejective ways. He explicitly excludes Shakespeare from his study of influence, since 'Shakespeare is the largest instance in the language of a phenomenon that stands outside the concern of this book: the absolute absorption of the precursor.'[7] Bloom is willing to exclude others, like Goethe and Milton, on the same grounds (ibid. 50). In short, he recognizes that not all authors view their literary ancestors with anxiety. Some – I would say many – invite their predecessors into their texts and, by establishing allusive parallels and oppositions, use them to enhance their own creations. In general, these allusions focus on a particular theme, character, or development.

Giraudoux's cavalier treatment of the Electra story shows no sign of anxiety. From the beginning he insists that his *Electre* occurs in an aleatory world of instability. The gardener describes the Argos palace and notes that it 'laughs and cries at the same time' (1.1). One of three malicious little girls, whom the gardener thinks resemble 'three small Parcae' (1.1), believes it looks like a widow's palace. Another that it looks like the stuff of childhood memories. A nearby stranger clearly does remember the place. When these juvenile Euménides announce that though they specialize in recitations they invent as they go, the spectator is left to wonder whether the ending is as fixed as it should be after several millennia (ibid.). One of the Euménides says that her story is like a rondeau, which repeats the first verse at the end; she will catch up with the beginning when she gets to the conclusion (ibid.). By the time the audience comes to the Mendiant's hedgehog tale, which illustrates the lesson that the animals are like men in that they die randomly, even those who know the myth well may suspect that the playful tone prepares rather startling inventions on the ancient model. Egisthe has just announced that he energetically discourages people who signal the somnolent gods, since when awakened, their reaction is haphazard. '[T]here is no question that the first rule of any chief of state is to ferociously see to it that the gods are not shaken from lethargy and to limit their damage to what they do while asleep, whether thunder or snoring' (1.3). Consequently, whenever anyone gets up on a high promontory and begins to wave his lantern or flag, Egisthe deals ruthlessly with them: 'No exile. I kill. . . . And I don't make a show of my punishment. While our poor neighboring cities betray themselves by erecting their gibbets at the tops of hills, I crucify in the depths of valleys' (1.3).

Giraudoux's *Electre* is a lesson in introducing suspense to a work whose outcome is preestablished. Although Oreste remembers that Electre's step 'was always measured, prudent, restrained by an invisible chain' (1.1), he sets up the possibility that by marrying a peasant she will no longer have the stature to permit a resounding act that might waken the gods. The idea is that as a married woman she would no longer have the unadulterated purity of youth. Furthermore, she would have left Agamemnon's famous family to become the wife of a mere Théocathoclès. 'In a level-three zone,' Egisthe explains, 'the most ferocious destiny only brings third-rate devastation' (1.3). A simpler solution is indicated by the Mendiant when he observes that Egisthe is thinking about killing the girl. The most effective means of insisting on the play's ambiguity, however, occurs with the bird that suddenly appears above Egisthe's head (2.6). When Agathe and Clytemnestre notice it, Egisthe mentions that it has been with him since morning. It actually caused his horse to kick. Clytemnestre wonders whether it is a vulture or an eagle (2.7). Agathe cannot take her eyes from it, though her husband tells her to stop looking. 'You really annoy me,' he says (ibid.). Finally, Electre announces, 'The bird is coming down, Mendiant, the bird is coming down,' and the Mendiant notes, 'My, my, it's a vulture' (2.8). The vulture finally attacks Egisthe (2.9).

As the ancient image of Electre overlays the modern, the deviations that are consequently emphasized hold nothing up to ridicule. Instead, they imply that there may be significant changes to come in the new version. Giraudoux has created a world where chance is the rule, where justice is rewarded with injustice, where a city will be destroyed by invading Corinthians just after its king experiences an epiphany that invests him with his office: 'Oh powers of the world . . . at the very moment when the fog dissipated. . . . I had gotten off my horse . . . , and suddenly you showed me Argos, as I had never seen it, new, recreated for me, and you gave it to me' (2.7). Almost surprisingly – perhaps as one more proof of an aleatory world – just as the wolf cub turned on the woman Narsès, so Oreste and Electre follow the archetypal model and turn on Clytemnestre. In the end, 'everything is lost . . . the city burns' (ibid.), and the little girls, who marked the chronology by growing up like mushrooms (1.1) during the play, become decidedly unbenevolent Euménides that more closely resemble the furious Erinyes. Electre, however, exults because she 'has justice' (2.10). She announces that the city will be reborn. 'And those who are slitting each others' throats in the streets?' asks the third Euménide. 'If they are innocent, they will also be reborn,' opines Electre. Perhaps. But this is a world where 'the plague breaks out precisely when a city has sinned through impiousness or madness, but it devastates the particularly holy city next door. War erupts when a people degenerates and debases itself, but it devours the last of the just, the courageous, and saves the most cowardly' (1.3). Who knows the meaning of the dawn that the Mendiant announces at the end?

Parallel allusions like that in Anouilh's *Antigone* emphasize the common elements through persistent focus on the parallels, while oppositional allusions like that of Giraudoux change the focus to emphasize the differences. Anouilh insists on an assured destiny in *Antigone*. Giraudoux calls on another kind of allusion in *Electre* to make one wonder whether anything at all is assured. In other works, an allusion of opposition may weight parallels as a means of preparing a contrasting conclusion. Anouilh's allusion in *La Répétition* (*The Rehearsal* [1950]) provides a good example. Numerous explicit and implicit references to Marivaux's *La Double Inconstance* (*Double Inconstancy* [1723]) throughout Anouilh's play arouse the audience's expectation of continuing parallels. Because we are prepared to enjoy the typically joyous conclusion of marivaudage, where all ends well, the disappointment of the bleak ending of *La Répétition* is exacerbated. Anouilh's allusion is as metaphorical as that of Giraudoux, or indeed of more straightforward parallels, but the image in the reader's mind is one of opposition, whether it causes exhilaration or despondency or the intensification of one trait or another.

La Symphonie pastorale (*The Pastoral Symphony* [1919]) provides a somewhat different example of oppositional allusion. From the second sentence, Gide warns the reader that he has situated the *récit* in a rarefied environment: 'I was unable to go to R—— where for fifteen years I have customarily led the worship twice a month. This morning just thirty of the faithful were gathered in the chapel of La Brévine.'[8] An isolated region of Switzerland's mountains is the more isolated because of fresh snow – 'this claustration' (877) – and the Protestant faith. Jean-Jacques Thierry calls the Calvinist environment of Gide's childhood a 'stifling milieu' (Gide, *Récits* 1582). Gide points to other aspects of the microcosm when he states that this particular work, as well as *L'Immoraliste*, *La Porte étroite*, and *Isabelle*, 'denounce in turn the dangers of extreme individualism, of a certain form of very precisely Protestant mysticism . . . and, in *La Symphonie pastorale*, of the free interpretation of Scripture' (ibid. 1583). Such communities still exist: small, ingrown, isolated, steeped in the Bible, subject to the authority of father and pastor.[9] Congregations like this may be outside any system of hierarchical authority that provides a system of checks and balances and prevents the more extreme forms of deviation from the norm. That is the case with this pastor, who apparently depends uniquely on his personal understanding of the Bible to lead his flock. When he begins to listen to other voices, if only those of his own perverted desires, considerable damage results to Gertrude, to his family, and to himself. In a place far away in time and space and on a miniaturized scale, Gide warns of Jonestown or Waco.

To insist on the tradition of a small Bible-based community, Gide gives the pastor a language full of biblical images and turns of phrase. 'Thanks be to God for having confided this task to me' (877), to take an example from the first few lines of the book. The task is of course Gertrude, the blind girl he brought home. When his hard-pressed wife, Amélie, wonders not unreasonably what he plans to do with her, he responds solemnly, 'I am bringing back the lost sheep' (881). Such passages serve a number of functions. On the most obvious level, they add to the realism, for they are typical of the speech of such communities, as are the references the pastor frequently provides for his quotations from the Bible. Equally important, however, is the establishment of an external text that will be brought into his creation. The biblical language and the frequent references to Scripture can scarcely fail to insert the Bible into the reading experience and establish parallel allusions. Indeed, one might suspect that, following biblical injunctions, the pastor is going to imitate Christ, as any good pastor should. Gertrude rather resembles a lost sheep. And the pastor is clearly anxious to serve as the girl's 'good shepherd.'

I do not know what will finally sound a false note for the reader and stamp the work with Gide's habitual impress, *caveat lector*. Perhaps only those ideal readers who read the way Gide did: 'I read as I would like people to read me: that is, very slowly. For me, reading a book is to go off alone for two weeks with the author.'[10] Even the less devoted should perceive the pastor's confusion of *agape* with *eros* when he says, 'She did not make a move to defend herself, and since she raised her forehead toward me, our lips met…' (924), discreetly using ellipses to hide the obvious sequel. But there can be no doubt that Gide left many signs that the pastor does not imitate Christ, that he is not a Christ figure or type, that there is no parallel allusion.

From the beginning, the pastor pushes the more disagreeable aspects of Gertrude's salvation off onto his wife, to the tune of his spiteful commentary, while he devotes himself, he would like us to believe, to her soul. One might well imagine that he could take part in a ceremonial foot washing, but just as cleaning up the vermin-laden child is beyond him, so also are the humility and self-abasement that are supposed to accompany the act. For our purposes, however, the pastor's use of the Bible is most interesting. Certainly, the pastor's version of the Gospels would astonish any but those absolutely innocent of Scripture.

Jacques is quite right to reproach his father 'for choosing "what pleases me" in Christian doctrine' (914). While it may be admirable that he 'did not choose this or that word from Christ,' he is on unacceptable ground when he goes on to state, 'It is just that between the Christ and Saint Paul, I choose the Christ' (914). Conservative Christian theology would never permit one to separate the recorded words of Jesus from those of Paul, as the pastor does.[11] In the pastor's tradition, all Scripture is believed equally inspired by the Holy Spirit. Consequently, Jacques's position, as described by his father, is absolutely orthodox: 'For fear of having to put them in opposition, he refuses to dissociate one from the other, refuses to sense a difference of inspiration from one to another, and protests if I tell him that at this point I listen to a man while there I hear God' (ibid.). There are, of course, exegetical traditions that would welcome the pastor's distinctions, though that is not the case in the setting Gide describes. Likewise, one may not ignore the law and remain faithful to the love of Christ, as, once again, the pastor prefers (ibid.). In fact, of course, he picks and chooses among Jesus' words as well. Those who remember Jesus' denunciations of the Scribes and Pharisees will be surprised to read, 'I search across the Gospels, I search in vain for commandments, menaces, prohibitions... All that is only from Saint Paul' (ibid.).

The explicit references to the Bible and the mentions of scriptural context invite the reader to go to the New Testament itself. Almost immediately the problems surface. The first time the pastor provides a reference, it is wrong: 'neither be ye of doubtful mind' is found not at Matthew 12:29, as the text says (898), but at Luke 12:29 (or Matt. 6:25). The error has been ascribed to Gide's haste,[12] a suggestion I hesitate to accept. While one might not assume that the author is always right, one should at least entertain the possibility that what at first might seem an 'inconsistency' or a 'mistake' is purposeful and designed to take the reader beyond the surface. In this case, the erroneous reference joins other indications to suggest that the pastor's acquaintance with the Bible has become somewhat inexact, colored certainly by his desires and perhaps by a changing world view. If one takes the trouble to consult the passage in which the quotation actually occurs, one discovers that the pastor not only gives the wrong reference, he quotes out of context, as well. In context, the faithful are instructed not to worry about food and clothing, but rather to trust in God, while the pastor is exhorting himself to worry about real rather than imagined complaints – '[A]h! how beautiful life would be, and how bearable our misery, if we were content with real injuries instead of lending an ear to the specters and monsters of our minds...' (898).

Similarly, the pastor's first mention of biblical context – 'Does not Christ teach us to forgive offenses immediately after the parable of the lost sheep?' (888) – is also inaccurate. The parable of the lost sheep appears at Matt. 18:12–14. It is followed by some of those commands the pastor later misses that provide instruction for correcting a brother who has sinned against you (Matt. 18:15–22). Only then do we come to the parable of the unmerciful servant or, in the pastor's terms, teaching on forgiveness. The context of the pastor's reference to the lost sheep is interesting for other reasons as well. It is preceded by Jesus' explicit and pertinent menace: 'But whoso shall offend one of these little ones which believe in me, it were better for him that a millstone were hanged about his neck, and that he were drowned in the depth of the sea. Woe unto the world because of offenses! for it must needs be that offenses come; but woe to that man by whom the offense cometh!' (Matt. 18:6–7). Of course, the pastor somehow misses this warning, even though he later quotes again from Matthew 18, this time verses two and three (915). The parable of the lost sheep is followed at the beginning of chapter nineteen by Jesus' condemnation of adultery (Matt. 19:1–11).

The pastor has blinked on other occasions in his study of the Bible. Though he quotes several passages from Romans, for example, he has apparently passed over another appropriate text: 'And art confident that thou thyself art a guide of the blind, a light of them which are in darkness, an instructor of the foolish, a teacher of babes. . . . Thou therefore which teachest another, teachest thou not thyself? thou that preachest a man should not steal, dost thou steal? Thou that sayest a man should not commit adultery, dost thou commit adultery?' (Rom. 2:19–22a).

Conservative exegetes might permit figurative interpretations of certain biblical passages, but only when the text explicitly indicates its appropriateness, as in John's Revelation. Otherwise, they would expect a literal understanding of the Word. The pastor does not follow such guidelines, nor is he consistent in his practice. His interpretation varies from strict literalism to the wildest-eyed of figural readings depending, not on the text, but on the meaning he wishes to adduce. When, for example, Gertrude assumes that there must be lilies in the field in front of them because the Lord once said, 'Consider the lilies of the field' (909), the pastor explains their absence, not by suggesting that Jesus does not claim that there are lilies in all fields, but by accepting Gertrude's literalist premise: 'For Him to say so, there doubtless were in his day, but men's farming practices caused them to disappear' (909).

Elsewhere, the pastor's interpretations are absolutely unbridled. The most egregious example of misinterpretation comes when he attempts to get in the last word after a discussion about his manner of using Scripture, and he and Jacques trade verses. The exchange resembles the technique of comedy where characters talk at cross purposes but, to those in the know, revealingly. The pastor's family understands that he is far too interested in Gertrude and that his interest is by no means purely spiritual. Though wives and children are limited in what they may say in such conservative communities – we remember his wife Amélie's protests that 'certainly, she had nothing to say to me . . . and that she had but to submit herself as always to whatever unusual, impractical, and foolish idea I could come up with' (882) – they do develop ways of communicating that are as clear as the most explicit words. Amélie, certainly, knows one of the passages in Matthew 18 that the pastor has passed over in silence: 'If thy brother shall trespass against thee, go and tell him his fault between thee and him alone: if he shall hear thee, thou hast gained thy brother. But if he will not hear thee, then take with thee one or two more' (Matt. 18:15–16). Though we are limited to what the pastor chooses to tell us, clearly Amélie has gone to him. 'You never paid so much attention to any of your own children,' she tells him (889). Later, after the pastor has taken Gertrude to hear Beethoven's Sixth Symphony (the *Pastoral*), Amélie 'found the means of making me feel that she disapproved of the way I had used my day. . . . "You do for her what you would never have done for any of yours"' (897). And Amélie does not whisper her reproaches to the pastor alone. This time, as the pastor reports, she takes the second biblical step: 'What distressed me most was that Amélie dared say that in front of Gertrude; for although I would have taken my wife aside, she had raised her voice enough for Gertrude to hear her' (897). Later, when the pastor has not noticed the budding love between Jacques and Gertrude and remonstrates with his wife for not warning him, she becomes more pointed: 'If I had to warn you about everything you are unable to notice!' (906) The pastor does not understand, but, more important, he does not want to understand – 'What did this insinuation mean? That is what I did not know or want to try to find out, and passed on' (906).

Amélie tries yet again. When he still does not mend his ways, though both she and Jacques have in their separate manners taken him to task, Amélie advances to the third level of remonstrance: 'And if he shall neglect to hear them [the two or more], tell it unto the church' (Matt.

18:17). Her method of communication would for most people be rather subtle: neither she nor Jacques takes communion on Easter Sunday. It is important to recognize, however, that although it took him a while the pastor grasps the substance, and eventually the detail, of what she is trying to communicate: 'I know Amélie too well to have not been able to see all the indirect reproach that entered into her conduct. She never openly disapproves of me, but she is anxious to have me note her disavowal by a sort of isolation' (913). He claims not to have understood that he loved Gertrude at the time he took communion alone, but he has perceived both the essence of the remonstrance and the reality of his love by the time he writes of the event, which is of course well before the series of tragedies that close the volume.

With this background as context, we are perhaps better able to plumb the depths of Gide's irony in the exchange of verses. When the pastor leaves the verse, 'Let not him that eateth not judge him that eateth: for God hath received him,' he gives, of course, the reference, 'Romains, XIV, 2' – so that Jacques and the reader will feel the full weight of scriptural authority (916). Knowing readers will be less impressed, for the pastor has once again given the wrong reference (the correct one is Romans 14:3). The pastor believes he is making a definitive point in his argument over his right to extract authoritative Scripture from the biblical context. In fact, this particular selection is surprisingly inappropriate, at least on this level, but there can be no question that Jacques finds it to the point. He apparently reads it as a commentary on the pastor's relationship with Gertrude, in essence, *If you aren't enjoying Gertrude, don't judge the one who is.* The pastor knows he is on shaky ground: 'Obviously, it is a question here of food, but for how many other passages of Scripture is not one called to attribute double and triple meanings? ("If your eye…"; multiplication of the loaves; miracle at the marriage feast of Cana, etc.). [Note that traditional Christianity would refuse unequivocally to take these examples as anything but straightforward teaching or reporting.] It is not a question here of quibbling; the meaning of this verse is broad and deep: the restriction must not be dictated by the law, but by love' (916–17). Jacques responds with another verse from the same chapter: 'Destroy not him with thy meat for whom Christ died (Romans 14:15)' (917). Jacques's reference is correct.

The distortion of the external text reaches its apex with the two quotations of John 9:41 (915, 929). Once again, the pastor's quotation is very partial: 'If ye were blind, ye should have no sin.' He uses it to justify keeping Gertrude physically and spiritually blind. As he puts it, 'Sin is what darkens the soul; it is what is opposed to its joy. Gertrude's perfect happiness, which radiates from her whole being, comes from the fact that she does not know sin. . . . I put the four Gospels, the Psalms, John's Apocalypse and three Epistles in her vigilant hands, because if, blind, she does not know sin, what does it serve to disturb her by allowing her to read: "That sin by the commandment might become exceedingly sinful" (Romans 7:13) and the whole dialectic which follows' (915). In its fuller context, Jesus is warning a group of Pharisees: 'For judgment I am come into this world, that they which see not might see; and that they which see might be made blind. And some of the Pharisees which were with him heard these words, and said unto him, Are we blind also? Jesus said unto them, If ye were blind, ye should have no sin: but now ye say, We see; therefore your sin remaineth.' The Pharisees have just seen and heard the evidence that Jesus has healed a man blind from birth and have nonetheless thrown the man out of the temple (9:1–38). Jesus tells them that they would have some excuse if they had not been able to see. In no sense is He suggesting that the blind are without sin. On the contrary, in spiritual terms they are no different from anyone else. Both Christ and Paul insist that whether or not one knows what sin is, one sins. By knowing what sin is, one can avoid or go beyond it. This is the lesson of Romans 14, the chapter the pastor says he 'reread[s] once again' (917). Amélie's belief that Christianity domesticates our instincts (898) is doctrinally correct. The pastor is explicitly going against Scripture when he wishes to find new virtues through instincts or feeling.

The title of the work admirably emphasizes the themes. On one level, it is a pleasantry of questionable taste: the pastor is making music with Gertrude. One is implicitly invited to consider the kind of music he should be playing and the tune we actually hear. On another level, we are reminded that Beethoven's symphony represents an idyllic countryside rather like the one in which this account is set; perhaps we are encouraged to think of the idyllic loves of ancient pastoral poetry. But I suspect it is more important to remember that Beethoven was stone deaf when he wrote the work, for it not only reminds the reader of the far-from-idyllic reality of this particular love but, as well, it links the concepts of blindness and deafness, as does the Bible in both the Old and the New Testament. Isaiah cries, for example, 'Hear, ye deaf; and look, ye blind, that ye may see. Who is blind, but my servant? or deaf, as my messenger that I sent? . . . Seeing many things, but thou observest not; opening the ears, but he heareth not' (Isa. 42:19–20). Indeed, *La Symphonie pastorale* tells the story of a man who hears and does not hear, who sees and does not see. As it says in Matthew 15:14, 'If the blind lead the blind, both shall fall into the ditch.' When Gertrude receives her sight, she sees a beautiful world and the two things that bring her death: Amélie's 'poor face' filled with sadness and Jacques, whom she recognizes as the one she loves (928–9). 'Sin revived, and I died,' she quotes from Romans 7:9. Jacques converts to Catholicism, whose system of authority will protect him from the dangers of the unfettered freedom that destroyed his father and Gertrude: '[T]he example of your error guided me,' he says (930).[13]

Unlike synoptic allusions of opposition – an Odysseus who stays home, a pessimistic Pollyanna – extended allusions such as those in *La Symphonie pastorale* gain power by their extension and consistency. They require a relatively fixed external text, usually as in this case indicated by the suggestion of a parallel. Oppositional allusions, however, require considerable knowledge on the reader's part, much more than in a text composed of an extended parallel allusion like that of *Le Journal d'un curé de campagne* (*The Diary of a Country Priest* – [1936]), for the reader must keep in mind both the lessons of the external text and the distortions occurring within the reading experience. *La Symphonie pastorale*'s allusion is not satire or parody, for the passages neither mock nor ridicule the Bible. It directs the reader's attention to the work in hand, rather than to an offending person, object, or text outside the actual reading. The test I propose here grows from that suggested by the Russian formalists to distinguish fiction from nonfiction. One needs to determine whether the image created by the text as a whole has importance primarily because of something outside the text or whether it is important in and for itself. In *La Symphonie pastorale*, Gide's emphasis is by no means on the Bible, but rather on what the pastor does with it. One is expected to keep present both acceptable and unacceptable readings of Scripture in order to appreciate the full implications of the work. Similarly, to take another example, in *Le Retour de l'enfant prodigue* (1907) those readers who are not aware that Gide's prodigal son is not following biblical precedent when he encourages a younger brother to imitate his profligacy will remain insensitive to the full ramifications of the Gidian creation.

La Symphonie pastorale establishes a parallel allusion early on in the reading. As Genette said in *Figures II*, 'In fact, the opposition between two terms gains its meaning only in relation to what establishes their rapprochement, and which is their common element: phonology taught us that difference is pertinent, in linguistics as elsewhere, only on the basis of resemblance.'[14] Readers are however expected to go beyond the similarities to sense the misreadings and the warnings. If Gertrude really were a sheep, there would be no problem. Unfortunately for everyone concerned she is a young woman. And while the pastor preaches his own version of Christ (not Paul), neglecting the law in isolated preference for the Gospels, insisting on 'love' (not righteousness), the reader is encouraged to pick up the pattern and reject the pastor's intellectually dishonest refusal to distinguish Christian charity from the flaccid acceptance of any behavior at all. In the place of such sloppy *agape*, the novel impels the reader to reject moral blindness and cling to its opposite: at the very least, clear-sighted awareness.

For the really knowing, the oppositions turn back in again and emphasize similarities. The key image of blindness offers the most obvious example. When Jesus says, 'If ye were blind, ye should have no sin' (John 9:41), he was, as already pointed out, emphasizing the Pharisees' hypocrisy. Not only are they 'blind guides. . . . fools and blind' (Matt. 23:15-16), they load others with excessive burdens: 'For they bind heavy burdens and grievous to be borne, and lay them on men's shoulders, but they themselves will not move them with one of their fingers' (Matt. 23:4). This is, of course, precisely the practice of Gide's pastor. As he leaves the unpleasant tasks to Amélie, as he turns Jacques out of the house, as he finally seduces Gertrude, he burdens those for whom he has both parental and pastoral responsibilities with grievous encumbrances. 'But woe unto you, scribes and Pharisees, hypocrites! For ye shut up the kingdom of heaven against men; for ye neither go in yourselves, neither permit them that are entering to go in' (Matt. 23:13). The oppositions between the pastor's faulty interpretations emphasize the chasm between his and the biblical meanings, but on looking more closely at the context, as Jesus sets the Pharisees' self-serving hypocrisy in a glaring light, so the context of the pastor's misreadings stresses his similarly appalling pastorship. Emphases shift, components are rearranged, patterns are redistributed, and the formal integrity of each significance is violated. Identical words, then, establish allusive oppositions from a basis in similarity, and a new coherence is created.

Eugénie Grandet (1833) provides a useful example of parallel allusion serving as a foil for allusive opposition. Although *Eugénie Grandet* continues to be extraordinarily popular, and frequently studied, the secondary literature concerning the novel reveals many equivocal or flatly negative judgments. Pierre Citron, for example, normally one of Balzac's more enthusiastic readers, calls it 'a lusterless novel.'[15] The establishment critic Sainte-Beuve may offer a clue to the mysterious divergences in critics' reactions to *Eugénie Grandet*. He chose it for exaggerated praise, by implication holding it up as a classical exception to the rest of Balzac's ungainly production – praise that Bardèche terms 'perfidious,' since it congratulates Balzac for all the qualities that he does not have: delicacy, measure, sobriety, gracefulness. Bardèche here is echoing Balzac's own discomfort. Both realized that readers who like *Eugénie Grandet* often do so for the wrong reasons.[16] For those who believe that Balzac's 'good and his bad alike were entirely conspicuous and unmistakable,'[17] the novelist's 'badness' (Lubbock 204) resides in his 'abominable' taste (ibid.) and in his uneconomical complexity. Such readers appreciate that Balzac was able to tell the 'very slight story' (ibid. 225) of Eugénie's 'simple emotions' (ibid. 230) 'straightforwardly' (ibid. 227). Fervent Balzacians see it rather as lacking the magnificently pulsating details that give other of the novelist's works depth of meaning and passionate life.

It is known as a love story, but its love is unfruitful; we quit the story when the sweet young maid of the beginning has become the widow of an unloved husband in an unconsummated marriage. Not surprisingly, she has developed an old maid's stiffness and the pettiness encouraged by the narrowness of provincial life (3.1198). For the title figure of a novel, Eugénie does very little, and in fact, for all the words that have been written about *Eugénie Grandet*, it is the girl's father, Félix Grandet, who has attracted the most attention. Nicole Mozet goes so far as to suggest that the novel's symbolic structure is constructed on the character of the father.[18] One might wonder whether Balzac mistitled the work. But even M. Grandet does little during the course of the story. 'The novel is new,' comments Citron, 'because nothing novelistic happens' ('Préface' 12). Grandet, well on his way to an enormous fortune at the beginning, consolidates his financial position with a few astute coups. Mme Grandet passes away, but she has been almost inconsequential since her husband took her dowry and used it to begin his pursuit of riches. Though Eugénie does fall in love with her cousin Charles, and though they exchange vows, Charles's love is not strong enough to last the seven years it takes for the boy to make his fortune. (On repaying the money Eugénie lent him, he calls their early love 'our childishness' [3.1187]). And when Grandet finally dies, his household continues to operate as it always had: Eugénie, an excellent steward of her enormous fortune, lives almost the same way she did when her father was alive. She lights the fire only on those days when it was permitted in her youth, she dresses as her mother did, and she remains in the dark, cold, melancholy house where she was raised. Balzac picks up the images of the beginning and repeats them in the end, thus insisting on a continuation of the cycle of provincial behavior. Seemingly, though there has been some small turbulence in the placid pond of Saumur, it has passed, and equilibrium has returned.

While I do not wish to contradict the claim for *Eugénie Grandet*'s economy, I would argue that it differs from much of Balzac's work in that the economy he always sought was achieved with less apparent prolixity. At base, the master's stories are usually quite simple and straightforward – Balzac was a narrational minimalist. The descriptive complexity comes from his desire to fit his characters and their lives into a physical and metaphysical world that would satisfactorily highlight the point he wanted to make.[19] The apparent simplicity of *Eugénie Grandet* comes from Balzac's decision to use an allusion to an extremely well-known story to open onto a larger dimension. Here, in creating his fictional world he did not need to create his own myth and thus did not need a plethora of detail. Under the descriptions of seemingly trivial events and objects, there has been a development of considerable significance, though it only becomes clear on reading the account with an awareness of the fuller potential of the story's images. *Eugénie Grandet* recounts the story of the heroine who, in spite of being surrounded by gross materialism, is quite successful at establishing and pursuing spiritual values. Furthermore, the novel provides an excellent example of an oppositional allusion to the biblical drama of Christ's departure and promised return, and, as well, it plays out the divine/human comedy more fully than any other of Balzac's works.

Some time ago, Léon-François Hoffmann and his students called attention to an extensive pattern of religious themes and images in *Eugénie Grandet*. They concluded that passive Christianity and an aggressive nineteenth-century religion of Mammon establish an ironic dialogue around Eugénie, who is herself committed to a third god, Eros.[20] Although I disagree with these conclusions, it seems to me possible to pursue in more depth the pattern of allusions pointed to in this excellent study and to understand that Eugénie has moved well beyond her father's faith into a system of belief that, though perverted by influences surrounding her, is nonetheless recognizable. From the opening lines, which mention how much Saumur's houses resemble

cloisters and monasteries, to the terminal announcement that Eugénie
is moving toward heaven accompanied by quantities of good deeds
(3.1198), frequent references establish an allusion to the divine comedy
of Christ and His church subsequent to the passion. Jesus promised His
people that He would return. In the meantime, He sent the Holy Spirit
to help the congregation of His saints, the church, in the tribulations
and persecutions that would take place before His second coming.
Balzac was to use the account again in *Mercadet* (1851), but only in
Eugénie Grandet does it assume such importance.

The church, in the France of 1819, had been seriously weakened. Elsewhere, Balzac terms it 'without strength' (4.505) and 'impotent' (4.664).
Most obviously, as the novel reminds us, the revolutionary government
had seized the church's lands and thus much of its wealth. Grandet, for
example, bought a previously confiscated old abbey and some of the region's best farms and vineyards from the government for a pittance
(3.1030–1). In many ways, including decimating the clerical ranks
through execution (4.392), the state had attempted to subordinate the
church to itself. Balzac's narrator goes to considerable length to illuminate another religion that had been established and was flourishing
outside the church in the provinces. As for Grandet himself, 'Was he
not the only modern god in whom people have faith, Money in all its
power, expressed by a single physiognomy' (3.1052). It is worth mentioning that Grandet is an anagram of *d'argent* (money).[21] A mirror
image of the Father in Heaven, Père Grandet (e.g., 3.1030, 1033, 1034)
lives at the top of the former Grande-Rue, which as Fischler suggests is
surely to suggest 'a heavenly abode.'[22] In addition, Grandet 'sees everything' (3.1060, 1090) and distributes the daily bread (3.1041, 1077–8),
though otherwise the novel stresses his negative rather than his divine
traits. While the Judeo-Christian God is the generous 'I am' (Exod. 3:14)
of eternal life in whom 'all the promises . . . are yea' (2 Cor. 1.20),
Grandet's four standard responses are essentially negative: 'I don't
know, I can't, I don't want to, and We'll see about that' (3.1035).

Superficially, many of M. Grandet's positions seem modeled on
biblical principles. God the Father proclaimed, for example, that 'all the
earth is mine' (Exod. 19:5). As the parable of the talents suggests, however, all of His gifts are held in trust and His people are accountable for
them until the Christ returns to take them back. While it is clear that
Grandet's gifts to Eugénie are not free gifts either, the strings he
attaches are more like steel cables. Furthermore, although God 'maketh
his sun to rise on the evil and on the good, and sendeth rain on the just

and on the unjust' (Matt. 5:45), Grandet's generosity is limited to his own household and, for anything significant, to Eugénie. What he gives to his wife, he quickly takes back, and she is only too happy to give it, since she knows from experience that it produces peace in her household (3.1108). The gold he 'gives' Eugénie is to be displayed regularly for his own enjoyment. In a somewhat different vein, both Grandet's religion and Christianity are essentialistic (essence precedes existence, to use a distinction of the existentialists). For Grandet, though, the value that gives essence comes only from the material possession of money: 'Charles is nothing to us,' he points out pertinently; 'he hasn't a cent; his father went bankrupt' (3.1094). Likewise, his cavalier treatment of his wife, after he takes her dowry and inheritances for his own purposes, sets up a significant pattern that is repeated when he learns that Eugénie no longer has her gold. At that point, Eugénie is sent to her room and locked up 'in prison' on bread and water (3.1156). Later, after it is brought to his attention that much of the wealth he has been using as though it were his own continues legally to be his wife's, and that he may be forced to divide 'his' property and allow Eugénie to receive her mother's inheritance, he suddenly alters his behavior and plays the toady. When the day arrives that Eugénie becomes the heir and owner of her mother's wealth, Grandet 'hovers over her as though she were made of gold' (3.1171).

The biggest difference between Grandet and God has to do with eternal life. If Grandet is the 'High Priest' of the gold cult (Hoffmann 212), his belief in eternal life is conversely very slight. After his mind weakens and he spends hours with his eyes fixed 'stupidly' (3.1175) on the gold coins that the heroine spreads before him, he attempts to seize the gilded cross extended for him to kiss. He tells Eugénie that she will give him an accounting 'over there,' thus proving, the narrator maintains, that Christianity must be the religion of misers (ibid.). Previously, however, the narrator says flatly that misers do not believe in eternal life (3.1101), and goes on to warn ominously:

This reflection casts a horrible light on our era, when, more than in any other period, money dominates law, politics, and general behavior. Institutions, books, men, and doctrines, everything conspires to undermine the belief in a future life on which the social edifice has been founded for eighteen-hundred years. Now the casket is a little-feared transition. The future that used to wait for us on the other side of the requiem has been transposed into the present. To arrive *per fas et nefas* at an earthly paradise of luxury, vanity, and enjoyments, to petrify one's heart and mortify the flesh with a view toward ephemeral possessions, as people were once martyred with a view toward eternal treasures, is the general idea! . . . When this doctrine has passed from the bourgeoisie to the lower classes, what will become of our land? (3.1101–2)

The passage is important, for it places in explicit opposition the worship represented by the church and the reverence of gold. If gold in the person of Grandet is the new god, he provides a clear opposition to the eternal God of the Judeo-Christian tradition.[23] Grandet, after all, dies.

Balzac indicates that Grandet is but one part of an unholy trinity. Just as the Christian God includes a Holy Spirit, who is essentially the arm of God, through whom His power, knowledge, and wisdom are manifested in the world, so Grandet has Nanon. She is Grandet's 'prime minister' (3.1077). He trusts her more than the members of his own family. Though she does not manifest herself as fire itself, as does the Holy Spirit (Acts 2:3), she lights the fire (3.1044) and carries candles (3.1053) or torches (3.1107) to illuminate the way. And while the Holy Spirit only speaks what He hears in accordance with God's will (John 16:13), Grandet has to remonstrate with Nanon on several occasions for saying things that do not correspond to his desires: 'I'm not speaking to you, Nanon! Hold your tongue' (3.1083). One of the most important of the Holy Spirit's functions was to be the Comforter for God's people after Jesus rose and went to heaven (John 16:7). Nanon serves a similar function during Charles's long absence, especially while Grandet is persecuting his daughter, and after Eugénie is alone. Finally, given the fact that the Holy Spirit represents earnest or down payment on all the promises of God (2 Cor. 1:22), it is perhaps worth mentioning in respect to Nanon that *nans*, *nant* in Old French meant 'earnest,' 'down payment,' or 'surety,' and *nanter* 'to provide a surety.'[24]

The other member of the Trinity is Jesus, who referred to himself as the Son of Man (Matt. 8:20) and as a shepherd (John 10:11). The etymon of Charles means 'man,' and while his pseudonym in the early versions of the novel was Chippart (possibly constructed on *chiper* 'to steal'), Balzac replaced it in the Furne edition with Carl ('man') Sepherd (which may suggest 'shepherd') (3.1182). Jesus raises Lazarus from the dead; Grandet condemns Charles because he cares more about the dead than about money (3.1093). Jesus leaves for heaven; Charles for the Indies. Both promise to return for their brides, but Charles, inoculated with egotism (3.1126), becomes callous and skeptical (3.1181). He leaves Eugénie in the lurch.

Eugénie's identification with the church, that is, the congregation of the saints, is emphasized by the traits that relate her to those particularly holy examples of the faithful who have been admitted to sainthood.[25] Her masculine attributes (e.g., 3.1075) have several functions. On the one hand, they prepare her impressive strength of purpose in opposing her father,[26] and on the other, they might remind us of St Eugenia of Alexandria, who dressed as a man and passed for many years as a monk. On joining the monastery, Helenus, who was supernaturally informed of her true sex, said, 'Thou dost well to call thyself a man, for woman though thou art, thou doest manfully'.[27] It is perhaps more important to note that the Cruchot whom Eugénie eventually marries is termed a *cruche* ('pitcher' or 'fool') by his uncle: 'My nephew is a fool [*cruche*]' (3.1051). St Eugenia of Alsace is normally represented with a pitcher or *cruche*.[28]

Eugénie's appropriateness as a symbol for the Christian church, however, is most obvious in what she actually does. The significance of her actions also helps to explain why she, rather than her father, is the title character. The Bible refers to the church as the bride of Christ and uses the betrothal customs in the intertestamentary and early Christian era to illuminate the image. As Joseph's decision to break with Mary on learning of her pregnancy indicates, although a betrothal did not absolutely have to lead to marriage, it was in fact a binding contract that was expected to move with well-regulated deliberateness to the actual marriage ceremony and consummation. When Jesus rose to Heaven, He promised to return for His bride, that is, for His people, at which time the actual marriage would be performed (e.g., Matt. 26:64; Rev. 19:7). In the meantime, the church is expected to love (2 Thess. 3:5), to remain obedient (1 Tim. 6:14), charitable (1 Cor. 1:7), faithful and ready (Matt. 24:44; 25:1–13), while functioning as a good steward (Luke 19:11–27).

In this context, many puzzling aspects of Eugénie's behavior are resolved. There is no question that the heroine looks upon her kiss and promise as betrothal: 'I will wait' (3.1139). And so she does, though as it finally turns out she awaits a bridegroom who changes his mind. The solemnity of the occasion where the two commit themselves to each other is perhaps highlighted by Nanon's sudden appearance. 'Amen! [*Ainsi soit-il!*]' (3.1140), she says. As a witness, the servant not only makes the agreement official, she also brings in the religious element. Nanon is elsewhere said to be 'conserved as though in brine' (3.1177), which may recall Jesus telling His people, 'Ye are the salt of the earth' (Matt. 5:13). (I have even wondered whether the novel's setting, Saumur, and its salty homonym 'saumure,' might have suggested Balzac's exploitation of the biblical drama of Christ's departure and promised return.)

As she waits, Eugénie's life is dominated by love. '[S]he could only exist through love, through religion, through her faith in the future' (3.1178). She is so obedient that at her father's demand, she signs away her rights to her mother's inheritance. Although her charitable spirit blossoms only after Grandet's death, she becomes an excellent steward of the family fortune. And, despite the lack of communication from Charles, she remains faithful during the long years after his departure. When she learns the truth of his inconstancy, she begins what is to be an important shift in her affections. Earlier, the narrator explains that the love she bears Charles 'explained eternity to her. Her heart and the Gospel signaled two worlds to look for. Night and day, she meditated on these two infinite ideas, which for her were perhaps brought together in one' (ibid.). While there is no doubt that the 'inextinguishable sentiment' (3.1193) preventing her from consummating her marriage is her love of Charles, she later seems to have made an important change. Much as Dante shifted his focus from Beatrice and Petrarch from Laura, so Eugénie turns from Charles to God. She has all her mementos of Charles turned into a gold monstrance and donated to her parish.

As the narrator would clearly wish, given the previously cited passage where he bemoans his society's commitment to money in an earthly paradise, rather than to living as did early martyrs 'with a view toward eternal treasures' (3.1101), Eugénie turns toward heaven. Although she has from the beginning lived in the midst of a 'gathering of people whose life was purely material' (3.1053), Balzac's heroine is indifferent to gold. We are told that she 'aspired to heaven' (3.1198) and 'lived, pious and good, filled with saintly thoughts, [and] constantly helped the unfortunate in secret' (ibid.). Eugénie 'walks toward heaven accompanied by a long procession of good deeds' (ibid.). She is a *beati*, one of the blessed. She stands in opposition to her father, Félix. Both *beati* and *felix* occur in the Vulgate, and both words can mean happy, but *felix* (e.g., Sir. 14:2) leans away from holiness toward material benefits and good fortune. It is surely no accident that M. Grandet's first name is Félix, given the pagan and materialistic Roman deity Felicitas, the goddess of happiness. Charlotte Yonge tells us that this name was frequently given to particularly fortunate individuals.

I take no position on Balzac's religion, but there seems no question that Balzac recognized the literary advantages to be reaped from a stable, reasonably well-known text like the Bible. Most of the biblical passages referred to above were familiar to most readers of the day, since they were included in the Mass at some point in the liturgical year. Balzac's charming, innocent, defenseless heroine looks for guidance to a weak church represented by a priest who for the sake of his family's fortune will entertain the thought of adultery (3.1167) and agree to permit a marriage that he knows will remain unconsummated (3.1192). The reader then watches Eugénie live at the heart of a cult of committed materialists worshipping gold and earthly success as she plays out a perverted and failed drama that alludes to Christ's departure and promised return, before committing herself to heavenly goals. Balzac believed that at one time the pattern of Christian belief and action within a strong church served the salutary end of protecting and nurturing society, but that it was being overwhelmed by an egocentric, destructive worship of Mammon. In one instance, at least, the heroic Eugénie resists Grandet/*d'argent* and suggests another possibility, where a socially functional stewardship, charity, and faithfulness remain operative.

Such extended allusions as in *Eugénie Grandet* gain power by their extension and consistency. They require a relatively fixed external text – usually, as in this case indicated initially by the suggestion of a parallel. Oppositional allusions, however, require considerable knowledge on the reader's part, much more than in a text composed of an extended parallel allusion, such as *Le Journal d'un curé de campagne,* for the reader must keep in mind both the lessons of the pattern of meaning alluded to and the distortions occurring in the text in hand. This example in *Eugénie Grandet* is not satire or parody, for the passages neither mock nor ridicule the Bible. It directs the reader's attention to the work in hand, rather than to an offending person, object, or text outside the reading experience. The test of determining an outward or inward thrust that I propose here requires the determination both of whether the image created by the text as a whole has importance primarily because of something outside the text or is important in and for itself, and of how that image relates to the rest of the reading. In *Eugénie Grandet,* Balzac's emphasis is not on the Bible, but rather on what his novel does with it. One is expected to keep in mind both the Christian drama and an opposing materialistic perversion of it in order to appreciate the full implications of the work.

Eugénie Grandet establishes a parallel allusion early on in the reading. Almost immediately, however, one begins to notice the differences between the genuine article and the monstrous perversion, and one consciously or unconsciously seeks a way of reconciling the two. Readers are expected to go beyond the similarities to sense Grandet's perverted theology and the warnings implicit in it. Eugénie serves as the fulcrum. Her role remains essentially the same, though the roles of others change radically. Grandet dies, Charles fades away, and Nanon marries, thus securing a life of her own. While she is still a servant and a comforter to Eugénie, her previously total allegiance to the godlike Grandet has been weakened. Eugénie remains the same, though her orientation changes. She turns from the perverted religion of Mammon, which has disappointed her, and, while storing up treasures in heaven by her good deeds, waits for the return of her Lord. In the process, as Balzac's touching heroine plays out the divine comedy in a human context, *Eugénie Grandet* demonstrates the potential power of oppositional allusion.

7

Allusive Oxymoron: *La Faute de l'abbé Mouret*

Was Barbey d'Aurevilly correct in proclaiming Emile Zola's *La Faute de l'abbé Mouret* (*Father Mouret's Sin* [1875]) a base attack against religion, or is it instead, as another critic suggests, Zola revealing through the abbé his sublimated desire to fall on his knees before the church?[1] To take another tack, could it be a 'paean of praise to nature,' a 'vigorously neopagan' hymn to irrationality and Eros,[2] or – less enthusiastically – the exaltation of fecundity,[3] or – downright insultingly – the nasty evidence of Zola's love of filth?[4] However encouraged we may be by the common denominator in these last three opinions, the accord unfortunately lacks universality. Still another critic discovers a 'fundamental ambiguity in Zola's attitude to sexual love. . . . The consummation of love in all Zola's early novels from *La Confession de Claude* to *La Faute de l'abbé Mouret* is invariably presented as at best a sad compromise, at worst a crime, and is usually attended by the sniff of brimstone to come.'[5] One writer goes even farther and maintains that when Serge talks of the 'abominable necessity of sex,' he is serving as Zola's mouthpiece.[6] And, to break this string of oppositions, another scholar sees the novel as a Schopenhauerian craving for peace and death.[7] It is apparently for good reason that Richard B. Grant has written of 'Confusion of Meaning in Zola's *La Faute de l'abbé Mouret*.'[8] Indeed, after having read what these and other scholars and critics have said about *La Faute*, one is tempted to claim with Taine, Maupassant, and Huysmans that the book is less a novel than a lyrical poem.[9] The next step would be to avoid the whole problem of interpretation by adopting the orientation of some recent critics, to assume that poetry's significance is nothing but its visual and sonorous texture, and to conclude, then, that *La Faute de l'abbé Mouret* is interesting but meaningless bric-a-brac.

Still, the very number of critics who have continued to struggle with this novel (where some of Zola's other efforts – such as *Le Rêve* [1888] – have been virtually ignored since their publication) indicates a widespread, perhaps unconscious conviction that the words Zola used to construct *La Faute* do indeed work together meaningfully to produce a coherent whole. I believe this is the case. It seems to me that the novel centers on the metaphorical union of two complexes of allusion, one turning around the Judeo-Christian tradition and the church, the other around nature and nature myths. Though the two allusive systems appear to be in violent conflict, in fact they work like an oxymoron – that is, the conjunction of *seemingly* contradictory elements. In precisely the same way as tropes like 'audible silence' or 'bloodthirsty pacifist,' Zola's allusions not only do not cancel each other out, they actually work together to suggest a third term: neither church nor nature, neither pure mind nor pure body, rather a unity of both – a human being. *La Faute de l'abbé Mouret* is an extraordinarily lush novel that allows me to recapitulate the structures of allusion that have occupied me up to this point, while considering an even richer pattern.

I

The primary themes of *La Faute de l'abbé Mouret* had long interested Zola. From a shrewd analysis of the dossier (a collection of the notes, character sketches, outlines, and manuscripts that remain from the author's preparation and writing of the novel), Henri Mitterand hazards the guess that Zola had a clear notion of the plot of *La Faute* by 1873, even before he worked out *La Conquête de Plassans* (1874).[10] The latter novel was written first, however, and there we are introduced to Serge Mouret and his family. This is not to say that one has to read them in order of publication. Zola repeated the information introduced in *La Conquête* that is essential to *La Faute*. Of that there is precious little: just a few details about Serge's unhealthy heredity. Insofar as the characters, the scene, and the plot are concerned, *La Faute de l'abbé Mouret* is reasonably autonomous.

On the surface, the novel hardly qualifies as 'action-packed'; it would require only a few sentences to summarize the actual happenings. I shall go on at more length, since the novel demands an awareness of seemingly unimportant details. Rather than cluttering up its pages, such elements make *La Faute de l'abbé Mouret* more than the vulgar account of a priest innocently seducing an ignorant girl; it becomes the story of man.

When the novel opens, Serge has completed his seminary and assumed the parish of Les Artaud, a village inhabited by a huge, inbred family of Artauds. The name is perhaps significant. It suggests the German *hart* (hard, difficult, crude) or *harthäutig* (thick-skinned, callous), though it probably derives from the Latin *arator* (ploughman or farmer). Zola's choice of a patronymic admirably highlights both the land and its inhabitants, for Les Artaud is a barren, desolate, rocky land, from which the local farmers extract a living only by dint of the most unrelenting labor. Archangias, an Ignorantine Brother in charge of the local school, adds another dimension to the villagers. He says they 'conduct themselves like animals. . . . They are like their dogs who don't go to mass, who make fun of the commandments of God and of the Church. They love their pieces of land so much that they fornicate with them' (1237).[11] Perhaps Archangias's name was meant to suggest a latter day reincarnation of the Archangel Michael. As Balzac's Father Grancey points out, Michael was considered 'the angel of executions, the inflexible angel,'[12] and Archangias, a worshipper of the Old Testament God of vengeance, would like to see Him wipe out the lot. Whether or not one agrees with the cure proposed by the ardent brother, there is no question that the children and young people of Les Artaud are considerably more interested in having a good time than they are in either school or church. The older Artauds seem a less sympathetic version of the peasants Zola portrayed in *La Terre*. Mother Brichet, a whiny, self-seeking leech, is the only 'pious' person in the village. She uses her 'religion' to wheedle food from the priest, his sister, Désirée, or La Teuse, Serge's crippled Norman housekeeper (Teuse is a Norman word meaning 'twisted'). Mother Brichet's son, Fortuné, has succeeded in getting Rosalie pregnant, to the delight of everyone but Serge, Archangias, and Rosalie's father, Bambousse. The representatives of the church would be satisfied if they could marry the two young people, but Bambousse will not stand for it. He is the wealthy man of the village, his daughter belongs to him, and he sees no reason to let her marry a penniless young scamp. 'If you were to ask me for a sack of wheat, you would give me some money,' he points out to Father Mouret. 'Why do you expect me to let my daughter go for nothing?' (1245). He hopes Rosalie will abort the baby, a solution that would enable him to marry her properly and increase the family wealth. And he is not above helping things along by pelting her with clods of dirt.

At first the plot seems destined to turn around Rosalie, Fortuné, and the child. Their trials soon become peripheral, however, only to resurface later in an extremely significant development. More and more, Serge's growing personal crisis draws our attention. After the death of his parents, the young priest assumes responsibility for Désirée, his retarded but extraordinarily healthy sister. Serge wants a desert retreat where he can shut out nature and concentrate on God (Quinet says Jehovah is the 'spirit, the eternal inhabitant of the desert'),[13] and initially, the little village satisfies his desire. On the first few pages of the novel we find Serge preparing for the Mass, which is said in a church empty except for La Teuse, a local urchin who serves as altar boy, and a merry group of sparrows. According to La Teuse, Serge is a saint, but she goes on to add that 'he hasn't lived, he knows nothing, he hasn't any trouble being as good as an angel' (1229). Although Serge is almost twenty-six years old, he is ignorant of life. He thinks he disdains nature and believes he has blocked his senses to physical sensation. In fact, a surge of life is about to awaken him from the 'sleep of the saints' (1232).

It starts when his uncle Pascal takes him off for a visit to Paradou, a privately owned park in the area. The place, left under the less than diligent guard of Jeanbernat, has been allowed to become overgrown. Jeanbernat, who is also called the Philosopher, lives just outside the wall surrounding Paradou and spends his time, like Candide, with his little garden. Only his niece, Albine, goes inside, and she seems as uncontrolled as the park's vegetation. While Pascal and Serge chat with Jeanbernat, a door in the wall suddenly opens, allowing Serge to catch a glimpse of the park. In the midst of rampant verdure, there rises an enormous tree, filled with a flock of birds (1253). Medieval legend has it that when St Brendan arrived at an island paradise he found a similar tree, likewise covered with birds. St Brendan's island differs from Paradou, however, for it had only two rivers (Paradou has four streams). One was the river of life and the other of death. Nonetheless, perhaps Serge's vision foreshadows the choice he will soon have to make between life and death. But the door closes and Albine, a sixteen-year-old dressed like a Gypsy in bright colors and flowers, stands laughing before them. Only seven years before she was a highly polished little lady. That was prior to her father's bankruptcy and suicide, after which she became the responsibility of Jeanbernat, who let her finish raising herself in the middle of Paradou. All vestiges of civilization seem to have dropped by the wayside. Now, she is a savage, perhaps worse. As she follows Pascal and Serge on their way back, the latter thinks he hears 'an animal running . . . behind' (1256).

Serge's senses have begun to awaken, and he is upset. He might well have succeeded in suppressing his natural impulses once again had not his sister, Désirée, dragged him off to look at her animals. There in her farmyard, surrounded by ducks, chickens, geese, rabbits, a pig, and a goat, Désirée is in her element. Serge is frightened, disgusted, even sick. Memories of a stone gargoyle representing a goat fornicating with a monk, hallucinations of fecundity and of Désirée's ample hips, and a vision of Paradou assail the defenseless priest, who can no longer stifle his growing awareness of surrounding life. Later, while walking before the church in the pleasant May evening, he sees and smells the human beings of the village. It makes him think he is once again in Désirée's realm, inundated by the heat of generation.

Without causing the laughter Candide's vicissitudes arouse, Zola could scarcely have a protagonist fall out of a train, be bitten by a lion, and scalped by Indians all in the same day, but the sources of Serge's malaise are so banal that the author could safely heap one upon another. Poor Serge is literally finished by the events of the evening. Rather than the month of September, with its exaltation of the cross, which as Pierre Ouvrard points out later dominates Serge's calvary (Ouvrard 79), it is the Month of Mary (May), and the big, healthy, sensual girls of the neighborhood come bearing olive, laurel, and rosemary boughs to decorate the altar of the Virgin. They leave the lamplit altar looking like a green thicket with 'a pale moon rising at the edge' (1285). Memories of his happy years in the seminary make Serge all the more miserable, and he prays vainly for peace.

Mary conceived without sin, annihilate me in the depths of the immaculate snow falling from each of your members. . . . Take my senses, take my virility. . . . Dry up my organs and leave me sexless, incapable of evil. . . . I want to be a thing, a white stone at your feet. . . . Yes, I deny life, I say that the death of the species is preferable to the continuing abomination that propagates it. Sin dirties everything. It is a universal stench spoiling love, poisoning the marriage bed, the cradle of the newborn. . . . Give me the death of everything! . . . Oh Mary, chosen Vessel, castrate humanity in me, make me a eunuch among men so as to fearlessly deliver the treasure of your virginity to me! (1312–15)

And, shivering with fever, the abbé faints. The apparently fruitless prayer is stilled.

Book two opens with Serge in Paradou. Uncle Pascal, a doctor, has spirited him away from the church and left his cure to fresh air and

Albine. Of his former life, prior to the symbolic death, Serge can remember only his fever and a dream of superhuman perfection that led
him to crawl through an interminable, underground tunnel. Cave-ins
frequently impeded his progress. But the nightmare is over, and he
laughs: 'Say! it's crazy, I'm a child' (1319). Symbolically, he has died
and begins a new life (Ouvrard 71). Indeed, it is as though he has
begun his life again, with Albine as his mother. The sick young man
seems to depend primarily on the sun and on Albine, whose hand
warms him like the sun (1320). At his best, his senses are so stupefied
that he lives a vegetable's life. Really, as the narrator says, 'he was
nothing but a plant' (1330). And when the weather changes for the
worse, he falls into the somnolence of winter until the sun returns. Then
he again feels the delight of new life.

While Serge convalesces, Albine chatters about an 'enchanted refuge,
with its immense tree' (1357), a place where she would like to live forever (1330). Serge will have none of it. He fears an even greater happiness, and he dreads the charm of the tree's shade, which is said to cause
death (1357). Perfectly content with the nature around him, he grows
stronger 'in the warm egg of spring' (1330), and under Albine's tutelage,
he learns once again to talk and to walk. Initially, he looks like an
ambulatory tree (1333), but ease comes with practice: 'Serge was no
longer afraid. He was being born in the sun, in this pure bath of light
which inundated him. He was being born at twenty-five years of age, his
senses suddenly opened, delighted with the big sky, the happy earth, the
prodigy of the horizon spread out before him' (1334). Soon Serge becomes an adolescent (1332), and we follow the account of their innocent
love as he and Albine discover the park. At first, there are roses with
their smell of love. In the midst of them, Serge takes his new vows: 'If I
abandon you some day, may I be damned, may my body dry up like a
useless weed' (1339). They revel in the 'nuptials of the odorous woods,
leading the virginities of May to the fecundities of July and August'
(1341). Serge, 'no longer [a] plant subject to the agonies of winter,' pro-
tects Albine (1345), though she continues to be in command (1371–2).
They wander through the park looking at the vestiges of its past inhabitants. The vegetation 'seemed in a rage to overturn what the efforts of
man had made' (1346). They look at the faceless statue in the water of the
grotto and walk into the flower beds, past a mutilated statue of a lion,
past an armless cupid, and on into catalogs of flowers.

Some days they stay in Serge's room, which used to be Albine's, and
tell stories – for example, of the lord and lady who long ago lived and

loved in the park. Legend has it that the woman died there (Albine thinks it was in that very room). Not many people know it, but they were the ones who discovered the 'place of perfect happiness' (1356) of which Albine dreams. The lord and his mistress passed most of their time there where the lady was probably buried. Serge thinks it must be 'forbidden to sit beneath a tree whose shade gives such a thrill' (1358). Albine agrees. Most of the people in the area say it is forbidden.

Sometimes Serge and Albine pretend they are the lord and lady, but usually they are out in the park, crossing the four streams, raiding the fruit trees, picnicking, losing themselves as they walk together through the woods. Then they kiss and begin to talk of love. 'Something power-ful, sovereign invaded them; it was like a long expected meeting where they saw each other grown, made for one another, forever joined. For a second they were astonished; they raised their eyes towards the religious vault of the foliage; they seemed to interrogate the peaceful people of the trees in order to find again the echo of their kiss' (1382). That night Serge listens long to the sound of Albine getting ready for bed.

The following days they are embarrassed in front of each other. It is not shame, rather a fear that their joy may be spoiled. Even though the park makes them uneasy, as though something dangerous were lying in wait, they eventually climb up to the springs where it is warm even in the winter. Hot from their walk, heady from the perfumes emanating from the plants drenched with aphrodisiac sweat, they finally sit beneath a lovely cedar. Serge wants to hold Albine, but she is terrified, and they leave past a nightmare of plants shaped like obscene bellies, skeletons, living pustules. Then, in the heat, Albine stumbles and turns to Serge. 'Take me,' she says (1390). But their embrace is too full of anguish, and they flee homeward, each by a different path.

From then on, they can no longer stand the garden. In Serge's room a new kind of school opens. Frolicking cupids and a satyr with his female prize are depicted on the walls. Pictures of men resembling bandits and women with 'the dying eyes of people being killed' teach Serge and Albine the 'science of loving' (1395). After that they suffer, not only from the voluptuousness of the garden, but from Serge's room as well. Although they begin to avoid each other, Serge's health needs a 'supreme plenitude' (1397), and it is only a matter of time before Albine finds the secret place with its giant tree. She overcomes Serge's fears and leads him there. 'It isn't forbidden,' she repeats (1401). 'In fact, the whole park pushed them gently' (1403), and 'it was the garden that had wished the misdeed' (1407). *Faute* may mean 'misdeed,' 'error,' or in nineteenth-century France 'sin,' usually of a sexual nature. The couple listens to the park, to the 'fatality of generation surrounding them' (1409), and they yield. The park applauds.

Afterwards they 'experienced an absolute perfection of their being. The joy of creation bathed them, made them equal to the powerful mothers of the world, making of them very forces of the earth' (1409). Serge has found his manhood; he feels complete, no longer an adolescent, as though he has 'awakened a lion' (1410). 'Now she was the servant' (ibid.). She fears that he will one day resent her previous empire, that he will reproach her because he once declared himself her slave. He calms her: 'Come on, it can't be wrong [*faute*]. We loved each other as we were supposed to love each other' (1411). But her sadness continues, and her uneasiness grows until it overcomes Serge. Suddenly they realize that they are lost 'in the middle of a labyrinth of bushes' (ibid.).[14] Albine thinks the underbrush is full of mocking voices, she is sure someone has entered the garden, and soon, as a result, they begin to cover their nakedness with leaves.

This episode has caused considerable confusion. If Albine is the delightfully primitive nature girl she seems to be, why on earth does she feel shame? Her trembling insecurity (1410), her uneasiness (1411), and her shame (1412) seem uncharacteristic to say the least. Not even Albine's intuition of a foreign presence manages to explain satisfactorily the violent change in her personality. Though Zola would appear to have left himself open to a charge of unrealistic portrayal, if the truth were known, he probably would have been more than willing to defend this episode as the most realistic of the novel. I suspect it represents another of those quaint beliefs of Zola's that have led him to be considered rather condescendingly as something of a smart ignoramus. His main crime, which, like Maupassant's venereal disease, is never forgiven or forgotten, consists in his having failed his baccalaureate examinations. When we add to that his (to our eyes) naive scientific beliefs and his acceptance of what we know now to be quackery, poor Zola has little chance of a reappraisal. We should perhaps not forget, however, that enormous numbers of people shared Zola's bizarre superstitions, and some of them had not only passed their baccalaureates but were even considered learned. I think for example of Jules Michelet, the great nineteenth-century historian, whose importance to the formation and early works of Zola can no longer be doubted.[15] Roger Ripoll goes farther and suggests that Michelet's works may have directly inspired certain elements of *La Faute*: both the use of the extremely important plant imagery and the allusion to the story of the Garden of Eden in Genesis. To support his insight, he quotes a number of passages from Michelet and a text from one of Zola's *Causeries*, published in 1868, in which Zola mentions Michelet while describing his own feelings in front of nature.[16] In addition, I would also suggest that Albine's strange behavior is the direct result of Michelet's vision of Woman that Zola apparently accepted almost *in toto*.

The woman in question is Innocent Woman (Michelet scarcely mentions the other kind, who is, he pronounces, fit for emigration, though little suited for marriage).[17] Unlike her ancient counterpart, this Modern (and Innocent) Woman is more than a body; she has intelligence and a soul.[18] When the marriage is consummated and thus begins, the new wife gives herself completely to her husband.[19] She is filled with fear because she knows that the gift of herself may lead to death in child-birth. 'The sister of love [is] death,' says Michelet.[20] Perhaps the main reason for her uneasiness, however, is the intuitive awareness of the irreversibility of the step she has taken. She has been stamped with the image of her man. Michelet, like Zola, accepted Lucas's outlandish belief that 'the widow frequently gives to her second husband children who resemble the first' (*Amour* 17). Although the husband may go elsewhere, she cannot.

According to Michelet, a woman's whole life, her meaning, her self-esteem, and her definition center on her marriage. Not even a child can fill her most pressing needs, for the woman's goal in marriage is love and companionship rather than offspring.[21] She must please her man, and especially during the few hours after they first make love, she lives in constant fear that she will not. She is unsure of herself, certain that she has become ugly. The thoughtful husband will, and indeed must, reassure her. He must also give her a few days of solitude, safe from the prying eyes of others, to come to terms with herself (*Amour* 126–8). During this emotion-filled period, a total change takes place. The man gains fulfillment and becomes the master, and his thoughts turn naturally towards the outside world, though with an awareness of his wife's self-sacrifice and her resultant dependency. She, on the other hand, formerly proud and untamed and now joyfully subjugated, turns inward. She will establish a haven for her master's return. There he will find trust, love, and peace to strengthen him for a return to the fray.[22]

If Michelet's conception of womankind was Zola's model, as seems likely, everything begins as it should. Both Albine and Serge react properly after having made love. The same thing is true when they come out of the trees and find themselves before a breach in the wall. Louis Kamm considers this breach a symbolic demarcation between life and death (*Object* 88). Albine tries to pull Serge back, but he follows Michelet's pattern and resists. He gazes out into the world, over Les Artaud where he sees some peasants: the Brichets, Rosalie, Vincent and his sweetheart, and finally La Teuse and Désirée. Then everything goes wrong. The Angelus tolls, and Serge remembers his position and his religion. This time he reacts as he has been trained – he falls to his knees. Feeling his long beard, which gives him the 'beauty of a beast,' he gropes in vain for his tonsure, and with a despairing glance at Albine, he says, 'We have sinned [*péché*]' (1416). Serge, confronted by the visions of both his recent and more distant past, is terrified. He hears 'a heavy step behind the wall. . . . like the slow, rumbling approach of anger' (1416), and Archangias appears. Standing in the threshold of the breach, the brother surveys them. He shouts, 'Are you an animal? . . . There you are, all covered with hair like a goat. . . . In the name of God, get out of that garden' (1417). Serge pushes Albine away and walks toward the breach where Archangias brutally drags him from Paradou.

Book three opens in the middle of Rosalie's and Fortuné's wedding. The baby is there with them, but not Rosalie's furious father. Serge's sermon in praise of the sacrament of marriage moves the peasants, especially because of the priest's obvious emotion. Fortuné even weeps. The young priest is a tortured man, and Désirée compares him unfavorably to her animals who 'get along better than people' (1428). He never goes out, except for a few minutes in the evening, because the smells, the sun, the expanse of the horizon upset him too much. Instead, to keep himself busy, he repairs the church. Starting by pasting paper over most of the broken windows of the nave (Désirée makes him leave some open for the sparrows), he then replasters and paints. Everything shines, except for the Virgin's altar, which now resembles an abandoned tomb (1438). Serge has deserted Mary to worship the Cross. His prayers for grace are long agonies, relieved only by those periods when peace descends and anesthetizes him, body and mind.

Archangias proclaims himself 'God's gendarme' (1440) and watches to make sure that Serge does not weaken again. He would like to prevent all meetings with either Jeanbernat or Albine, but on the night of Fortuné's wedding, when Serge and Archangias are on their way to bless the couple's bedroom, Jeanbernat stops them. A rock fight between

Archangias and Jeanbernat ensues. When the latter finally overcomes Archangias, he tells Serge that he would be welcome at Paradou. Naturally the priest ignores the invitation, and Albine comes to the church to find him. Speaking as a child of nature, she wants to take him back to the garden, while Serge leans for support on the altar in front of the big bleeding Christ and refuses. After she has left, the hour of the priest's Calvary tolls. First he is tempted by the vision of her 'round waist, her superb shoulders, her odor of a passionate woman' (1477). He cannot even pray to Mary, for when she appears, she is in the guise of Albine. He needs 'a jealous God, an implacable God, the God of the Bible, surrounded by thunder, only appearing in order to punish the terrified world. There were no more saints, no more angels, no more Mother of God; there was only God, an omnipotent master' (1480). But Serge gives in to temptation and dreams of caressing Albine. Then he is tempted by wealth. It seems to him that the light fills the church with gold, and the priest decides the church will serve them as a palace. 'God wouldn't say anything, since He permitted loving. Besides, what did God matter! Wasn't it Serge now who was God, with his gold feet that the crowd kissed and who accomplished miracles' (1485–6). Sin triumphs as one temptation follows another. Serge gives in to them all. Finally, he damns God.

In the dark church, a hallucinating Serge watches while the whole of nature attacks and bursts the church apart, spreading the debris to the four corners of the sky. Christ falls. Serge applauds furiously, for the church is vanquished, and heaven has been terrestrialized. Then, when Désirée calls him, he awakens to discover that the little church still stands. 'He no longer understood, he remained in terrible doubt between the invincible church, growing back from its ashes, and all-powerful Albine, who shook God with a single one of her breaths' (1490).

That night Serge sleeps like the dead, and the next few days pass in a trance. Finally he leaves for Paradou, where he finds Archangias, who has fallen asleep while on guard at the breach in the wall. Serge steps over him to meet a joyful Albine. Soon, since she quickly realizes that something is wrong, she takes him into the park, past the grotto and its sleeping woman, past the lion, by the places of their former joy. In an attempt to warm him she leads him to the rocks and would like to go up to the cedar where they experienced the anguish of their first desire, but Serge is incapable of the climb. While he rests, she offers to accompany him into the modern world where she will use

the social graces learned so long ago; he will be proud of her. Serge
seems oblivious of her presence and reminisces about his experiences
with churches. Then, in desperation, Albine leads him to their place
beneath the giant tree. She takes him in her arms and kisses him, but
nothing happens. And since Serge is not a man, Albine drives him
from Paradou.

Archangias has awakened and is delighted. It takes only one look at
Serge for him to know what has happened: 'Heaven broke you as it has
broken others' (1509). And the abandoned Albine seeks advice from the
park. She collects flowers, not failing to include plenty of tuberoses and
hyacinths (the book has intimated on several occasions that they are
poisonous),[23] and fills her room. Shutting herself up there, she lets the
flowers kill her. The tuberoses and hyacinths work as only an author
could make them.

Pascal comes immediately. He stops to scream at the church that
Albine was pregnant and finds, on arriving at Paradou, that he can do
nothing. He does, however, calm Jeanbernat, who during a fit of temper
furiously waves a book by d'Holbach. Events then move rapidly. In the
last chapter, we see Désirée dancing around Mathieu, her pig, which
has just been slaughtered. Thinking of the cow, Lise, about to calve, she
says, 'One leaves, and another arrives' (1521). Then Albine's funeral
procession arrives at the cemetery, while another group waits its turn
to bury Rosalie's child. (Bambousse is outraged that the death did not
occur earlier, but Rosalie does not mind: 'What difference does it make
if the old man gets mad? . . . Now, we are married just the same' [1524–
5].) As Serge finishes the service, Jeanbernat suddenly appears and cuts
off Archangias's right ear. The cock crows, and Désirée comes running.
'Serge! Serge!' she calls. 'The cow just had a calf!' (1527). With those
words, the book ends.

Although I think this is a valid summary of *La Faute de l'abbé Mouret*, there remain a number of unanswered questions raised by the
book itself. Albine, for example, wonders, 'Why wasn't [Albine] loving, why wasn't she loved?' (1461). Later, while agonizing like a
'wounded animal' after having driven Serge from Paradou, she asks
in vain, 'Of what *faute* was she guilty?' (1510). Should we take the
title of the book as the answer? The *faute* was not Albine's, it was
Serge's. If so, what did Serge do wrong? In his marriage sermon he
says it is wrong to abandon one's woman. Was that his *faute*? This
conclusion might seem more reasonable, were it not for the very
obvious allusion to the Bible.

II

The name of the marvelous garden, Paradou, is itself suggestive of the biblical earthly paradise, but there are many other supporting elements. The Garden of Eden contained 'every tree that is pleasant to the sight, and good for food; the tree of life also in the midst of the garden, and the tree of knowledge of good and evil. And a river went out of Eden to water the garden; and from thence it was parted, and became into four heads' (Gen. 2:9–10). Paradou has a rich orchard, a marvelous forest, a river that separates into four branches, and two memorable trees. The first, a cedar, stands up on the rocks surrounded by a pine grove; the second towers above the middle of the garden. Little is said about the cedar. We know only that beneath it Albine and Serge are filled with anguish and flee. Judging from the horribly shaped plants nearby, it would seem that Zola meant this tree and place to represent pure evil. The other important tree is unequivocally referred to as a 'tree of life' (1402), but it has some of the qualities of the biblical tree of the knowledge of good and evil. On one occasion, Albine tells Serge that beneath the tree 'we will know everything, we will be the true masters' (1401). It also gives death to those who sit beneath it (1357), and they refer to its forbidden quality several times (e.g., 1358, 1367). Interestingly enough, since Serge and Albine suggest Adam and Eve and since their sin, according to the abbé, is sexual, they once mention that coitus is prohibited (1377). To associate sexual intercourse with original sin is, of course, well within the traditions of the Catholic church. Father Mouret makes a great deal of man's being conceived and born in sin, and his experience with Craisson's *De rebus venereis ad usum confessariorum* leaves an 'indelible stain' deep within him that threatens to grow and 'cover him with mud' (1307).

In Genesis, the snake tempts Eve, who then acts on Adam; but in *La Faute*, though the garden might well be a 'nest of snakes' (1249), it is the garden itself which 'was the tempter' (1407), and Albine, with 'a mouth and eyes of temptation' (1403), fills Eve's role as she leads Serge to the tree. When they arrive beneath it, 'The air tastes like fruit' (1405). Nonetheless, the clearest parallel with Genesis occurs in a few passing comments: for example, when Serge tells Albine, 'You come from my flesh. . . . And I woke up when you came out of me' (1339), and especially in the drama after they make love. Like Adam and Eve, they cover themselves. Then later, at the wall, they hear the rumble of anger, just as the first man and woman heard the voice of God in Eden. After Serge is pulled from Paradou, Archangias guards the entrance to the garden. One assumes that God's cherubim were more effective than Archangias. He dozes off, allowing Serge to return.[24]

Serge's reentry into Paradou constitutes but one of the elements that deviate from a parallel with Genesis. God, among other things, was walking *in* the Garden of Eden when he discovered the disobedience of his minions; Archangias apparently took no more than a few steps through the breach (1416). God thrust Adam and Eve out away from him; Archangias pulls Serge out toward him, leaving Albine behind. These deviations are important, and we shall return to them later, but it cannot be denied that the allusions to Genesis, the creation of man, Adam's sin, and the expulsion of Adam and Eve into the world of suffering and death remain perfectly clear.

In addition to evoking Adam, Serge suggests a Christ figure. This latter allusion, though faint, is nonetheless recognizable. It serves to expand the echoes of Genesis into an allusive complex that includes the traditions and teachings of the church. Serge's church in Les Artaud is twice compared to a stable, once to a barn, and once to a sheepfold.[25] True, if Serge's ministry begins with his departure from the seminary, the priest started at a somewhat younger age than Christ. Moreover, the period of time between Serge's final ordination and his symbolic death is shorter than the span of Jesus' ministry. Still, on noting that Serge confuses Albine with the Virgin,[26] that Désirée sees their resemblance (1456-7), and that Albine becomes his mother figure (e.g., 1331), the way is perhaps prepared for Father Mouret to follow Christ on Calvary. Of course, Jesus was much kinder to his mother than was Serge to Albine. Serge repulsed her, where Jesus left Mary in the care of one of his disciples. There was, however, that earlier occasion when Jesus refused to see Mary, claiming that those who obey God were his mother (Matt. 12:46-50). In addition, Father Mouret regarded Les Artaud as a desert (1257), and his temptations in the church resemble those suffered by Christ in the desert (Luke 4.1-13), the difference being that Christ did not succumb either there or at Gethsemane or on Golgotha. Serge gives in to each and every temptation, while echoing over and over again the anguished cry of the Son of Man: '*Eli, Eli, lama sabachthani?* which means, "My God, my God, why did you abandon me?"' (Matt. 27:46). Nonetheless, Serge has devoted himself completely to the Cross, and his favorite dream is to take Jesus' place (1448-9). 'From Jesus, he took only the cross. . . . He took up the cross and followed Jesus. . . . And when he was fastened to the cross, he had the boundless consolation of the love of God' (1480).

Serge's admission that he is damned (1486) corresponds to the death of Christ, for the church in Les Artaud seems to crack as the earth rises up violently. 'And, behold, the veil of the temple was rent in twain from the top to the bottom; and the earth did quake, and the rocks were rent' (Matt. 27:51). After this experience, Désirée comes to take him away. That night he falls into a leaden sleep, and the next morning he feels as though he is in a stupor, annihilated (1496). Seemingly unable to move, he stays in his room until the fifth day (rather than the third), when he leaves for Paradou and Albine. But now he feels his kinship with a saint of stone that has been censed for centuries: 'This embalming is the cause of my serenity, the tranquil death of my flesh, the peace I taste in not living... Ah! let nothing upset my immobility! I will remain cold, rigid, with an endless smile on my granite lips, powerless to go down among men' (1506). He is a 'corpse' (1507).

The clearest parallel with the Christ story occurs later, at Albine's funeral. Archangias, the self-appointed gendarme, is assisting Serge when Jeanbernat lops off the brother's right ear. Poetic justice, we might say, for Archangias likes few things better than to grasp pupils brutally by their ears. When one remembers that the brother worships the Old Testament God, the punishment seems even more appropriate, and terrible. Not only does Archangias stink like 'a goat that would never be satisfied,'[27] when he looks at Serge after the second exit from Paradou, his eyes shine 'with a terrible jealousy. The half-seen delights of Paradou tortured him. For weeks, he had remained on the threshold, sniffing the damnable enjoyments from a distance' (1509). The fury with which he pursues Serge indicates the degree of his jealousy and of his sin. In essence, it is of a sexual nature, and for a sin of the mind he receives a symbolic castration. Saint Jerome pointed out that mutilation of ears and noses has been employed to punish similar misdeeds, particularly adultery.[28] It is also true that Archangias, member of a Christian order, does not appear to have heard the word of Christ. One would think him the perfect example of Jeremiah's (6:10) and Luke's (Acts 7:51) 'uncircumcised' ears. According to Smaragdus, whoever is deaf to the Word and then loses the right ear will hear it through the left.[29] In any case, after being mutilated in this fashion, Old Testament law would henceforth prevent him from approaching the altar.[30] It is, of course, open to serious question whether Zola knew all this, but it seems scarcely possible that he could have failed to know that in cutting off the right ear of Archangias, who by his own admission is 'God's dog' (1492), Jeanbernat repeats the cruel act of Simon Peter who 'smote the high priest's servant, and cut off his right ear' (John 18:10). The New Testament story is and was told every Good Friday during Mass.

Where the discrepancies between Christ's and Serge's passions point effectively to the fact that Serge is not Jesus and perhaps not yet a saint (perfection is not, however, required of a saint, only proof of being an instrument of God), the allusion to Simon Peter and Malchus raises more problems than it resolves. Although Archangias's wrathful religious orientation and the fact that he is a brother make him a good double for the slave of the high priest, what does Jeanbernat have in common with Simon Peter? While preparing to write his novel, Zola wrote in the margin of a page in the dossier: 'Jeanbernat [,] Christian philosophy as far as practice is concerned,'[31] but the character we meet in *La Faute de l'abbé Mouret* has few beliefs or practices corresponding to Christianity, however much he may be the 'Philosopher.' A prior description seems closer to Jeanbernat's final incarnation: 'A ridiculous atheist, an old fellow sunk in Voltaire, etc., eating meat on Fridays, denying God, uncivilized. . . . Very old, moreover, 75. He cultivates his garden like *Candide*' (ibid. 91). The Jeanbernat of *La Faute* is not quite so ridiculous. (It should be noted, however, that he keeps his earlier name, which might be rendered in English as 'Simple Simon.' In Provençal, which Zola knew, *bernat* means 'simpleton.') His philosophy of life seems to boil down to a hatred for the church, an attitude of 'live and let live' (could this be the 'Christian' practice?), and the affectation of nihilism. He loves to say, with a large gesture sweeping the horizon, 'There is nothing, nothing, nothing' (1251–2). This constitutes the only visible result of what Jeanbernat has learned in twenty years of reading 'all the 18th century *philosophes* [and] a pile of books on religion' (1251).

Zola's reference to d'Holbach in connection with Jeanbernat (he spent the day after Albine's death reading one of his works [1519–20]), serves to stress the position of Albine's uncle as an enemy of the church and an adherent of natural morality. D'Holbach is famous for his unremitting attacks against the church and Christianity, for example in *Le Christianisme dévoilé* (1761), and for his advocacy of a morality based on enlightened self-interest, systematized most notably in *Système de la nature* (1770) and *La Morale universelle* (1776). Jeanbernat, of course, despised the church and its representatives. His statement 'I don't want any priests at my place. . . . Things like that kill people' (1250) is a not unacceptable vulgarization of one side of d'Holbach. And Jeanbernat seems to have believed in a version of natural morality. I think, however, that the reference should be carried no farther. Especially in respect to natural morality, Jeanbernat's beliefs lack the nuance and, indeed, the wisdom of d'Holbach.[32] Although, as already noted, it is not uncommon for such a reference to accompany extended allusion, this time it leads no farther than to prepare Jeanbernat's dramatic vengeance against Archangias by emphasizing his educational theories and his antichurch feeling.

It is in considering Jeanbernat as the philosopher of nature that the allusion to Simon Peter adds a significant resonance to *La Faute*, for Jeanbernat, in taking his knife to the Ignorantine brother, opposes the institutional church and announces a new faith. In this he resembles Peter. When one reflects on the depiction Zola gives of Serge's and Archangias's theology, it is difficult not to cheer Jeanbernat. Albine compares the little church to a grave; to live there is to live 'in the midst of death' (1469). Serge agrees: 'You are right, death is here, death is what I want, the death that delivers, that saves from all rottenness... Do you understand! I deny life, I refuse it, I spit on it. . . . And do you want to know what will happen one day? The little church will become so colossal, it will cast such a shadow, that the whole of your nature will die. Ah! death, the death of everything' (1473–4). Hardly a pretty picture! By this time, Serge has long since abandoned the tender, loving Virgin. He suspects her of having led him off to the greenery (1415–16). Perhaps the fact that her statue once seemed to shiver with sap, 'as though death were vanquished by the eternal youth of the earth' (1226), had something to do with his neglect of her. The big Christ quivered at the same time, and it was not long before Jesus' gentleness began to make Serge uneasy. So He too is excommunicated. And Serge has returned to his 'hole of darkness' where he tastes 'terrible joys' (1344). He worships a Christless cross. 'Suffering, dying, these words rang ceaselessly in his ears, like the end [*fin*, which may mean 'terminus' or 'goal'] of human wisdom. . . . Death . . . was to his eyes nothing but an outburst of love' (1480). The abbé has already sacrificed his reason (1306). This further equation of love and death leads to his much-feared, much-admired, and much-emulated model, Archangias. From the beginning, Serge looks up to the brother, and as his fear grows, so does his admiration. At first, he merely reprimands himself sharply for the 'sin' of being disgusted by Archangias (1239–40). Then, in emulation, Serge 'felt pious joy at plunging into baseness. . . . Heavenly peace seemed to be at the end of this contempt for the world, of this degradation of his whole being' (1278). Finally, he begins to envy Archangias and despairs of ever being able 'to raise himself to this uncouthness' (1479).

Brother Archangias kills the warblers; he would like to twist the blackbirds' necks; he thinks the people of Les Artaud should be broken, and he would not mind seeing God clean up the area by sending fire as He did to Gomorrah; he hates women; and he advocates strangling all girls at birth. If love is death, then Archangias overflows with love. Not surprisingly, he proclaims that God prefers baseness (1237). Serge, of course, agrees.[33] Personally, although Bossuet once suggested that there could be a glorious baseness, I believe even the great French prelate would have had difficulty using Archangias as an example. But Serge is not Bossuet. Furthermore, we are told that he is a saint. La Teuse says so, as does Pascal, in both *La Faute*[34] and *Le Docteur Pascal*. Elsewhere, Zola described another saint, Christodoulos, who provides an excellent summary of what it means in *La Faute de l'abbé Mouret* and, thus, in *Les Rougon-Macquart* to be one of the blessed.

There is in him an eternal negation of life, a savage and unthinking hatred of humanity. . . . What he wants is to live apart on his desert rock. . . . Women and children, the smooth faces, cause him continual fright; they are the family, life in the sun, fruitful peace, and he damns them . . . because he is a priest of death and a fervent disciple of frigid solitude. How sad his ideal is! . . . And yet what grandeur in Saint Christodoulos's ferocious exile! What an anathema cast at creation! This monk is a somber and desperate figure . . . breaking the bonds of blood and declaring his brothers leprous. The world is evil, he does not want any of it. He seems in a hurry to go up to God in order to complain of His work. He has passed through the world, without understanding it, and he leaves, having had nothing human, avid for a glorious nothingness, this nothingness of a paradise where we would not find our dear loves, our smiles and even our tears   (OC 10.309–10).

I do not wish to give the impression that Zola attacks Serge, for that is not the case. The book carefully points out that the young man cannot help himself; his nature is simply the result of hereditary degeneration (1451–2). If only he had had a little more blood, Pascal laments, things might have worked out (1454), and as far as Zola was concerned, Serge's belief that his impotence resulted from God's answering his prayer would constitute but one more proof of his malady. Still, with all due regard for Serge's bloodlines, it continues to appear pertinent to wonder whether, saint though he be, the impotent Serge is now more than a man or less, and whether Archangias's church should command our loyalty. But the opposition between Jeanbernat and Archangias serves another purpose, for it effectively puts two systems of upbringing at odds. Jeanbernat stands for the unrestrained, 'natural' development of instincts, a vulgarized extension of the noble savage. When he cuts off Archangias's ear, he acts, not as the disciple of Christ, nor of Serge, but as a follower of his own variety of natural morality. The episode then brings to a conclusion the theme of education that traverses the novel. Archangias, the repressive schoolmaster, appropriately represents his order, whose teaching practices were so notorious that they were called the 'whipping brothers.' He confronts the representative of, shall we say, *very* progressive education. Dr Pascal mentions Jeanbernat's methods very early in the book. 'If you ever have a daughter to raise, I don't advise you to confide her to Jeanbernat. He has a completely primitive way of letting nature act [on his niece]. When I ventured to talk to him about Albine, he answered that you shouldn't prevent trees from growing as they wish. He said it's for the normal development of temperament' (1256). Pascal's disapproval is evident, as is Zola's from Albine's tragic end.

Elsewhere, in newspaper articles written from 1868 to 1878, Zola considered at some length the way girls should be raised. He vigorously opposed convent education and praised the salubrious effects of an open-air life in the country, but he insisted over and over again on the necessity of parental guidance and encouragement toward a life of useful, creative activity. He even suggested that country girls be kept in school as long as possible: 'It is not in school, but outside of it, in total freedom, in the fields, where girls and boys are corrupted.'[35] Jeanbernat, of course, yanks Albine out of school when she sneaks off there to join the other children her age; but it should not be forgotten that Jeanbernat is not necessarily Zola's mouthpiece. Granted, Zola's sympathies would be for the 'Philosopher' over the Ignorantine, though this is not to say that Jeanbernat should be emulated. His methods apparently produce a 'Sleeping Beauty' – Paradou, once in *La Faute* (1251) and once in *Le Docteur Pascal*, is referred to as 'Sleeping Beauty's park.' This image satisfactorily supports the theme of dormant human life, a theme to which I shall return. In addition, it stresses Jeanbernat's failure to give parental guidance to the motherless girl. By 'Sleeping Beauty,' Zola meant a girl raised in absolute ignorance, occupied at meaningless tasks, and who consequently passes her time in unhealthy dreams of a kiss from the first passing cavalier.[36] Because Jeanbernat leaves Albine to shift for herself, she has no choice but to follow her instincts. Because he never leaves his garden to intrude on the developing idyl, he abandons a defenseless Albine. She is too ignorant to understand the complications implicit in Serge's position, and unfortunately for her, the wrong prince happens by first. Unlike the prince's kiss, which resuscitates Sleeping Beauty, Serge's kills Albine.

Serge exemplifies the result of the opposing system of education as found in church schools. According to Zola, it is guided by the same idea that justifies Archangias's brutality: an attempt to stamp out nature. 'It doesn't matter if you pull their ears until they bleed, the woman grows in them just the same' (1239), Archangias observes. Because of 'the fatal mark of [Serge's] early education' – a point Zola made in the dossier[37] and one that, I suppose, one might infer from the novel – the abbé is unable to throw off the church, no matter how much he wants to. In addition, although there are no instances cited of Serge's having been beaten, he obviously was encouraged to indulge in self-laceration. His schooling has then prepared him to repress his very natural inclinations to marry Albine. As the dossier puts it, 'They made a eunuch of him.'[38]

The resolution of this antithesis between the two educational methods is to be found in a statement by Albine: 'And I want my daughter not to leave me. You may, if you think proper, send the boy to parochial school.[39] I'll keep my little fair-haired darling in my skirts. I will teach her to read' (1506). Though she believes in guidance, she is closer to Jeanbernat than to Archangias. Her teaching is based on love and an understanding of the natures of little girls, not on repression.

III

If we reject Archangias's God – and the book gives us little choice but to do so – where does that leave us? The most obvious alternative is nature, which opposes the church from beginning to end. And here again there exists within the framework of the novel a galaxy of allusions to help the reader understand and evaluate the incorporated ethic. Although many of the elements that form the biblical complex of allusions will reappear as integral parts of allusions to nature myths – rather like signposts giving alternate routes – the most salient figure is unalterably committed to nature. Indeed, the allusions to Cybele are so pervasive that one might well suspect her, rather than God, of being responsible for Serge's emasculation. It would not be the first time Cybele unmanned one of her followers. Back in Phrygia, there was the handsome young Attis whom the goddess loved. He promised to be forever faithful. 'If I lie,' Ovid quotes him, in Frazer's translation of the *Fasti*: 'may the love for which I break faith be my last love of all.'[40] But young men being what they are, he soon had an affair with one of the local nymphs. Some say he even planned to marry her. When Cybele discovered his faithlessness, she caused Attis to go insane. Screaming, he ran to the top of a mountain, and there, beneath a pine, he emasculated himself. Ovid quotes him in his death throes: 'I have deserved it! With my blood I pay the penalty that is my due. Ah, perish the parts that were my ruin' (*Fasti* 4.239–41). From his blood sprouted a violet, but somehow the goddess found this poor compensation. She would have liked to undo her work and tried to persuade Zeus to resuscitate the errant young man. The father god refused. He did permit, however, that Attis should not decay. His hair would moreover continue to grow and his little finger to move. Apparently it was in this state that Attis accompanied Cybele as she drove her lion-drawn chariot around the world. The myth supposedly explains why pine trees were sacred to Cybele, and why her priests, the Galli, henceforth unmanned themselves before beginning to serve her.[41]

In antiquity, Cybele's bloody cult was for the most part repulsed by the Greeks, but it found a home with the Romans and spread into Gaul and Germany. In Zola's Les Artaud, Cybele is very much alive. At night, 'this ardent countryside assumed a strange sprawl of passion. She slept, disarrayed, one hip slightly raised, twisted, her limbs spread apart, while she exhaled big warm sighs, the powerful aromas of a sweating sleeper. You would have said it was some powerful Cybele, fallen on her back, bust thrust forward, her stomach beneath the moon, drunk with the sun's ardors, and dreaming of fecundation' (1308). The Great Mother rests. And Désirée, 'a girl nourished by the earth, with wide shoulders and the narrow forehead of a young goddess' (1262), was 'like the mother of us all, the natural mother, letting the sweat of generation fall from her fingers without a shiver' (1263–4). She presides over her barnyard animals, loves her goat (sacred to Cybele because it nourished Attis), adores birds, and looks upon animal savagery as the most natural thing in the world. Not surprisingly, La Teuse compares her to Cybele (1261). Indeed, Désirée-Cybele[42] must feel right at home in the Artaud area, for according to Maury and Larousse, Cybele was associated particularly with harsh, rocky land.

Even when Serge is away from Désirée in Paradou with his woodland nymph, Cybele's influence continues. On one of their walks, Serge and Albine look into a grotto where they see the statue of a woman in a spring. 'The clear sheet of water flowing over her had made a smooth stone of her face, a whiteness without a face, while her two breasts, as though raised out of the water by an effort of the neck, remained intact, still living, swollen with ancient voluptuousness. "She isn't dead . . ." said Serge as he descended. "Someday we'll have to pull her out of there." But Albine, who shivered, led him away' (1347). Albine has good reason to shiver if, as it seems, the statue is the vengeful Cybele. The most famous of the *Magna Mater*'s representations had, instead of a face, an unworked stone.[43] Once a year, it was purified in the Roman Almo. Cybele seems to be receiving another annual *lavation* in one of the many grottos and springs sanctified to her. Should there be any doubt of the statue's identity, Serge and Albine walk away through two and a half pages of flowers, most notably Attis's violets: 'violets which kept coming back, a sea of violets flowing everywhere' (1348). Then they come to the statue of a lion spitting blood. Perhaps it is Atalanta whom Cybele changed into a lion for making love to Hippomenes in one of the goddess's shrines. On the way up to the rocks where Serge and Albine are almost overcome by passion of frightening ferocity, they pass near this grotto, cross a pine woods (both pine trees and pine woods were sacred to Cybele), and finally sit at the edge of the springs, under a giant cedar. Knowing the bloody sacrifices that Cybele's Galli used to make beneath her pines, one is scarcely surprised to discover Zola comparing the pines to 'sacred stones, still black from the blood of victims' (1387). But this description concerns fir trees, not pines. In the extension from Cybele's pines to firs, the author seems to have wished to incorporate the whole range of the more savage nature cults. According to Larousse, firs were worshipped in the Black Forest. It may even be pertinent to recall Zola's dossier notation, 'Conifers see Loise 44.'

On this page of Ferdinand Loise's *De l'influence de la civilisation sur la poésie* begins the chapter including discussion of druidism 'with its bloody sacrifices on the stones of the sacred forests.'[44] The cedar tree, beneath which Serge and Albine sit, has similar associations, for it was sacred to Isis (it represented Osiris) and to Ishtar. Even the cypress standing near the young people adds to the connotative thrust of the scene. Maury states that it was consecrated to Astarte. Pines, firs, cypress, and cedar, all symbolize generation and death in these traditions.

The allusion to Cybele remains significant, however. After Serge abandons Désirée the second time, he discovers his impotence. Up there on the rocks, the runaway priest remarks, 'It seems to me that all my blood is leaving my veins' (1504). Later he gives thanks to God. Perhaps he should have addressed a few words to Cybele.

The allusion to Cybele is without question the most important of those that oppose Genesis and the Old Testament God. Still, Cybele, however important, is not the only allusion to nature mythology. Just as the Jehovah allusions are accompanied by others to the Christian tradition, so too Cybele is accompanied by numerous touches that recall other nature myths. Zola seems to have wanted to confront Eden, inhabited by Adam, Eve, and Jehovah and guarded by angels, with another kind of paradise, peopled by a whole series of gods who sprang from nature itself. These secondary allusions are subtle, as are those to Jesus and Mary, but they effectively fill in the tapestry, giving nuance and sheen to the dominant Jehovah-Cybele oxymoron, while concomitantly enlarging it to take in – and thus establish an opposition between – church and nature. When Serge first awakens in Paradou surrounded by nature, he not only begins his life over again, he goes back in time to another world, a world where gods walked on earth, where men became gods. Paradou is the Judeo-Christian Eden, and it is also the mythical realm of Ovid's *Metamorphoses*. The satyrs, the cupids, the lion, and the statue of the faceless woman constitute the clearest indications, though there are others. Paradou continues a world in which oaks were once nymphs, hyacinths and anemones boys, lotuses, heliotropes, and reeds girls. Consequently, Albine begs Serge not to hurt the plants. 'You would break the branches, you would crush the leaves,' she says while holding him back. 'Since I've lived here, I've been very careful not to kill anyone.'[45] Later she says much the same thing while wondering why her life and love are frustrated. 'I grew up very happy. I used to look in the nests without touching the eggs. I didn't even gather flowers, for fear of making the plants bleed' (1466). Albine herself 'looks like a big flower' (1326). And she lives in the midst of a park where Serge sees 'the big, superb bodies of goddesses' (1324–5) and where 'Titan-trees' grow (1379).

Albine is a fascinating creation. Like Serge, she fills many roles, perhaps too many. She fits nicely into the Adam and Eve account and into other myths and legends. There is, for example, the allusion to one of Sun's romances, which is prepared by Serge's awakening in the spring sun: 'How good the light is!' he says. 'And you would have said his words were the sun's very vibration' (1335). Somewhat later, while they walk in the park, the whole garden bows to Serge as though he were a king. Albine herself seems no more than the white appendage to her companion, 'a sovereignly handsome being' (1345). Together the two young people 'passed slowly, dressed in the sun; they were the sun itself' (ibid.). These images are perfectly consistent with the Attis myth, for the god was often identified with the sun, but it also seems appropriate to think of one of the myths in Ovid's *Metamorphoses*. Much as Serge overwhelmed the innocent Albine, Ovid tells us that Sun once dazzled Leucothoe. (The girl's name means 'swift whiteness.' Albine's simply means 'white.')[46] Now Clytie was jealous of Sun's mistress, and she betrayed Leucothoe by revealing the love affair. While Sun was away, Leucothoe was punished by being buried alive. By the time Sun returned, there was little to be done. Lacking a better alternative, he sprinkled a rain of nectar over her body, and the mythic maiden was transformed into a shrub of frankincense. As a corollary, the pregnant Albine buried herself in a flower-filled room, so that the following season she could become either a rosebush or a willow or a birch.[47]

Perhaps Albine's faint but recognizable allusion to Diana Nemorensis is even more important. Like Albine, the goddess was associated with white. In one of her forms, she was Artemis Alpheia ('whitish Artemis'). Occasionally, she took on the qualities of Hecate-Silene and was identified with wolves, a cat, a bear, and the moon, among other things. When, in *La Faute*, Archangias tells Albine to go back to her wolves (1508), when he says she is a sorceress (1277) and a cat (1278), and when Albine is compared to the glint of a moonbeam (1275), we may be justified in thinking of Diana. Of course, Diana was primarily known as the goddess of the mountains and woodlands. For a while Hippolytus was her hunting companion, but Poseidon had him killed. The heartbroken Diana then called on Aesculapius, who saved the young man. Hippolytus was subsequently spirited away to a grove in the Alban hills, where he assumed the form of an old man and the new name of Virbius. This grove, known from then on as Diana's, had once been the trysting place of King Numa and his nymph-mistress, Egeria. The nymph did not die (as did the lady who once inhabited Paradou);[48] she simply wandered too far into the woods and became lost, and thus was unable to return to Numa. Diana took pity on the disconsolate Egeria and changed her into a stream. Afterwards, Diana continued to inhabit the grove, accompanied by Virbius and protected by a series of slave-kings. In order to qualify for the latter position, which was open only to slaves, a runaway had to come to the grove and break off a branch from Diana's tree. As with the gigantic Paradou tree, we do not know what kind Diana's was, only that it was very large (Frazer suggests it might have been an oak). Successfully breaking a branch from the tree entitled the slave to single-handed combat with the current king. The one who survived became, or continued as, king of the forest and Diana's companion, and he reigned until he was in turn vanquished.[49]

I have already mentioned the passage where Paradou accords Serge 'admiration similar to that of crowds saluting long awaited kings' (1345). True, he was spirited away by Dr Pascal, whereas Aesculapius only healed Hippolytus, but he resembles one of Diana's slave-kings in other ways. He proclaims himself Albine's slave, for example. In fact, he, Archangias, and Jeanbernat (an old family retainer given the position at Paradou to get rid of him [1251]), all qualify as modern-day slaves. And not long after Archangias breaks off some branches from the trees in Paradou by throwing rocks into the park (1509), Jeanbernat comes toward him out of the night, 'straight as an oak tree' (1442). In the ensuing fight, Archangias is soundly trounced. Jeanbernat presumably remains king of Paradou.

This episode prepares later struggles. The first occurs between Albine, a woman with an 'air of fecundity' carrying dormant life in her enlarged flanks (1465), and the priest, reveling in the delights of self-martyrdom. Serge's hallucination of nature engaging the church is, it seems, more significant. As previously suggested, this battle serves to mark Serge's death as a Christ figure, but it functions even more clearly to allude to the Titanomachy, as recounted in Hesiod's *Theogony*. It consists of a parallel allusion that sets off and builds a discrepancy into an opposition of enormous importance. There were two phases in the war between the Titans, those unruly forces of nature, and the Olympian gods of light and justice. The first was inconclusive, and the wily Zeus enlisted the aid of the Titans' brother-monsters of nature, the Hecatonchires. In the second phase, the three Hundred-Handers

stood against the Titans in grim strife, holding huge rocks in their strong hands. And on the other part the Titans eagerly strengthened their ranks, and both sides at one time showed the work of their hands and their might. The boundless sea rang terribly around, and the earth crashed loudly: wide Heaven was shaken and groaned, and high Olympus reeled from its foundation under the charge of the undying gods, and a heavy quaking reached dim

Tartarus and the deep sound of their feet in the fearful onset and of their hard missiles. So, then, they launched their grievous shafts upon one another, and the cry of both armies as they shouted reached to starry heaven; and they met together with a great battle cry. . . . It seemed even as if Earth and wide Heaven above came together; for such a mighty crash would have arisen if Earth were being hurled to ruin, and Heaven from on high were hurling her down; so great a crash was there while the gods were meeting together in strife. Also the winds brought rumbling earthquake and dust storm, thunder and lightning and the lurid thunderbolt, which are the shafts of great Zeus. . . . And amongst the foremost Cottus and Briareos and Gyes insatiate for war raised fierce fighting: three hundred rocks, one upon another, they launched from their strong hands and overshadowed the Titans with their missiles, and hurled them beneath the wide-pathed earth . . . as far beneath the earth as heaven is above earth.[50]

The Titans were vanquished.

In Zola's La Faute, the first phase of the battle of nature against the church is inconclusive. Consequently, the hills, rocks, ponds, fields, rivers, plants, vines, grasses, trees, the very dust involved in the first attack, they, rather than the church, enlist some allies. The animals come running, along with the inhabitants of Les Artaud and the peasants' off-spring, 'a forest of men' produced by coupling with the land. Then, with Désirée's rooster, Alexandre, trumpeting the assault, 'this whole tide of overflowing life swallowed the church in an instant.' Finally, the church crumbles. 'It was victorious riot, revolutionary nature raising barricades with overturned altars.' The 'tree of life' marches in and grows to burst the roof and heaven. And 'the big Christ,' rather than the Titanic forces of nature, 'torn from the cross . . . was carried off, rolled, lost in the dark night, to the bottom of which he fell with a resounding crash. . . . The church was vanquished' (1487–90). Where Zeus was too clever to allow himself to be isolated and thus allied himself with nature, in the persons of the Hecatonchires, the church of La Faute stands alone. Throughout the novel, it is presented as the champion of the soul and the enemy of the body, of nature, of life itself. The church is not merely spineless, it is disembodied. How could it possibly prevail against a world of matter, of nature, of physical life? The outcome is a foregone conclusion. The church falls, but – and this is an important detail to which we shall return – in reality the little church building still stands.

IV

Though in person or through their representatives nature and the church meet four times in battle, only once does the church prevail, and that time, when Serge sends Albine away, the book's sympathies clearly lie with the defeated. Surely, it would be difficult to find a more pathetic scene than Albine's departure, unless it is her later depiction as she wanders in Paradou, alone, tormented, and lost. No matter how one conceives of the struggle between nature and the church, nature appears, on the basis of the evidence we have thus far considered, clearly the winner.

Even Pascal seems to echo a decision on the side of nature. On one occasion, he judges the relative advantages of being, like Serge, a sickly saint, or, like Désirée, a healthy moron. He opts for Désirée (1248). Later he goes farther: 'If everyone in the world were like my big animal [that is, Désirée], the earth would be too beautiful. . . . Yes, brutes, there should be nothing but brutes.'[51] When Serge denies God, he makes a similar choice. 'He only believed in himself, in his muscles, in the appe-tites of his organs. He wanted to live. He needed to be a man. Oh! how he longed to run in the open air, to be strong, to have no jealous master, to kill his enemies by throwing stones at them, to carry off . . . the girls who pass by' (1486–7). There can be no misunderstanding the import of these words. Serge in rejecting the church, chooses brutish nature. He wants to be one of those women-killing bandits he studied on the walls of his room in Paradou. The anguished desire to return with Albine to Paradou, which, according to the young lady, 'was life' (1469), reveals his wish 'to create life' and, thus, he says, 'to be God!' (1482). Of course, he will have to share his divinity with all others who have the same ability to procreate. There is, for example, Désirée's cow, Lise, who is about to give birth to a calf. It seems scarcely accidental that Lise derives from a form of the Hebrew noun *Eli*, which means God.[52]

Lise is indeed as much a god as Serge could be, for Serge's concep-tion of nature makes no distinction between men and animals. As for Cybele, it does not matter if Albine dies, for she will produce lush vegetation to feed Désirée's rabbits the following spring. Albine and the pig, Mathieu, die, and they are replaced by Lise's calf. Zola used Dési-rée's pig to insist on the ethic implicit in the worship of such a nature. The animal got its name because its mistress thought he looked like the 'fat man who brings the letters' (1428). Zola knew that in iconography, where Mark is represented as a lion, Luke as an ox, John as an eagle, Matthew (the French form is 'Matthieu') is portrayed as a man.[53] In *La Faute*, Zola simply reversed the symbolism. The pig represents a man, and Désirée, who extols her animals over human beings, feels no sorrow when Mathieu is slaughtered. This conception of nature makes no distinctions between men and animals. One even wonders if family bonds matter. As an indication of an answer, *The Golden Legend* provides the interesting information that the pope who chose to be called Serge had previously born the name of Buccaporci, which means 'pig's snout.'[54] Before becoming pope, Sergius IV was also a Buccaporci and, more important, given Serge's problems with celibacy, Pope Sergius the First is known primarily for his rejection of the Quinisext or Trullan Council's reforming decrees that would have sanctioned a married clergy.

Even the all-powerful Désirée-Cybele is mounted by the rooster, Alexandre, who digs his claws into her (1460). He seems to be saying, in imitation of his famous namesake, 'Earth I have set under foot; Zeus, keep Olympus for yourself.'[55] After all, the cock will soon lead the victorious attack against the church. Indeed, Désirée's pet has an all-too-appropriate name, for if we are to believe Michelet, Alexander the Great was responsible for 'precipitating man to the level of animals' (Michelet, *Humanité* 353).

Did Zola really wish his readers to choose nature, to worship the land, the Great Mother, the *Magna Mater* of all living things? Was he truly in favor of peasants like Bambousse, who equate their daughters with sacks of grain, or like Jeanbernat, who maintains that 'Girls are like hawthorns: when they make flowers, they do all they can' (1446)? Allusions to the Judeo-Christian tradition face off against allusions to nature mythology.

Overshadowing the church and its neighboring cemetery stands a tree that in the Western tradition symbolizes death, a 'gigantic cypress. . . . known by the whole country under the name of the *Solitaire*.'[56] It towers above Paradou, 'colossal,' 'dean of the garden, the father of the forest,' from whose foliage falls 'the joy of creation' (1404). The connotations of this tree are equivocal. I have discussed those resonances that might make one think of the Edenic tree of the knowledge of good and evil, but it cannot be denied that it resembles even more closely the tree of life, as indeed it is specifically called, whether Edenic, Egyptian, Druidian (I think of the oaks Caesar felled), or Persian. The latter tree, like the one in Eden, also produced fruit and stood at the source of four rivers.

Indeed, as Victor de Laprade says in the 'Invocation' of *Psyché*, 'Every people has dreamed of this marvelous garden.' In relation to Albine's contention that beneath the Paradou tree they will know everything, it may be pertinent to mention Quinet's similarly gigantic tree. It is likewise a 'father of the forest,' and it also possesses wisdom, which it imparted to the first Druid, and secrets, which it reveals to Merlin.[57] All in all, Paradou's tree seems primarily a tree of life. It confronts the tree of death. Around the former are grouped brutish life, Jeanbernat, Albine, Diana, Cybele, and the lubricious, debilitating Syrian Sulamite.[58] Around the tree of death gather passive whining for grace, purity of soul, physical and emotional suffering, the vacillating, defenseless Father Mouret, Archangias, and the ferocious, arbitrary, death-dealing Jehovah. Forced to choose between them, if there were no alternatives, who would not clamber into Cybele's bed?

V

Fortunately, alternatives exist. The terms of Zola's allusive oxymoron join and create a meaningful option. As Cybele and Jehovah struggle fiercely against each other, we suddenly realize that they are relatives, rather close ones at that. Nature, of course, represents the well-known devil, and Archangias's fingers, twice referred to as hairy, mark him as Satan's servant.[59] It may even be that his name alludes to the archangel who fell away from God – Lucifer. Furthermore, if Bambousse, in refusing to let his daughter go for nothing, is an uncivilized brute, then Archangias who agrees with him (1272) is no better. And, although enough has been said about the connotations of death surrounding Archangias and the church, it should be pointed out that not only does Paradou have a cemetery (1351), Jeanbernat says it *is* a cemetery (1252). As already established, even the benevolent tree of life casts a mortal shadow, and the place on the rocks reeks of lustful death. Cybele herself stands as much for death as she does for life, since her worshippers viewed death as a part of the process that produces new life. Significantly, Serge reacts with the same obedience to both Archangias and Désirée.[60] However violently the latter two hate each other (1279, 1439), in the end they represent but slight variations of the same ethos. Both negate humanity. Archangias wants to kill the physical, which is generally considered essential to human life; Désirée dances while she bleeds Mathieu and laughs while her bloodthirsty chickens tear each other to shreds ('If you were to give them a Christian,' she once told

Serge, 'they would manage to finish him' [1268]). She does not seem aware that the human spirit exists. And we know how Cybele bled her male adorers. Cybele's bleeding Attis, like Désirée's bleeding Mathieu, when read through the lens of biblical symbolism, provides one reason for rejecting Zola's nature worship as definitively as we have discarded his church. Blood, in the Old Testament, is the soul of the flesh.[61] Without soul, in this tradition, life is impossible.

Throughout his life, Zola insisted over and over again, in his fiction as in his theoretical work, that man is not just body, or just spirit. Soul or spirit when set apart is the equivalent of isolated flesh or body; it is not human. Man without humanity is like man without blood, he is dead, at least as a human being. That explains why Zola so vigorously opposed much of the literature prior to him. 'The literary spirit of preceding centuries is . . . a conception of literature separated from any idea of scientific inquiry. It constitutes pure literature, taking as its philosophic base the initial idea of a soul clearly distinct from the body and superior to it.'[62] '*Our* reality, nature as science has revealed it to us, is not similarly cut into two slices, one white, the other black. It is the whole of creation, it is life, and the whole of our task is to seek it at its sources, to seize it in its truth, to paint it in its details. We do not say there is a soul and a body; we say that there are living beings, and we watch them act.'[63]

These statements emphatically place Zola in opposition to any system that attempts to suppress the physical, natural side of man. 'You put man in the brain,' he said in his polemical letter to Jules Lemaître on 14 March 1885, 'I put him in all of his organs. You isolate man from nature, I do not see him without the earth, from which he comes and to which he returns. The soul that you enclose within a being, I sense it spread everywhere, in and out of [human] beings, in the animal, who is his brother, in the plant, in the pebble.' The point is, of course, as Zola put it in a letter to his friend Baille on 22 April 1861, 'Man partakes . . . of the nature of brutes and of angels, and it is precisely this mixture which constitutes what people have agreed to call the human element.' But just as man is not an angel, neither is he naturally an animal, though he may indeed become one: 'When [a country-girl's] parents withdraw her from school to help them with harvesting. . . . She scarcely knows how to read. . . . Her knowledge of the work around the house is not elaborate. . . . [and] if you add the work in the fields where she grew up to that, the whole of her knowledge will be exhausted. That is why the intellectual level of the majority of peasants, who let themselves be guided almost exclusively by instinct, is very low. To improve themselves, they have to leave their village and become a servant in the city. By staying in the country, they acquire a mind which becomes more and more obtuse, and, as they get old, they return to the animal state, which they left in childhood.'[64]

The most complete exposition of the hierarchy Zola saw extending from stones, up through plants, animals, and finally to human beings is to be found, however, in his creative work. In a myriad of forms across the *Rougon-Macquart*, Zola presents the tragedy of those characters who are unwilling or unable to raise themselves, without denying reality, above the level of brutes. In *Germinal*, as distinct from *La Faute* where Désirée's pets seem egregiously vicious, animals are capable of compassion for the suffering of others, but in none of Zola's works are animals capable of aspiring after a life better than has already been experienced. They cannot dream of and work for what are normally called humanitarian goals. No animal could be a Pauline or a Mme Caroline. Animals are, as the protagonist of *Le Docteur Pascal* puts it, 'like the rough sketch of man.' In some cases, as I have suggested in *Novel Configurations* (73–93), Zola's message becomes an open threat. The creation of human beings requires effort and education. When this is denied, men will act like animals, for that is what they will be. And the results of such arrested development could, as Zola vividly intimates, destroy us all.

The hierarchy comes through, as well, in *La Faute de l'abbé Mouret*. Within the complexes of allusions at each end of the opposition between church and nature, there are incorporated others that move away from the extreme ends of Archangias and Désirée-Cybele toward the center. Adam and Eve faced their life of trials together. Diana, however uncivilized the practices for choosing her slave-kings may seem, is considerably more humane than her earlier incarnations, than the Taurian Artemis, for example, and without any question more humane than Cybele. But even the early Greek Artemis, who mercilessly destroyed Actaeon, raised such serious doubts about the steadfastness of her virtue that Apollo felt compelled to trick her into killing Orion. By the time Diana arrives in Zola's Les Artaud, she has had an affair with Endymion (in the guise of Silene), with Hippolytus-Virbius (an affair that achieved a certain, and for our purposes important, permanence), and with a whole succession of slave-kings. For Diana, although one may not admire all its qualities, a somewhat more human love is possible.

On the other side, the Virgin Mary represents 'a beginning of human passion' (1286), and her cult is responsible for humanizing the rigorous austerity of Archangias's church. Naturally, the brother violently opposes any tenderness. According to him, the rural regions are losing their religion because it has been made too much like a nice little old lady (1238). With Serge, the cult of Mary goes even farther. 'Often, on serene nights, when Venus [the star of love] was shining very blond and dreamy in the tepid air, he would forget himself, he would drop from his lips, like a light song, the *Ave maris stella*.'[65] And we have already noted the Virgin's incarnations as Albine. When Serge repulses the Virgin, when he likewise rejects Jesus because of his gentleness, the priest then worships a dehumanized, lifeless church. Christ gave the church his body and blood, as Serge points out (1422). Without Jesus, the church has no flesh, no blood, and no soul; it is not even an empty shell; it is nothing. Appropriately, Father Mouret's next parish is Saint-Eutrope. Eutropius was an Armenian slave, a eunuch, who sought sanctuary in a church and was subsequently put to death. Serge, the bloodless eunuch, however much a saint, is dead. He almost falls into Albine's grave when the dirt gives way (1524); then he finds a more lonely – and thus an even more suitable – final resting place.

Mary-Diana and Jesus–slave-king–Virbius serve as the point at which the oppositions converge. Adam and Eve provide, however, an even better juncture – a new Adam and Eve, to whom all alternatives are open. They may choose to worship Jehovah or nature. Or they may choose to *be* human beings. These allusions working against and with each other could perhaps be represented in the following fashion:

As can be seen, I place the emphasis on Adam and Eve. I do so because it seems to me that Pascal is absolutely correct when he says in *Le Docteur Pascal* that Serge and Albine begin the 'Adamic adventure again in legendary Paradou.' Zola put his version of a first man and woman into a garden that differs from the biblical Eden in that no man or god reigns there. As one wishes, one can see Jehovah or a pantheon of pagan gods, but within the garden itself only nature rules. Nonetheless, the material is there ready to construct a religion. In this fashion, Zola emphasizes that man, starting essentially at the same point, constructed two completely different types of religion. In the Judaic tradition, man was subordinated to spirit, and in the pagan to the physical world of nature. Once again, Zola puts Adam and Eve before the prehistoric choice: Jehovah, Cybele – or humanity. Tragically, the results are no better than they were before. Serge and Albine go their separate ways along well-trodden routes and neglect the alternative that they themselves represent.

VI

That, I think, is as far as the allusions take us. The opposing terms move together and unite, but they do not reveal the exact character of Abbé Mouret's *faute*. For that information we must turn to the whole text, to which the allusions are subordinate and of which they form but a part. The fusion of body and soul that they suggest is also indicated by the book's images. At the outset of the novel, for example, the bread and wine and the 'intimate union' Serge contracts 'with God through the communion' (1224) vividly portray a similar unification. But the most dramatic figure appears in the little church building itself. We remember that after Serge's hallucinatory vision of nature's attack on the church, he wakes to find that the parish church still stands. From the standpoint of realism, there is no difficulty understanding why. It is now able to withstand somewhat longer the slow incursion of nature because Serge has repaired the worst of the damage inflicted by the wind, weather, and plants. From the point of view of the images, the church does not collapse because it has not shut out nature. At the beginning of *La Faute*, the sun, the sparrows, the service-tree enter the church freely. Later, even after Serge has made the repairs, some of the windows are left open so the sparrows can still enter. The little church has not been cut off from nature. Where Serge's dream image of the church differs from Zeus, a Greek personification of wisdom, the real parish church resembles the god; both Zeus and the little church of Les Artaud join with nature. In Paradou, nature reveals a similar breadth, for it is likewise a church (1378, 1382).

There are also the ramifications of Rosalie's and Fortuné's love affair. This secondary plot rises again to prominence in the first chapter of book three when Father Mouret marries the pair. If the reader pays close attention to the sermon, something Serge unfortunately did not do until he was incapable of acting, the problem posed by the novel's title begins to be resolved.

My dear brother, my dear sister, you are joined in Jesus. The institution of marriage is the figure of the sacred union of Jesus and his Church. It is a bond that nothing can break, that God wishes to be eternal, so that man may not separate what heaven has joined. In making you the bone of your bones, God has taught you that you have the duty to walk side by side, like a faithful couple, in accordance with the ways prepared by the All-Powerful. And you just love each other in the very love of God. . . . Remain then forever united, in the image of the Church that Jesus married in giving to us all his flesh and blood. (1422)

And if Rosalie does not fulfill her duties? 'The punishment would be terrible, you would lose your love. Oh! living without love, tearing flesh from its flesh, no longer belonging to the one who is half of yourself, agonizing far from what you have loved' (1423). Then, for Fortuné, there is a warning: 'May you be damned if you ever forsake her! That would be the most dastardly desertion for God to punish. As soon as she has given herself, she is yours, forever' (1424). But perhaps the most important phrase is lost among the priest's words: God 'did not mean for man to live alone [*solitaire*]' (1424). Serge repeats this phrase, word for word, during the series of temptations (1485).

Serge's sermon contains an enormous amount of essential information. Not only does he date the marriage from the point at which the woman gives herself to her man, but he goes far toward explaining his *faute* while vividly describing his punishment. Albine is his. She gave herself to him and he accepted her. For deserting her, he is damned to loveless solitude. Later, when he stands before Albine and denies her, his cassock will resemble 'a black shroud' (1464). It takes little imagination to see him beside the enormous cypress, the *Solitaire*, in the cemetery.

But there is more to his *faute*, which, we recall, 'the garden. . . had wanted' (1407). Paradou wished them to couple – a word I use deliberately. The big tree, that 'father of the forest,' and Paradou itself care only that the species continue. Whether or not love is involved makes no difference, and the minute Serge and Albine have had intercourse, the garden loses interest. Albine even senses that it makes fun of them. 'The brushwood is full of voices. . . . You would say some people are mocking us,' Albine says (1411). The garden has won. 'It was a victory for the animals, the plants, the things, that had wanted the entrance of these two children into the eternity of life' (1409). Later, when she wanders alone in the park with the realization that there is no hope for her love, '[S]he held out her hands despairingly, she screamed in protest. It couldn't finish like that. But her voice was stifled beneath the silent trees. Three times, she begged Paradou to answer, without an explanation coming from the high branches, without a single leaf taking pity on her' (1511). Désirée could lead Lise off to the bull and bring her back. The cow remains unaffected (1428–9). But Albine is not a cow. She is a woman, a human being, and she has given herself to her man for life. Henceforth she 'can live nowhere but in his arms' (1463). Numa may be pertinent (if I am correct in sensing an allusion to the early Roman king). Plutarch says Numa believed marriage was not primarily for the purposes of procreation, rather it was for the advantages of conjugal life and companionship (*Numa* 26.4.1–3). Zola said the same thing through the mouth of Rosalie. That their child has died does not really matter, for the important bond remains: 'We are married just the same.'

Serge also serves as a mouthpiece: 'Was it damnation to love Albine? No, not if this love were to go beyond the flesh' (1476). Serge interprets his own words to mean it is not a sin if love begins where the flesh leaves off. But that is not what he says. Where animals mate and separate, human love includes intercourse, and it goes beyond to continuing love, compassion, and companionship. However deep may be the feeling of Serge and Albine when they make love beneath the tree, only Albine reacts like a human being, with an understanding of the implications their love holds for the future. Serge loves her and abandons her, leaving Albine with no recourse but death. Serge's *faute* was to act like an animal.

VII

In *La Faute*, Zola apparently wished to recount the history of humanity. He begins back when human beings lived in tribes. According to Edgar Quinet, 'In this age, antiquity is everywhere similar; humanity lives in tribes. . . . Physical man has been born; moral man continues to sleep' (*Génie* 149–50). The 'tribe' (1231) of Artauds inhabiting the area where Zola situated his story are 'a people apart, a race born from the soil, a humanity of three hundred heads who began time again' (1232). Although the inbred Artauds are 'civilized' insofar as they have their rich and their poor, their robbers and their murderers, the overall impression they produce is of extreme primitiveness. It is more than a simile to say that the region is a 'country of wolves'[66] or that the children are like sparrows (1239). Little distinguishes the Artauds from animals. In book two, Zola reverts to an even more distant past in the history of mankind. Through the slowly awakening senses of Serge, the author follows evolution from plants to the point where Serge and Albine make love in the guise of nascent human beings surrounded by 'the beautiful tenderness of the first days of the world' (1393). This corresponds to the early plans for the novel. In the dossier, Zola wrote, 'This second part is nothing but a long study of the awakening of humanity.'[67]

The above passages point to the novel's deeper subject. *La Faute de l'abbé Mouret* tells the story of the development of man from his beginnings to the moment where he becomes capable of human love, a love Serge refuses and that Fortuné and Rosalie apparently accept. Perhaps Albine constitutes the book's central image. Until Serge's arrival, she is a savage, a nature girl, but not a human being. Pascal hoped to 'humanize' her by sending Serge there (1452). White Albine represents Sleeping Beauty, dormant life. Had the erstwhile priest who kisses her awake been an acceptable husband, she could have fulfilled a human destiny. But Serge will not have her, and once awakened, Albine can no longer return to the somnolent state of animals or of the majority of the peasants in the area. The only sleep available is permanent. The equivocal allusions in Paradou, centering on the big tree, effectively point to the alternatives confronting the young people. Jehovah's Edenic tree or nature's tree of life. Or they could have refused the extremes and chosen humanity. They do not. Albine subordinates herself to nature and Serge to the church. For both it means death.[68]

VIII

Zola's desire to write such a novel was of long standing. In a letter to Baptistin Baille, dated 14 January 1859, he mentions a similar project: 'A great and beautiful task, a task that Michelet undertook, a task I occasionally dare consider, is to make men return to women.' Not quite a year later, on 30 December 1859, he wrote to his other close childhood friend, Paul Cézanne:

You probably know that Michelet, in *L'Amour*, only begins his book when the marriage has been concluded, speaking thus only of spouses and not of lovers.

Well, puny me, I plan to describe nascent love, and to lead it to marriage. You can't yet conceive of the difficulty of what I want to undertake. Three hundred pages to fill, almost without plot; a sort of poem where I'll have to invent everything, where everything must work together towards one single goal: loving! And besides, as I've told you, I've never loved, except in dreams! . . . It doesn't matter, since I feel I'm capable of a great love, I'll consult my heart.

As time passed, the indications of Zola's interest in the subject continued: If he could change the world, he told Cézanne on 16 January 1860, 'He who would not love, would be condemned to death.' And on 14 February 1860, he wrote to Baille:

The sickness [of our century] depends especially on this: young people lead polygamous lives. . . . In love, the body and the soul are intimately bound, true love cannot exist without this mixture. It's a vain wish for you to want spiritual love, a moment will come when you will love with your body, and that is just, natural. Now, polygamous love completely excludes love with the soul, consequently [it excludes] love. . . . Put any young man and woman together. They are beautiful, they love with their bodies; it isn't yet love. Soon they will discover each others' qualities (and who doesn't have some), and, if only their characters are not opposed to each other, if only they have no major faults, they will love with their souls.

Doubtless, *La Faute de l'abbé Mouret* benefited considerably from the long period of germination, which included less successful attempts like *La Confession de Claude* (1865). For the time being at least, Zola had outgrown his tendency to sermonize. And in the meantime, he had apparently achieved a love that accorded with his definition. By 1874, when, Mitterand suggests, he began to work seriously on this novel, he had long been 'married,' though the marriage was not formalized by an appearance before the church and state until 1870. He had developed the maturity and experience to infuse an enormous amount of strength, an almost inexplicable force into the project. In addition, he had deepened his knowledge and understanding of mythology. This acquaintance was by no means superficial, as Philip Walker has demonstrated in his excellent study 'Zola's Hellenism.'[69] Not only had Zola been a first-rate student of Latin and Greek while in high school,[70] but he had followed the publishing scene very closely for years. While supplementing his income by writing for the newspapers, he reviewed works by Michelet, Quinet, and Beauregard, among others. Some of his information may, as Ripoll suggests, have come from Michelet, who was clearly aware of the developments. In truth, however, as Walker points out, Zola had numerous sources available to him, and we do not know which ones were the most formative. The many references to Greek and Roman mythology that are to be found throughout his letters, his news-paper articles, reviews, and stories, as well as his novels make it clear, however, that Zola was far from a stranger to this material. This is, of course, not surprising, for Hellenism was and had been for some time in the air.[71] As for Zola's knowledge of the Bible, we have proof that he reread Genesis while preparing to write this novel.[72] In addition, the Adam and Eve story appeared frequently in the literature of the period.[73] Of the many possible examples, I should perhaps make special mention of Victor de Laprade's poem *Psyché* (1841), which Zola dis-cusses in a letter of 22 April 1861 to Baille. The fact that Laprade mixes Adamic imagery with imagery chosen from several ancient mythological traditions makes it particularly interesting.[74]

Because this material was of considerable interest to both the writers and audience of the period, Zola could reasonably have expected a fair percentage of the reading public to understand the most important of the allusions fused into his novel. Taine even recognized the more subtle resonances. In the letter cited above (n9), he mentioned the indebtedness of *La Faute* to Indian and Persian poetry. A knowledge of its ancestry is not really necessary for an understanding of the novel, although the debt may have been more widely recognized than the contemporary reviews of *La Faute* indicate. It is relevant that, as I men-tioned earlier, the novel was conceived, written, and published in a period when all over Europe both scholars and ordinary educated people were becoming interested in mythology and comparative reli-gions. George Smith fed the interest in 1872 when he announced to the scholarly community his discovery of a Chaldean account of the Flood that provided graphic support for the contention Indo-European scholars had long been making, that Genesis might well have derived from an already existent body of non-Hebraic myths.[75] Alexander Heidel states that Smith's announcement 'created a tremendous enthusiasm throughout Europe.'[76] However that may be, interest in Indo-European and Egyptian mythology clearly existed in France, and the material Zola used was widely available. Much of it appears in the volumes of Pierre Larousse's *Grand Dictionnaire universel* (1866–78), which had been pub-lished before Zola began to work seriously on *La Faute de l'abbé Mouret* and which Zola owned at his death.[77]

Of course, in the end, whether or not Zola's contemporaries were sufficiently knowledgeable to understand his allusions should not affect our own judgment of *La Faute*. I said earlier that the novel has an almost inexplicable force. That is not to say, however, that *La Faute de l'abbé Mouret* is a great book; it is not. Even leaving aside considerations of verisimilitude – a novel that blithely kills off its heroine with tuberoses and hyacinths clearly has refused realism as a standard of judgment – there are other flaws. Those excessively long catalogs of plants, flowers, and trees,[78] for example, must surely rank among the most tedious passages in the whole of Zola. The animation of similar pages in *Le Ventre de Paris* or *Au bonheur des dames* is almost totally absent. In addition, these long lists must certainly bear most of the responsibility for the fact that so many distinguished scholars and critics have passed over some of Zola's essential cues to both the complexes of allusions and the system of images. Far too many of the catalogs' constituent elements are insufficiently motivated, and the important indicators tend to get lost in the profusion of detail. Nonetheless, I would say that the primary weakness occurs, not because Zola 'put in too much,' as he feared in a letter to Turgenev dated 29 June 1874, but because of the excessive power of one of the allusions. Had he not alluded to any myth or legend, the meaning of the book would, I believe, be perfectly clear. If the allusions to both Eden *and* Cybele were equally forceful, the novel likewise would present few problems. Unfortunately, Zola miscalculated and emphasized his allusion to Genesis to such a degree that it overshadows and obscures not only the allusion to Cybele but also the reasonably coherent system of meaningful images as well. As a result, the book seems to contradict opinions Zola expressed elsewhere about sex, nature, and man. Because of Zola's error, *La Faute* has appeared unbalanced and confused.

This does not detract from the novel as far as my present needs are concerned, for it provides another excellent example of the potential of allusion. Where Proust established his allusions in a circular fashion around the shadowy figure of Albertine, slowly brushing in aspects of her personality, gradually highlighting the protagonist's impressions, until finally the reader's mind completes the closure and thus joins the protagonist in the conception of an extraordinarily complex characterization, Zola deployed his masculine allusions in orderly ranks, backed them up with reinforcements, and then set them against feminine forces of (almost) equal strength. Rather than establishing a simple parallel, as Barbey did in 'Le Rideau cramoisi,' or an opposition to play against the plot thread, as Gide did with his allusions to the Bible in *La Symphonie pastorale*, Zola created in *La Faute* a text that suggests numerous opposing allusions working together metaphorically to direct attention toward a third term or synthesis. To return to the analogy of the battle of the sexes, peace is established and marriage results. The text then forces readers back into the story for a fuller understanding of the alternatives involved. There, they discover that although the allusions extend from beginning to end, they are subordinate to the major symbols of church and nature. Zola's allusions are a mere part of the entire, coherent (or relatively so) novel. Oppositions pervade virtually every level of the text: Cybele against Jehovah, Désirée against Archangias, Paradou's tree of life against the cemetery's tree of death, body against soul. Opposites marry and they produce, not a child, but the vision of what it means to be a human being.

8

Allusive Permutations:
La Nausée, Les Gommes

Whether the elements of allusion are profuse or scarce, complicated or elementary, extended or synoptic, allusion functions in a rather direct way, as I hope the preceding pages have demonstrated. The text being read elicits an image in the reader's mind that is then brought to bear on the central image of impressions being formed during the reading, and as the interpretation builds, the overriding image constantly changes, integrating new details of more or less density and depth. The reader's basic mental process varies little whether the allusions are extended over long passages or are limited to a single reference. Du Bellay's mention of Ulysses in 'Heureux qui, comme Ulysse...' brings little more than homesickness into the reading of the poem. Likewise for most synoptic allusions of opposition – a Good Boy named Peck or a wimpy Hercules. More lengthy allusions – for example, when Balzac's *L'Histoire de la grandeur et de la décadence de César Birotteau* (1837) alludes to the story of Julius Caesar – are not significantly different, though the external, historical image probably remains tentative until the resonance of the onomastic repetition of Caesar, the premonitory dream rather like that of Caesar's wife, Calpurnia, Montesquieu's *Considération sur les causes de la grandeur des Romains et de leur décadence*, and so on, leave no doubt that they signal an allusion. At that point, the image of Julius Caesar's downfall should be integrated into the reader's experience of Balzac's César and, as Mileham points out, the numerous, shared elements stress themes of filial rebellion and paternal indulgence.[1] Though the allusive image grows gradually from a number of referents as the reading proceeds, its incorporation into a relationship is quite straightforward, whether it resembles a parallel, an opposition, or an oxymoron.

Allusion may extend over many volumes without changing the basic relationship. Zola made frequent use of more extended allusions of opposition to emphasize his belief that France was disintegrating morally and spiritually. He implicitly calls us to recognize the difference between Rastignac's famous *défi* from Père Lachaise and Aristide Saccard's similar challenge from the Butte Montmartre. While Rastignac was by no means an admirable character (Bixiou calls him 'a profoundly depraved gentleman'),[2] generations of readers witness to his continuing attractiveness, a quality that Saccard lacks. This particular opposition joins others that mark a further change highlighted in Zola's *Rougon-Macquart* (1871–93). In Balzac's world, Eugène de Rastignac, Du Tillet, and others are nothing but jackals feasting on the remains of Nucingen's gargantuan repasts. They would never dare challenge the 'Napoleon of the financial world.' In the Second Empire as chronicled by Zola, however, Gundermann (Zola's successor to Balzac's Nucingen) is almost toppled by Aristide Saccard. Through much of *Les Rougon-Macquart*, Zola used *La Comédie humaine* (1829–48) to emphasize the degradation of France and the French as they passed from the July Monarchy to the Second Empire.

Of course, the allusion may be superficially very complex, either in the subtlety of its reference or in the intricacy of the relationships established. Even during the first performance of Molière's *Ecole des femmes* (1662), for instance, not everyone would have recognized the allusion when Arnolphe says, 'That is enough. / I am the master. I speak; go, obey' (vv 641–2). Arnolphe is quoting Corneille's tragedy *Sertorius* (1662), which had just been performed. As Frédéric Hillemacher points out, Pompey the Great utters the lines near the tragedy's conclusion, when he sends Sertorius's assassin, Perpenna, to his death. Unlike the low-born Arnolphe, however, Pompey immediately excuses himself for having spoken so imperiously.[3] While there is no question that the quotation establishes an opposition between the humility of an illustrious general and the arrogance of Agnès's guardian, it additionally casts an extraordinarily brilliant light on Arnolphe and emphasizes his ridiculousness. Molière's use of the quotation stresses his character's inappropriate pride and continues to prepare the catastrophe coming, not to Arnolphe's servant, or even to his ward, but to himself. Despite the subtlety of the allusion, the pattern of relationship remains straightforward.

The complexity of the allusion may come from the amount of material that must be integrated. When in *La Faute de l'abbé Mouret* and *Le Doc-*

teur Pascal[4] Zola refers to the Paradou as 'Sleeping Beauty's park,' he brings to *La Faute* an idiosyncratic Sleeping Beauty who signifies a particular concept of education. As we have seen, by 'Sleeping Beauty' Zola meant a girl raised in absolute ignorance, occupied at meaningless tasks, and who consequently passes her time in unhealthy dreams of a kiss from the first passing cavalier. Because Jeanbernat leaves Albine to shift for herself, she quite naturally follows her instincts, and because he never leaves his garden to intrude on the developing idyl, he abandons a defenseless Albine. She is too ignorant to understand the complications rising from Serge's position, and unfortunately for her, a profoundly impotent priest happens by first. Unlike the prince's kiss that resuscitates Sleeping Beauty, Serge's kills Albine. Zola's allusion to the legendary princess then stresses Jeanbernat's failure to give parental guidance to Albine.

Such complications notwithstanding, as the images within the reading experience come together with the images from other texts (but, of course, within the reader's memory), whether they seem initially to establish a parallel or an opposition, the allusive relationship stresses the identical elements and produces a sense that would not have been possible for either of the constituent images.

Would that it were always so! There is, of course, nothing to impel writers to provide such relatively clear applications of allusion. Indeed, while the examples I have chosen have the advantage of focusing on allusion's essential relationship, and thus, I hope, of clarifying the device and the way it functions, the various kinds of intertextuality may slide into one another. I think, on the one hand, of a work's transposition through time and space – as Homer's *Odyssey* in Joyce's *Ulysses* – or, on the other, of that kind of inspiration exemplified by Virgil's admiration of the same work in his creation of *The Aeneid*. Some would call the latter example imitation, some *refacimento*; as Genette sees, however, both intertextual relationships require a preceding text, which, though perhaps not used in its particularity, forms the basis for a tradition and which enters the new text by a plurality of explicit and implicit relationships. One of the more useful aspects of Genette's categories comes from his understanding that they are not necessarily discrete.[5]

When parody slides into allusion or some other intertextual device, for example, the distinctions that I have tried to establish with clarity become considerably more problematic. Jean-Paul Sartre's *La Nausée* (*Nausea* [1938]) provides an illustration. His references to concepts and sequences that are essential to the aesthetics and epistemology of

Proust's *A la recherche du temps perdu* continue throughout *La Nausée*. Unlike Sainte-Beuve, who, though personally acquainted with Balzac, Baudelaire, and Stendhal, was unable to appreciate their stature as the major writers of his day, Sartre had absorbed Proust in a period when few French people recognized his importance. He makes reference to Proust and *A la recherche du temps perdu* sometimes only in passing, sometimes in extended essays that discuss what Sartre felt to be Proust's weaknesses and misconceptions, and sometimes, as in *L'Etre et le néant*, *Situations II*, *Les Temps modernes*, and elsewhere, through an ongoing debate about the concepts explored in *A la recherche du temps perdu*. The relationship has been studied repeatedly, generally with the recognition that significant differences separate the two.[6] Rather than extend these considerations, it seems to me more interesting to see how Sartre used Proust in *La Nausée*. Unquestionably, Proust's masterpiece played a major role in the novel from start to finish. According to Grossvogel 'Sartre's *Nausea* provides a postscript to *Remembrance of Things Past*, since it is so clearly a restatement of a number of Proust's themes.'[7] I believe, however, that Proust has a far more visceral part in Sartre's first novel.

Throughout *La Nausée*, Sartre raises issues of language, of memory, of perception, of art, of being, of love – all issues close to the heart of Proust. Newman-Gordon thinks of pastiche,[8] an artistic imitation of manner and style that is used often for purposes of ridicule. Although Sartre unquestionably introduces Proustian themes, images, names, objects, and attitudes, there is little attempt to echo the syntactic rhythms and lexicon so important to pastiche. Instead of stylistic echoes, he establishes oppositions, and I would consequently prefer other terms: parody or, more precisely, burlesque. Sartre's parody is for the most part accomplished in a flat, spare style that contrasts markedly with that of *A la recherche*. It is nonetheless pointed. It simply ridicules by opposition, maintaining both images of a double vision – implicitly calling for 'this' rather than its opposite, 'that' – instead of fusing them, as allusion does, in stereoscopic vision.

The matter is complicated, since *La Nausée*'s initial burlesque changes in the concluding pages, and the beginning mockery becomes the terminal allusion. Early in the novel, Roquentin has gone to the Rendezvous des Cheminots, a café near the railroad station, the only place where he had previously been free from nauseous feelings and that he had then come to look upon as a place of refuge. Nausea accompanies his occasional but overwhelming crises of anguish and becomes a symbol for a terrible feeling growing from an awareness of his own uselessness and alienation in a world that lacks a preexistent purpose. This time he scarcely arrives at the café when he is overwhelmed by nausea. To his enormous distress, he no longer has a sanctuary. He asks the waitress, Madeleine, to put on a recording of 'Some of These Days' in the hope that it will give him respite. Some might think immediately of Proust, but despite the well-known passages turning around the 'involuntary memory' experienced by Proust's protagonist when he dipped the little cake, a madeleine, into his tea and resuscitated the childhood world of Combray, the fact that the serving girl has the same name would surely not be significant were it not for other features. The waitress's name, Madeleine, the jazz piece's title referring to time, the repeated refrain, and the fact that Sartre's hero is looking for a woman give more assurance that *La Nausée* is referring to *A la recherche du temps perdu*.[9]

Still, one must also recognize the significant differences. Proust's 'little phrase' comes from a masterpiece by Vinteuil, the Sonata for Violin and Piano. It is 'serious' music and set off against the sung refrain of an old ragtime piece, 'Some of These Days';[10] thus, a live performance faces off against a scratched recording, a salon and its modish orangeade against a café where Roquentin drinks tepid beer (*N* 206), the elegant Odette de Crécy, the object of Swann's lust, against the object of Roquentin's, Mme Françoise (or Mme Jeanne, as she is elsewhere called [*N* 11, 203]), and the euphemistic 'making orchids [*faire catleya*]' (*R* 1.230) against Roquentin's coming to the café 'to fuck [*baiser*]' (*N* 24). Swann hears the Vinteuil composition at the refined home of Mme Verdurin, 'la Patronne [the patron]' (e.g., *R* 3.755); Roquentin hears the scratched record in the seedy café run by 'la patronne [the boss]' (*N* 24). Proust's protagonist is served by Françoise, the family retainer who has her own ideas about virtually everything, and Roquentin by Mme Françoise, the café's proprietor who 'never says no' (*N* 11).

Despite the conflicting levels, where the lush Proustian poetry is replaced by Sartre's descriptions that emphasize the banal and the trite with short sentences and few adjectives, the similarities are striking. Swann had heard the sonata 'the year before, at a reception' (*R* 1.205); Roquentin remembers hearing 'Some of These Days' 'whistled in 1917 by American soldiers in the streets' (*N* 28). For Swann, 'suddenly charmed' (*R* 1.205), 'it was . . . a great pleasure when, beneath the little line of the thin, resisting, dense and directive violin, he had suddenly seen the mass of the multiform, coherent, even, jostling part for piano try to rise in liquid lapping like the mauve agitation of waves that moonlight charms and pitches in a lower key' (ibid.); for Roquentin, the refrain 'throws itself forward like a cliff against the sea' (*N* 28), and he 'begins to warm up, to feel happy. . . . a little happiness that stretches out at the bottom of the viscous pool of water' (ibid.). Swann 'had tried to capture the phrase or the harmony' (*R* 1.205). He experiences 'one of these impressions that are perhaps . . . the only purely musical impressions, limited in extent, entirely original, irreducible to any other kind of impression. An impression of this variety is momentarily *sine materia*' (*R* 1.206). Roquentin 'would have liked to hold onto the melody' (*N* 28), but he understands that he cannot stop the flow of notes. 'I have to accept their death, even to wish it. I know few impressions that are stronger or more bitter' (ibid.).

Later Roquentin will recognize that the refrain 'does not exist,' by which he means, 'It is on the other side – always on the other side of something, of a voice, of a violin note. . . . It is behind [things that exist]' (*N* 206). Clearly, this nonexistence closely resembles the existence of Proust's 'little phrase.' Swann felt that 'the sonata's phrase really existed' (*R* 1.345). '[S]he belonged however to an order of supernatural creatures that we have never seen, but that we nonetheless recognize with delight when some explorer of the invisible succeeds in capturing one, in bringing it back from the divine world to which he has access, so as to shine for a few moments above ours' (ibid). Swann is like a valetudinarian who begins 'to make out the unhoped for possibility of beginning . . . an entirely different life' (*R* 1.207–8). In the music, he finds 'one of these invisible realities that he had stopped believing in and . . . he felt once again the desire and almost the force to consecrate his life' (*R* 1.208). Swann associates Vinteuil's sonata with Odette and the various places where they pursued their love (e.g., *R* 1.339-45). Roquentin likewise remembers places and adventures: 'I am filled with emotion. . . . I have had true adventures. I don't remember any detail, but I perceive the rigorous links of circumstances. I have crossed seas, I have left cities behind me. . . . I have had women, I have fought with guys, and I could never go backwards, no more than a record can turn in reverse' (*N* 30).

The Proustian protagonist is later overwhelmed by Vinteuil's septet, which was discovered after Swann's death. First, Proust's hero recognizes the 'flushed promise of dawn' (*R* 3.755), though he will soon realize that it is quite simply a call to art (*R* 4.456), a vocation that he accepts when he commits himself to writing his own masterpiece.

Behind the septet, the narrator recognizes the particular, unique being of the composer, Vinteuil (R 3.757–61). The protagonist is about to become the narrator. He will devote the rest of his life to the demanding task of his work; he will sacrifice current pleasures to this new obligation, however difficult it may be (R 4.621–5). As Roquentin waits for his train, listening for the last time to 'Some of These Days,' he too makes numerous associations: 'Thoughts about Anny [his former mistress], about my wasted life. And then, further below, Nausea, as timid as a dawn' (N 205). He imagines the composer, an 'American with black eyebrows, panting, with sweat rolling down his cheeks. He's sitting in shirtsleeves before his piano. He has . . . vaguely, vaguely, the phantom of a tune in his head, *Some of these days*. . . . But first he had to jot down this tune. *Some of these days*. His moist hand grasped the pencil on the piano. *Some of these days, you'll miss me honey*' (N 208).

For Proust, Vinteuil's compositions represent the noblest of human endeavors, while Sartre holds such pretentiousness up for ridicule. Indeed, in the harsh light of *La Nausée*'s opening burlesque, as the major elements of the episodes related to the madeleine, the sonata, and the septet are repeated, so to speak, in vulgar dress and echoed in a minor (if not off) key, it is difficult not to see the absurdity of the Proustian dream. But the tone and context change through the course of Sartre's novel. By the end, 'Some of These Days' is less important as popular music and an opposition to serious compositions than as the sign of something worthwhile. The emphasis shifts from the contextual, circumstantial elements – the *patronne*, sexual intercourse, the seedy café – to the central work of art, which indicates the possibility that Roquentin's life can acquire purpose and that he can avoid the existential anguish identified with nausea. Of course, no student of Sartre's philosophy would believe in the authenticity of Roquentin's decision to write a book and thus create a sort of metaphysical escape hatch. Roquentin's decision to create art is for Sartre the philosopher as mistaken as his previous decision to write history. *La Nausée*, however, is neither a philosophical disquisition nor, despite the number of times Sartre refers to it in subsequent compositions such as *L'Etre et le néant*, a valid illustration for his philosophical writings. One might suspect that Sartre used the shift from parody to allusion in order to bring the novel closure by highlighting his character's belief that he has found a means of salvation.[11]

When the novel begins to focus on the significance of the ragtime piece, the parodic elements have been moved to the background. '[A]nd at this precise moment, from the other side of existence, in this other world that can be seen from afar, but without ever approaching, a little melody begins to dance, to sing' (*N* 207). 'I feel something brushing timidly beside me and I don't dare budge because I am afraid that it will go away. Something that I don't know, a sort of joy' (*N* 209). Soon he, like Proust's protagonist, begins to think about creating a work of art.

Couldn't I try?... Naturally, it would not be a question of a musical melody... but couldn't I, in another genre...? It would have to be a book: I don't know how to do anything else. But not a history book: history talks about what has existed – something existing cannot justify existence by another existing thing. . . . Another kind of book. I don't know very clearly what – but it would be necessary for people to make out, behind the printed words, behind the pages, something which wouldn't exist, which would be above existence. A story, for example, which can't happen, an adventure. It would have to be beautiful and hard like steel and make people ashamed of their existences. . . . A book. Of course, it would at first be a difficult, tiring job, but it would not keep me from existing or feeling that I exist. But a moment would come when the book would be written, would be behind me, and I think that some of its light would fall on my past. Then perhaps I would be able to remember my life across it without repugnance. (*N* 209–10)

The Proustian imagery and themes remain in focus, and the novel concludes with the terminal hope of a solution for Sartre's hero: 'I think that a little bit of its light would fall on my past' (*N* 210). Roquentin's conclusion is unexpected, a *deus ex machina* that occurs in a sudden, terminal epiphany, since it offers a surprising, unjustified hope occurring in a novel that has moved progressively through an increasingly clear understanding of the character's contingency, gratuitousness, and superfluity. Nonetheless, for my purposes, however poorly prepared Roquentin's illumination and faith in salvation through art, the parody has become an allusion.[12]

'Some of These Days' has not changed. It is still a popular melody in a vulgar café; the *patronne* continues to serve and service clients; the record's scratch remains. While the parodic resonances should maintain the reader's suspicion of the unacceptability of Roquentin's decision, which thus creates some ambiguity, *La Nausée* as a whole builds an experience where the main character chooses to seek authenticity through art. Such, at least, is one reading.

Gerald Prince appropriately points out that, while for many of us 'Sartre's first novel goes from certain initial questions (what is nausea? how will I transcend it?) to certain final answers ("it is Existence revealing itself"; I will become an artist),' these terminal responses constitute only one of several possible closures.[13] Another version grows from what 'we might call a closure of uncertainty (making sense of or exploiting inconclusiveness, hesitation, and contradiction) as opposed to the earlier closure of certainty' (Prince 188). He goes on to suggest that because *La Nausée* proposes alternate accounts, it 'constitutes an apprenticeship in uncertainty' (ibid. 189). He would distinguish between what the Russian formalists termed the 'story' (events in their normal chronological and causal order) and 'plot' (the artistic arrangement of those events). Prince considers the 'Editor's Note' the indication of another version, since the discovery of some notebooks containing a diary among Antoine Roquentin's papers followed the events recounted in the diary and is thus out of chronological order. Moreover, the fact that no mention is made of a novel may mean that Roquentin never wrote the book he planned. This variety of indications and questions are common in novels, however, and are readily accepted by most readers. If one accepts them as attempts to enhance verisimilitude, as Prince does, they probably work minimally in establishing the work as realistic. The other contradictions are equally unobjectionable. Was the incident with the stone really Roquentin's first such experience, when he elsewhere tells of nausea in front of a Khmer statuette? When did he really last see Anny? Likewise for all the hesitations in the beginning, as the diarist begins to jot down his thoughts, and in the end, as he wonders whether salvation might come through art. Diaries tend to be 'discontinuous, heterogeneous, or disorderly,' and such confusions are well within the practices of authors who wish to increase verisimilitude in fictional journals.[14] To call them 'paradoxes' (Prince 187), much less 'another account' (ibid.), is to give them more importance than they should have, although the fact that I do not accept Prince's justifications for his central intuition – that *La Nausée* focuses on uncertainty, irresolution, and ambiguity – in no way impugns the validity of his insight.

The act of reading demands that readers make active choices in the process of interpretation. We give weight to what is significant and neglect what is not. Importance cannot be determined without comparison or, to put it another way, without a context. The most important context is that of the work itself, though language, literature, society, history, and so on provide other contexts that may be decisive. Readers decide which of the possible contexts are important, and this decision determines whether a work is read for itself as literature or for insights of a philosophical, biographical, historical, sociological, linguistic, or other nature. Of course, there is nothing wrong with orienting understanding according to these other disciplines. It is just that *La Nausée* as philosophy is very different from *La Nausée* as literature with philosophical interests. In the first case, the novel takes its place in a progression that includes subsequent philosophic texts; in the second, the philosophy informs Roquentin's movement from dissatisfaction with his life, to despair, and to the closing hint of a possible salvation through art. Readers may not have the background necessary to give the proper weight to whatever textual phenomena they notice. When they nod off and miss significant features, they may misinterpret, or they may be saved by textual redundancy that uses other means to highlight and direct their attention.

The answers proposed in response to literary questions must be submitted to the whole of the text. The fact that, like most French clauses, most of *La Nausée*'s sentences have nouns or pronouns as grammatical subjects is insignificant, for example, and should be ignored. In other instances, examination of such morphological features may be essential. Spitzer argued that the high frequency of causal constructions in Charles-Louis Philippe's *Bubu de Montparnasse* (1905) grows from a feeling of fatalism arising from the social disintegration of his day.[15] Similarly, I argued above that the paucity of *La Nausée*'s adjectives is important when contrasted with the descriptive richness of Proust's novel. Or for a different kind of context, some readers might translate Bouville, the site of Sartre's novel, as Mudville and think of the Mudville in James Wilson's poem 'Casey's Revenge' where the great Casey finally got a hit. Knowing readers would immediately reject such an association, however, for the novel has no other markers pointing toward either Casey or Wilson, and the association adds nothing to an understanding of *La Nausée*. Instead, intelligent readers will link Bouville to the images of grime, viscosity, and repugnance that accompany Roquentin's experience of nausea.[16] Significant associations, in short, will be validated by plural, textual markers that direct the reader more or less consistently toward an acceptable interpretation.

Trouble arises, however, when several sets of markers point in different directions. The first indication of ambiguity perhaps comes, as Contat and Rybalka suggest, when one notices that though *La Nausée* is purportedly the diary of a man named Roquentin, it bears Sartre's name as author (*N* 1721). Indeed, when modern readers come across a statement like the putative editor's assurance, 'we publish [these notebooks] without changing anything' (*N* 3), it does the reverse of increasing verisimilitude. These days, in fact, the formula indicates the presence of fiction. It may be that when Marivaux's *La Voiture embourbée* was first published in 1714, readers accepted the introductory sentence at face value: 'Finally, my dear friend, I am keeping my promise to you; here is the little story that I promised; the tale will be faithful, and I give it to you as I heard it.' Many writers must have thought the device would be effective, for it appeared in legions of novels, so much so, in fact, that by 1902 when Gide wrote 'Yes, as you thought, Michel has talked to us, my dear brother. Here is the story that he told us' at the beginning of *L'Immoraliste*, the device was worn out. But although it could no longer serve to render a text believable, it could indicate artifice. It enabled Gide to distance his reader.[17] It strains credulity that Sartre, so attuned to the artificialities of Mauriac's fiction, would on reading *Le Nœud de vipères* (1932) have viewed with anything but disdain the introduction – 'You will be astonished to discover this letter in my strongbox, on a packet of securities' – or the conclusion – 'My dear Geneviève. . . . [y]ou know that our father died at his work table and that Amélie found him on the morning of November 24th with his face in an open notebook, the very one that I am sending you by registered mail.' That he would then adopt the device in the attempt to make readers of 1938 believe that his *La Nausée* consisted of Roquentin's notebooks 'without changing anything' is quite simply inconceivable. I suggest that he meant these words to encourage readers to distance themselves, to refuse identification with Roquentin, to recognize him and his solutions as invalid.

The parody enhances and exacerbates the distance between reader and work, for it calls attention not to the reality of Roquentin's experience but to an author who is arranging a fiction. There are then two stories: Roquentin's fiction and the author's creation. In one context, Roquentin functions as best he can to come to terms with nausea. In the author's world, Sartre uses the fiction to comment on Proust and on the way one ought to look at life and love. As Hollier points out, 'Monday, 25 January 1932' (*N* 8), the date indicated for the beginning of the diary proper, is anachronic. In 1932, 25 January fell on Friday rather than Monday (Hollier 76). The two calendars, the one 'real,' the other anachronic, then proceed across the novel until Roquentin leaves Bouville on 25 February. It would be out of character for Roquentin to recognize Proust in the various elements that bring a debased *A la recherche* into *La Nausée*. It would likewise be out of character for him to recognize the Proustian flavor of his thought that there might be a sort of salvation through the creation of art, especially since he gives no indication of a background in Proust's novel. While many novels use such parodies and allusions to support and strengthen the thematic movements, the difference here consists in the degree to which Sartre's novel brings attention to them. It is not just the dedication to Castor or the epigraph from Céline – 'It is a fellow without collective importance, nothing more than an individual' – both of which would seem strange flowing from Roquentin's pen. Castor was Simone de Beauvoir's nickname, and Celine's words would appear awkward as Roquentin's self-characterization. Whether or not one accepts such accessories as an unobjectionable part of a literary work, *La Nausée* nonetheless brings its artifice to the attention of knowing readers. Hollier catalogs numerous inconsistencies and implausibilities across the novel (76–84).

There are other more startling indications of a manipulating author. What is the café manager really named? Is she Mme Françoise or Mme Jeanne? When Roquentin goes looking for sexual satisfaction, she is Mme Françoise (*N* 11). 'She never says no. . . . I don't pay her; we make love as equals. She gets pleasure from it (she needs a man a day, and she has many others besides me)' (ibid.). When he goes to the same café for the last time before taking the train from Bouville for Paris, she is busy with another customer and is called Mme Jeanne. As Wood points out, 'Roquentin (like Sartre himself) lives out of cheap hotels, restaurants, and cafés. Furthermore, he is clearly hostile to marriage and has a love life which, in its degree of freedom, would only become universally available to the middle classes in the 60s. (Indeed, Sartre . . . is in part responsible for the explosive demand for such freedoms . . .).'[18] Françoise derives from etymons meaning 'free,' and Jeanne from roots meaning 'gift (of God).'

Of course, there is another possible explanation for these inconsistencies: perhaps Sartre made a mistake. Although that is certainly possible, it is usually better to assume, at least at first, that the author was right and that the text is internally justified. A few moments' thought about criticism over the last few hundred years will remind us that when scholars ponderously proclaim authors' poor taste, insufficient insight, bad judgment, or whatever, the critics have generally been shown to be the greater fools. Critical poetic justice! In this case, there is a common thread to the inconsistencies, one that points to *La Nausée* as an important precursor of the 'undecidable,' indeterminate novels, plays, and films of the last generation.

Thesis novels generally establish a binary structure that encourages a mildly schizophrenic reading. Unlike allegories, whose first-level account has little importance other than to indicate the figural significance, didactic novels of the last several centuries tell a story that is supposed to have importance in and for itself. Although readers are expected to 'suspend their disbelief,' at least to some degree, and accept the story as real or potentially real, the characters and the events so clearly illustrate a thesis that readers are also disaffected and encouraged to distance themselves. The characters should then not be accepted as 'real' persons; they are rather figures with a message. If I am correct in believing that readers of *La Nausée* are encouraged to see a manipulating author who mocks Proust, then it follows that they would accept the shift to a positive presentation of Proustian salvation as an acceptable solution to the problems posed by the work. Parody and allusion then actively function not as an integrated pattern that constantly points back into the work; rather they point to a creating, manipulating author.

Indeed, the variations that writers can effect on the conceptions basic to allusion are limited only by the writer's imagination. Many authors regularly search for the unorthodox to produce the unexpected. Robbe-Grillet's *Les Gommes* (*The Erasers* or *The Gumshoes* [1953]), for example, frustrates the allusions that are unquestionably a part of the text, impeding their completion, and confounding their most obvious significance. Like *La Nausée*, which Robbe-Grillet had studied carefully, *Les Gommes* insists on a world where man has no preexistent meaning, where he is, as Sartre put it, extraneous (*de trop*) and contingent. For Sartre, and for Robbe-Grillet, when removed from human systems, 'the world around us becomes a smooth surface, without significance, without soul, without values, on which we have no claim.'[19] Robbe-Grillet objects not to the sense of Sartre's world, but to the philosopher's describing it as though the world were living and capable of impressing its alien nature on Roquentin. Robbe-Grillet refuses '*any* complicity. There is then a refusal of analogical vocabulary and of traditional humanism, a refusal at the same time of the idea of tragedy and of any other idea that leads to a belief in a meaningful and superior nature whether of man or nature (or of both together), in short, a refusal of all preestablished order' (ibid. 65).

As a novel, *Les Gommes* plays on the conventions of the detective story, though with significant differences. Robbe-Grillet explained in an interview that 'traditional detective novels. . . . are closed structures. That is to say that a good traditional novel begins this way: there are pieces in disorder with lacunae; someone, a detective, must put them in order and fill in the lacunae, and once the novel is concluded, there is no more obscurity anywhere. That is to say that the detective novel is a novel that is strongly marked by the realist ideology where everything has a meaning, one meaning. . . . Now, the narrative structures which interest me are precisely lacunal structures.'[20] *Les Gommes* purports to tell of the attempted murder of Daniel Dupont by a gang of terrorists that has caught the community's attention by killing someone at 7:30 every evening for more than a week. In fact, however, Dupont merely suffered a minor wound, and he managed to slip away leaving the impression that he had been killed. He takes refuge with Dr Juard, a gynecologist and friend, who may also be an abortionist and the gang's doctor; we are never quite certain about his other activities. Indeed, we are uncertain about many aspects of this novel and its characters and their roles. It is typical of the entire book when Laurent, the police chief, declares that the death certificate constitutes the 'single certain piece of evidence,'[21] whereas we know that it is a fabrication by Dr Juard.

Wallas, a special agent sent to investigate, is left to flounder in a world where he resembles both Garinati, the failed assassin, and André VS, the successful killer – on the following night – of Albert Dupont; where he carries the same 7.65-mm-caliber pistol as both victim and assassin; where both successful (André VS) and unsuccessful (Garinati) assassins wear raincoats with rips in the right shoulder; where both Wallas and Garinati bear names that may derive from etymons meaning 'war';[22] where Daniel Dupont and the murderer of Albert Dupont wear similar spectacles; and where there is some suspicion that the murders may have been committed by the very government that employs the investigator Wallas. Of course, it may be that the various characters' perceptions are simply erroneous. It is worth remembering that for André Gide, who is often cited as a precursor of the New Novel, a novel 'bears a diversity of points of view, submitted to the diversity of characters that it puts on stage. In essence, it is a deconcentrated work.'[23] As the frequently 'disoriented' (54) Wallas makes his way around town, he crosses places and people important to the investigation, though he does not see the connection until someone else brings it to his attention. He comes, for example, upon Daniel Dupont's former wife, the cleaning lady who worked briefly at the post office and may have given mail to André VS, the post office in question, and so on. This novel, like Gide's 'ideal' novel, is 'an intersection, a rendezvous of problems.'[24] And in the midst of Wallas's peregrinations, the reader comes across half a dozen different versions of what might have happened, often recounted authoritatively in the indicative rather than hypothetically in the conditional: Dupont committed suicide. Dupont died later on the operating table. Dupont was killed by his son. The one thing that seems assured is the calendar. The prologue begins at 6:00 a.m., and the epilogue at the same time the next day. The crime took place at 7:30 the evening before the epilogue, when Wallas's watch stops, and Wallas 'accidentally' kills Dupont twenty-four hours after Garinati had attempted to assassinate him. At this point, his watch begins functioning again.

Almost with relief, many readers have embraced Bruce Morrissette's seminal analysis of the allusion to *Œdipus Rex*.[25] Some have denied the importance of the allusion, but its textual reality is incontrovertible. From the epigraph attributed to Sophocles to Wallas's swollen feet in the end (259) – 'Œdipus' means 'swollen foot' – the novel teems with allusions to the Greek play. The fact that the book has five chapters may suggest a tragedy, given that French tragedies usually have five acts, but the reference is equivocal, since Sophocles' *Œdipus the King* is not divided into acts. Were it not for a few particularly appropriate details and for the sheer mass of evocative material, one might doubt the allusion to Sophocles' play. Wallas sees a curtain picturing shepherds finding an abandoned child and another with shepherds giving sheep's milk to a baby (50). Nothing, of course, says that it is the same child or that it is Oedipus. And nothing says that the bronze group in the square before the Prefecture representing a Greek chariot drawn by two horses (62, 85) has anything to do with Oedipus, at least not until Morrissette pointed out that the Sculptor's last name, Daulis, incorporates an anagram of Oedipus's father, Laius (*Novels* 56). Other evidence quickly accumulates. People get to the square most efficiently by Corinth Street, and a few pages after describing the chariot, Wallas sees a newspaper headline announcing that there has been a serious traffic accident on the Delf road (64). Oedipus killed his real father where roads to Delphi, Corinth, and Thebes crossed. Paralleling the Greek hero's effort to uncover the truth and so explain why Thebes seemed to be cursed, Wallas is sent to investigate the gang of terrorists that have already killed some nine people (34, 62). The concierge calls Wallas a prince when he goes to visit Mme Bax, and Oedipus was both the adopted son and the real offspring of the rulers of Corinth and Thebes respectively. When Wallas is drawn to a shop, it is hardly surprising that a photograph of the ruins of Thebes decorates the window. Wallas is attracted to the shopkeeper, Evelyne. Only later does he learn that she is Dupont's former wife. When the suspicion grows that Dupont might be his father – after all, Wallas had come to the city in his youth to see his father (136, 238) – one also has to wonder whether Evelyne might be his mother. The evidence is insufficient for any conclusions.

After a series of riddles proposed by a local drunkard – 'What animal is a parricide in the morning, incestuous at noon, and blind in the evening. . . . [P]arricide in the morning, blind at noon... No... Blind in the morning, incestuous at noon, parricide in the evening. Huh? What animal?' (234) – Wallas's vision of a sphinx in the canal (37), a little statue of a child leading a blind man (217), Morrissette's suggestion that the 'di' in the center of the eraser Wallas wants to buy could be the brand name Œdipe, French for 'Oedipus' (Novels 63), all leave no reasonable doubt that Les Gommes alludes to Oedipus Rex. Of course, other scholars have advanced other, less interesting six-syllable words that could have 'di' at the center: 'Di-di-er,' 'Ra-di-er,'[26] but the presence of alternatives in no way vitiates Morrissette's splendid interpretation. Nor is it significant that Oedipus killed his father before Sophocles' play begins and passes the time of the tragedy in 'unveiling' the truth (in Ricardou's recapitulation), while Wallas moves from the fiction of Dupont's death to the reality of killing him.[27] As the preceding pages have shown, it is neither necessary nor desirable for the alluding text to repeat all or even most of the text alluded to. The two texts of a successful allusion are different, and as their common elements bring them together they will create something that is new to both.

The question raised by Les Gommes's allusion to Oedipus Rex is not whether or not it functions, for it does. The problem arises when we wonder what the allusion brings to Robbe-Grillet's novel. Does it create a destiny for Wallas? Are we to understand that Wallas is fated to kill his 'father'? If so, such a reading not only conflicts dramatically with Robbe-Grillet's public pronouncements of a neutral universe with no transcendent meaning but with the rest of the novel as well, since Les Gommes stresses an aleatory world. Unlike such later novels as La Jalousie, the various patterns are not structures that are created and projected by the narrator onto the surrounding world.[28] They are rather embedded in the world of this northern city and discovered by Wallas, however little he has the cranial surface to understand (because the area of his forehead lacks one square centimeter of the 150 square centimeters required, he was given only a trial appointment as a special agent [165]). It is perhaps more disturbing, however, when other allusions having at least as much textual support raise irreconcilable conflicts with the figure of Oedipus.

Without denying the Oedipal allusions, P.J. Tremewan has persuasively argued that *Les Gommes* includes extensive references to the Christ story.[29] The café's owner rises early to take the twelve chairs down from the tables (11). '[D]rowned in his halo' (12), he prepares for his customers and 'the communion that they will be served' (16) by wiping off the tables that nonetheless remain stained 'like blood' (12). The proprietor goes up to Wallas's room only to find that he has already risen and left. He can still see where he lay, with 'the covers thrown toward the bottom' (14). When Garinati comes to ask about him, the proprietor says, 'The man has left' (14) and does not answer when questioned about the time he would return. These passages that identify Wallas with Christ continue to expand around Dupont, who as mentioned above, configures the 'father.'

A few pages farther on, there is a strange reference to Lazarus. Garinati tells himself that if he follows the directions laid down by Bona, 'the word will be accomplished and Lazarus will come out of his tomb wrapped in grave cloths' (23). This is of course true, but the meaning is the opposite of the biblical passages it calls up. If Garinati does as he is told, Dupont's office will be the place of his death, and he will not come forth alive. But the assassin does not follow directions, and Dupont remains among the living (23). The main function of the reference to Lazarus seems primarily to continue the series of allusions to the Christ story. At some point, we realize that although Dupont is apparently killed, like Christ, he is miraculously found to be alive. When Garinati says ironically, for he knows that he has botched the assassination, 'He is dead. Obviously. I had extinguished the light' (104), we recall that Jesus is called the 'Light of the World.' The fact that both Dupont and Wallas are identified with Jesus may be explained by the passage where Jesus says, 'I and the Father are one' (John 10:30). Like Peter, Marchat is a disciple (176), and while Peter was given the keys to heaven, Marchat is handed the house keys (33). Marchat tries to distance himself from Dupont (35, 153), before leaving the city (249). Peter denied Jesus and fled.

As Tremewan understands, the allusions to Christ have as many difficulties as those to Oedipus. 'Dupont, for example, is really resurrected before he dies, and in this way embodies a reversal of the story of Christ. . . . Wallas . . . has been sent from Heaven not to be crucified, but to kill: "As for the assassin, he fell from heaven". . . . Juard tries to save Dupont (145) instead of vice-versa' (Tremewan 46), and so on. But such reversals and confusions do not impugn the allusion proper. The references are too widespread and too clear to be denied. Nor can one suggest that Wallas has a Christ complex that he imposes on the world, for as with Oedipus, the markers of the allusive pattern do not occur uniquely in his own mind. They occur in the minds of others as well. In the same way as with the Oedipal allusion, the major difficulty comes in what the allusion brings to *Les Gommes*. Wallas/Oedipus came to discover the truth, save the people from the terrorists, and kill his father, though not necessarily in the same order. Wallas/Christ came to obey a higher command, discover the truth, and save the people. The thought that Wallas/Christ came to kill his father boggles the mind. Could the Oedipal pattern constitute an allusion and the Christic a parody?

There is one object that may bring the two patterns together. On Garinati's mantle there is a small statue of Apollo as an athlete crushing a lizard. We remember that Apollo was deeply involved in Oedipus's misadventures, and that Oedipus descends from one of the *Spartoi*, who were born of the sown dragon's teeth, though the 'lizard' in question is the 'serpent' (*drákon* in Greek) Python that Apollo killed. Perhaps the piece suggests another association. Medieval artists frequently represented Adam with a serpent. Occasionally the serpent has limbs and thus resembles a dragon or lizard, and art historians recognize the figural relationship of Adam and Apollo.[30] The biblical Satan appeared to Adam and Eve as a serpent who apparently had such appendages, since he was cursed to crawl thenceforth on his belly (Gen. 3:14). God's curse of the serpent continues in a passage that conservative scholars consider prophetic: 'And I will put enmity between thee and the woman, and between thy seed and her seed; he shall bruise thy head' (Gen. 3:15). Eve's seed is Jesus, the New Adam, who will eventually crush Satan, the serpent. Still, whether or not the binary reading of the statue has validity, *Les Gommes* regularly confronts the two sets of allusions, to Oedipus and to Christ. Because the allusions do not appear to serve any single overriding function, the result is a seemingly irreconcilable conflict or confusion that does nothing but increase with the addition of a third set of allusions – to the Tarot.

Morrissette and others have pointed out that Garinati's visit to Dupont's house includes an allusion to the Tarot.[31] 'The stairs are composed of twenty-one wooden steps, plus a bottom step of white stone that is noticeably bigger than the others. It holds a copper column with complicated ornamentations, capped with a finial in the form of a fool's head wearing a three-belled cap. . . . Above the sixteenth step, a small picture is hung on the wall at eye level. It is a Romantic scene representing a stormy night: lightning illuminates the ruins of a tower. At its foot you can make out two men lying down, sleeping in spite of the racket, or perhaps hit by lightning? Perhaps fallen from the top of the tower. The frame is of sculpted, gilded wood; the whole thing appears very old. Bona did not mention the picture' (24). The mention of Bona's name in this context is appropriate, since it is short for Bonaventure. A *diseur de bon aventure* is a fortune teller, and Tarot cards have long been used for little else. Later, Marchat wonders what the picture means (150), and farther on, when Wallas returns to Dupont's house, the novel adds additional information: 'It is a horrifying night. Two men lay at the foot of a demolished tower that the storm illuminates with sinister lightning. One wears royal clothing, his golden crown shines in the grass beside him. The other is a simple peasant. Lightning just killed them both' (243).

Most often, the Tarot deck has seventy-eight cards, of which one unnumbered and twenty-one numbered cards make up the Major Arcana or Trumps. For esoteric purposes these twenty-two cards are considered particularly important.[32] The unnumbered card, the Fool (in French, the *Fou* or the *Mat*), changes position in various systems of interpretation. Both variations in name and placement are important. As the *Mat*, he may suggest a checkmate. As the Fool, he may indicate either foolishness or the true wisdom that comes from beyond reason. Some esotericists place him at the beginning of the Trumps, some at the end, some between Trumps XX and XXI. His real importance comes in relationship with other cards and thus changes depending upon the environment. Depicted either with the innocence of youth, and about to walk blithely off a cliff, or with a confused, imbecilic demeanor as a cat or lynx sinks teeth into him, the Fool is something of a wandering knight or vagabond, on the fringes of civilization, suffering from remorse because of past errors, governed by capricious impulse, and subject to the unexpected. He may be shown with a dog, though whether the animal accompanies or attacks and drives him on his way is unclear. It is easy to see how the Fool might serve as an image for

Wallas (or Garinati). Certainly, it seems hardly accidental that when Garinati looks into the water of the canal he sees, on the one hand a sphinx, and on the other the 'grotesque face of a clown' (37).

The Lightning-Struck Tower, also known as the House of God and the Tower of Babel, is usually depicted with two figures falling from it, often with one of the two figures just hitting the ground. Lightning strikes the top of the tower, which signifies a man whose previous patterns are suddenly destroyed, the humbling of presumption and pride, and the softening of rigid dogmatism. Some consider the crowned figure to be the ruler of Babylon and the other his architect, some reason and instinct, some Manichean forces of good and evil. Morrissette connects the one in royal garb with Laius (*Novels* 60). The change Trump XVI represents may be entirely catastrophic, or it may open new opportunities. It depends on the subject's ability to learn from hard experience.

Hasty consideration of the picture might encourage one to assume that it simply provides a thematic support for the destruction of Dupont, and one might then be led to find other of the Major Arcana in the book. At the top of the stairs, Garinati and Wallas meet Dupont, a professor and a dabbler in unclear things. The first of the Trumps, the Magician, perhaps corresponds. This enigma depicts a man of knowledge regularly using tricks and sleight of hand to control new situations and accomplish things. Self-confident and self-reliant, he experiments until he finds solutions. As the first card in the numbered series, the figure is a prime mover; he causes activity. He may be clever and show initiative, or he may be a mendacious imposter. Still, if the landing of the staircase (37) constitutes the twenty-first step, one might rather associate Dupont with Trump XXI, the World. The latter represents the end of a period or cycle, the journey's end, and entry into the world of the spirit. Of course, each of these associations has less textual support than the one before, and like the telescopic vision of the canals on Mars, requires more effort from the reader; but one might continue and remember that the chariot described in *Les Gommes* sounds very much like that in the Major Arcana number VII: 'In the middle of the square rises . . . a bronze group representing a Greek chariot drawn by two horses, in which several personages, probably symbolic, have taken their places and whose unnatural poses are not in accord with the supposedly rapid pace' (62). It would take very little to see the café owner and his halo as the Hierophant, Trump IV, the channel of divine grace, the bridge between God and man, the one who can distinguish good and evil. The boulevard circling the city might represent Trump X, the Wheel of Fortune. And so on. The ease of making such associations casts doubt upon all, and one begins to suspect, as Laurent tells Wallas, '[Y]ou can always prove what you wish' (168).

At some point, readers should notice that Robbe-Grillet's picture is unlike any other Major Arcana Lightning-Struck Tower. Traditionally, this Trump represents change, violent change, and it is inconceivable that the two figures would be quiescent. There are variations. Of the more than 100 different decks I have been able to consider, a few have no falling or supine figures and some only one falling figure. One has four, and many have one falling and one apparently dead figure on the ground. But by far the majority show two figures falling from a tower that is in the process of being destroyed by lightning. Robbe-Grillet has of course the right to make up his own Tarot deck, as have Oswald Wirth, Arthur Edward Waite, and others, but to effect such a fundamental change in this enigma would be to abrogate the entire Tarot tradition. The difference between Robbe-Grillet's picture and the conventional representation takes on importance, and one must wonder about the reasons for such deviation.

On consideration, readers may note that something similar happens with every single allusive system in the novel. Either one notices an egregious deviation from the external text, or one realizes an irresolvable conflict between the systems implied by the novel, or one wonders about the significance of the allusions. While it may be true that '[t]he machinery is perfectly regulated' (23) and that 'very ancient laws regulate the details of [the café owner's] gestures' (11), we are never sure what those rules are and how the machine is regulated.

Perhaps readers should wonder whether the systems of allusion might resemble the bascule bridge Wallas crosses (53, 57). If the bridge-tender pulls certain switches, the bridge moves out of the way, and boats may pass on the canal; another adjustment, and the bridge swings back into place, allowing pedestrians to cross. Though the employee chooses whether to favor boats or land traffic, his choice of one does not negate the other. Just as both boats and people are present in or over the canal, so with the allusions to Oedipus, to Christ, and to the Tarot. Readers may choose to identify Wallas with Oedipus or with Christ or with the Fool, but the three do not work together in conventional ways. Wallas cannot be in the claws of destiny and, simultaneously, be playing the fool subject to his own undisciplined whims; he cannot be fated to kill his father (or a professorial father-figure), while intentionally

choosing to obey his father and thus benefit other men. Bona, the terror-
ist gang leader, cannot make effective, determinative decisions if whatever he decides is in fact subject to Apollo or if this is an entirely
aleatory world. Something very different happens in *Les Gommes* from
what happens with allusive complexes in such novels as *A la recherche
du temps perdu* or *La Faute de l'abbé Mouret*. The conflicts between various possibilities in Robbe-Grillet's novel are willfully unresolved. They
never come together to construct a complex. They are rather presented
as parallel but opposing views for purposefully alternate readings.

Critics have been brought by the contradictions in *Les Gommes* to
various conclusions. For Olga Bernal, there is a central void; for Jean
Alter, there is an absence of any extra-human foundation for tragedy;
for Ann Jefferson there is the absence of a *telos* [an end or goal].[33] One
could also say that in the world of Robbe-Grillet's novel there are no
transcendent truths. As he argued in his essay 'Nature, Humanisme,
Tragédie,' the objective world has no connection with man. Man may
invent what he calls a 'bridge' (*Pour un nouveau* 48) – an image that
recalls the character Dupont ('from the' or 'of the bridge') – between
man and the world of things, but it is man's invention. It has no external, objective reality. In short, as Ann Jefferson would have it, 'It is not
what the gods, or in this instance, Bona, decree, but what literature
writes. . . . "You only have to follow the text, speaking line after line,
and the word will be accomplished"' (*Nouveau Roman* 29). Philosophi-
cally opposed to making 'sense' of existence, the author leaves readers
free to make whatever connections they wish. In the end *Les Gommes* is
no more and no less than a series of printed words on paper. With this
conclusion comes, of course, the resolution to the conflicts. Readers may
avoid the bridge and fly over the city by understanding that *Les Gommes*
points to a single, integrated, transcendent interpretation: There are no
transcendent meanings.[34] There is no truth to discover. The allusions
then make Robbe-Grillet's novel resemble one of those creations nur-
series love to display: a single rootstock with several varieties of apples.
Les Gommes then stands as a peculiar sort of tree that is able to bear
apples and oranges and grapes. The three traditions, the three texts, are
brought together on a single stock. The novel then has meaning despite
all the contradictions, but that meaning consists in interpreting its world
as having no meaning. Of course, to reach such a conclusion a priori
before taking the text in hand vitiates the frustrating adventure that
comes on reading *Les Gommes* and confronting on page after page the
confusion of irreconcilable conflicts.

Allusion has then virtually limitless potential. In times where tradition is valued, it tends to enhance the tradition, but in periods when authors and public alike disdain the past, allusion continues to be able to enhance whatever is being communicated.[35] The only limitation comes from ignorance. When readers have not read, when their background is limited to pap, when readers and writers share no common tradition, then allusions may have been seeded in a text, but they will produce neither plant nor fruit. Of course, the potential remains. As long as the text exists, some day a reader may come with the proper, fertile background and permit a new efflorescence. When this happens, the seed sinks new roots and the reader's mind gives birth to a living text.

Notes

1 Introduction

1 Julia Kristeva, *Semeiotikè: Recherches pour une sémanalyse* (Paris: Seuil, 1969) 146. Here and elsewhere, unless otherwise stated, all translations are my own. For a brief but good introduction to intertextuality, see Jeanine Parisier Plottel's 'Introduction,' in J.P. Plottel and Hanna Charney, eds, *Intertextuality: New Perspectives in Criticism*, in *New York Literary Forum* 2 (1978): 11–20. Thaïs E. Morgan's more detailed discussion of the various theoretical approaches to intertextuality is outstanding: 'Is There an Intertext in This Text?: Literary and Interdisciplinary Approaches to Intertextuality,' *American Journal of Semiotics* 3 (1985): 1–40. For helpful bibliographic work on allusion and other forms of intertextuality see Carmela Perri, Giuliana Carnugati, P.W. Costa, M. Forndran, A.G. Mamaeva, E. Moody, Z.L. Seligsohn, L. Vinge, and F. Weinapple, 'Allusion Studies, An International Annotated Bibliography, 1921–1977,' *Style* 13 (1979): 178–225; and Udo J. Hebel, ed., *Intertextuality, Allusion, and Quotation* (Westport: Greenwood, 1989).

2 Julia Kristeva, *La Révolution du langage poétique* (Paris: Seuil, 1974) 60. For a brief but eloquent summary of the benefits of this way of thinking about literature, see, e.g., Jan Miernowski, 'L'Accès aux vérités spirituelles, continuités et ruptures des codes intertextuels dans *La Sepmaine* de Du Bartas,' *Continuités et ruptures dans l'histoire et la littérature, Colloque Franco-Polonais, Université Paul Valéry, Uniwersytet Warszawski, 9–14 février Montpellier* (Paris: Champion-Slatkine, 1988) 33–4.

3 Tzvetan Todorov, *Introduction à la littérature fantastique* (Paris: Seuil, 1970) 14–15.

4 Harold Bloom, *Poetry and Repression: Revisionism from Blake to Stevens* (New Haven: Yale UP, 1976) 5. The confluence of texts and the inability (or unwillingness) to make valid distinctions constitute the salient features of recent writing on intertextuality. Patrick O'Donnell and Robert Con Davis discuss this state of affairs in 'Introduction: Intertext and Contemporary American Fiction,' in their collected volume *Intertextuality and Contemporary American Fiction* (Baltimore: Johns Hopkins UP, 1989) ix–22; as does Thaïs E. Morgan in the same volume: 'The Space of Intertextuality' 239–79.

5 Roland Barthes, *Le Plaisir du texte* (Paris: Seuil, 1973) 58. For outgrowths of such theory, see, e.g., Mary Ann Caws, 'Suppression et sous-texte: Une Re-lecture d'Antonin Artaud,' *Le Siècle éclaté: Dada, surréalisme et avant-gardes* 2 (1978): 175–98; or, more recently, her 'Under-Reading at Noon: Leconte de Lisle's "Midi,"' in Christopher Prendergast, ed., *Nineteenth-Century French Poetry: Introductions to Close Reading* (Cambridge: Cambridge UP, 1990) 103–17.

6 Marcel Proust, *A la recherche du temps perdu*, ed. Jean-Yves Tadié, 4 vols, Bibliothèque de la Pléiade (Paris: Gallimard, 1987–9) 1.153.

7 Geoffrey H. Hartman, 'Forum,' *PMLA* 92 (1977): 308. For discussion of the confusion that now reigns, see, e.g., Heinrich F. Plett, 'Intertextualities,' in his collected volume *Intertextuality* (Berlin: Walter de Gruyter, 1991) 3; and, in the same volume, Hans-Peter Mai, 'Bypassing Intertextuality: Hermeneutics, Textual Practice, Hypertext' 30–59.

8 F.O. Matthiessen, *The Achievement of T.S. Eliot: An Essay on the Nature of Poetry* (New York: Oxford UP, 1947) 35–6. Susanne K. Langer is not so generous. For her, Eliot's demand for a reader of virtually flawless culture and exceptional memory is unreasonable: *Feeling and Form* (New York: Charles Scribner's Sons, 1953) 248. Allusions may, of course, be multiplied to the point of overload for the purpose of exemplifying confusion. For David H. Richter, Thomas Pynchon's *V* constitutes a case in point: *Fable's End: Completeness and Closure in Rhetorical Fiction* (Chicago: U of Chicago P, 1974) 130–1. Another approach to allusive multivalence is to stress the difference and suggest that the varying, often opposing, alluded images suggest irony. 'The problem,' as Jonathan Culler says, 'is that of "échos qui de loin se confondent [echoes that are confounded in the distance]," a problem about the signifying status of resemblances, about whether patterns we detect are meaningful or not' ('Intertextuality and Interpretation: Baudelaire's "Correspondances,"' in Prendergast, ed., *Nineteenth-Century French Poetry* 126). I shall be primarily interested in those texts that multiply univalent references and thus direct readers of goodwill toward

a pattern of allusive significance. See, however, my discussion of Robbe-Grillet's *Les Gommes* in the last chapter.

9 Michael Riffaterre, 'La Trace de l'intertexte,' *La Pensée* 215 (Oct. 1980): 5. Riffaterre has many fascinating studies of specific cases of texts that impose external texts on readers. For the most part they exemplify what I would call 'parallel allusion.' See, e.g., his 'La Syllepse intertextuelle,' *Poétique* 40 (1979): 496–501; 'Flaubert's Presuppositions,' *Diacritics* 11 (1981): 2–11; 'Ponge Intertextuel,' *Etudes françaises* 17 (1981): 73–85; 'Interpretation and Undecidability,' *New Literary History* 12 (1981): 227–42; 'La Trace de l'intertexte' 4–18; 'L'Intertexte inconnu,' *Littérature* 41 (1981): 4–7; 'The Interpretant in Literary Semiotics,' *American Journal of Semiotics* 3 (1985): 43–55; and 'Compulsory Reader Response: The Intertextual Drive,' in Michael Worton and Judith Still, eds, *Intertextuality: Theories and Practices* (Manchester: Manchester UP, 1990) 56–78.

10 Quoted from Susan Katz Keating, 'Perilous Pathways and Cold Trails,' *Insight* 6, no. 7 (12 Feb. 1990): 63.

11 Frank Kermode, 'Sensing Endings,' *Nineteenth-Century Fiction* 33 (1978): 147. The basic point that one must pay attention to intention has been argued by others. See, e.g., E.D. Hirsch, Jr, *Validity in Interpretation* (New Haven: Yale UP, 1967); and E.H. Gombrich, *Symbolic Images* (1972; London: Phaidon, 1975) 1–25.

12 The division I suggest depends on the meaningful (semantic) results of considering the two or more texts (and their varying combinations) rather than on the semiological fact of duplication and reduplication (whether syntagmatic or paradigmatic, textual or metatextual). For an outstanding semiological study of some of the forms that interest me here, though in other ways, see Lucien Dällenbach's *Le Récit spéculaire: Essai sur la mise en abyme* (Paris: Seuil, 1977). For him *mise en abyme* is 'any internal mirror reflecting the whole of a story [*récit*] by simple, repeated or specious [i.e., aporetic or ambiguous] duplication' (52). I am interested not so much in the singleness of the duplication – for example, when Pierre Froment confronts the Botticelli in Zola's *Rome* (ibid. 64) or when *As You Like It* occurs in Théophile Gautier's *Mademoiselle de Maupin* (ibid. 65) – as in how the confrontations complete the representations of the heroes' destinies. Rather than to the mobius-like ('specious') complication of Edouard's diary reflecting *Les Faux-Monnayeurs*, as seen in Gide's *Le Journal des Faux-Monnayeurs*, and indeed in Gide's diary (ibid. 50), I am drawn to Proust's use of a complex of external texts to highlight his hero's adventure.

13 I am aware that my use of the botanical image forces the reality well beyond what actually happens – and goes well beyond the sense of

'grafting' that Dominique Jullien uses in her consideration of Proust's modeling: *Proust et ses modèles: Les 'Mille et Une Nuits' et les 'Mémoires' de Saint-Simon* (Paris: Corti, 1989). In a real graft, when a cutting is bonded to a different rootstock, the essential character of the cutting does not change, though because the rootstock is more sturdy or efficient the resultant plant may be hardier and, in some cases, grow faster. As will become increasingly clear in my study, however, I want to suggest that allusively bringing an external text into the work being read will produce something essentially different.

14 Except, perhaps, allegory, which, if Maureen Quilligan is to be believed, became a genre long after classical genres were established; see her *The Language of Allegory: Defining the Genre* (Ithaca: Cornell UP, 1979). In ch. 4, I shall treat allegory as a device that requires interpretive responses quite different from allusion.

15 By this term, which I introduced in my 'Nouveau où Ancien Roman: Open Structures and Balzac's "Gobseck,"' *Texas Studies in Literature and Language* 20 (1978): 29, I mean an allusion activated by one rather than several more or less widely spaced references. Such brief references are capable of inciting allusions of considerable scope, though they are usually limited to intensifying one or two traits, as in this case with the theme of homesickness. For a fascinating analysis of what I would call a synoptic allusion, see Erwin Panofsky, '*Et in Arcadia ego*: Poussin and the Elegiac Tradition,' in his *Meaning in the Visual Arts* (Garden City: Doubleday / Anchor 1955) 295–320.

16 Enrico de' Negri, 'The Legendary Style of the *Decameron*,' *Romanic Review* 43 (1952): 166–89. At the end of his fine article de' Negri poses a problem that was seminal to my thought: 'The analogy [between the Book of Job and Griselda's trials] is evident. It remains to be seen which extension Boccaccio may have attributed to it, which symbol he may have assigned to his last legend.' In the present study, I attempt to provide a framework to facilitate the resolution of such problems.

17 In 'Autenticidad y crítica del *Romancero espiritual* de Lope de Vega,' *Revista de Bibliografía Nacional* 33 (1942): 64–70, Luis Guarner has argued convincingly that Lope was not responsible for the *Romancero espiritual*. He later repeated his conclusions in the prologue of his edition of *Romancero espiritual y Rimas sacras* (Madrid: Castilla, 1949) 18–25.

18 E. Allison Peers, 'Mysticism in the Religious Verse of the Golden Age: Lope de Vega Carpio,' *Bulletin of Hispanic Studies* 22 (1945): 42; José F. Montesinos, *Estudios sobre Lope* (Mexico D.F.: Colegio de México, 1951) 115–58, 193–9. Cf Bruce W. Wardropper, *Historia de la poesía lírica a lo*

divino en la cristiandad occidental (Madrid: Revista de Occidente, 1958) 195, and Guarner, 'Autenticidad y crítica' 74–5, for a more moderate view.

19 Jean Paulhan, *Braque le patron* (1952), in *Œuvres complètes*, vol. 5 (Paris: Cercle du Livre Précieux, 1970) 31. Paulhan is playing on the classic definition of allusion, e.g., 'Allusion . . . consists in communicating the relationship between something said and something not said, and whose very relationship reveals the idea': Pierre Fontanier, *Les Figures du discours* (1821–1830; rpt Paris: Flammarion, 1968) 125. In a similar vein, Earl Miner defines allusion as '[t]acit reference to another literary work, to another art, to history, to contemporary figures, or the like': 'Allusion,' Alex Preminger, ed., *Princeton Encyclopedia of Poetry and Poetics*, (Princeton: Princeton UP, 1974) 18.

20 Carmela Perri, 'On Alluding,' *Poetics* 7 (1978): 290; Ziva Ben-Porat, 'The Poetics of Literary Allusion,' *PTL: A Journal for Descriptive Poetics and Theory of Literature* 1 (Jan. 1976): 107–9. See, also, Perri's 'Knowing and Playing: The Literary Text and the Trope Allusion,' *American Imago* 41 (1984): 117–28. This is but one of a number of instances where my early thought – as reflected in 'Marcel, Albertine and Balbec in Proust's Allusive Complex,' *Romanic Review* 62 (1971): 113–26; and in 'A Study of Allusion: Barbey's Stendhal in "Le Rideau cramoisi,"' *PMLA* 88 (1973): 461–71 – has been affected, if not as in this case changed, by the excellent work of these two critics. Udo J. Hebel provides an excellent overview of current theoretical positions on allusion: 'Towards a Descriptive Poetics of Allusion,' in Plett, ed., *Intertextuality* 135–64.

21 When I use the term 'literary allusion,' I mean not that the referent is a work of literature, but rather that the referring text is literary. For a fine study of such a text, see Marion F. Freeman, 'Nabokovian Echoes in the Works of Ramón Hernandez,' *Anales de la Literatura Española Contemporanea* 14, nos 1–3 (1989): 65–78; and for an outstanding consideration of a text with several referents, see Patrick Henry, 'Cervantes, Unamuno, and Graham Greene's *Monsignor Quixote*,' *Comparative Literature Studies* 23, no. 1 (1986): 12–23. For an example of 'mythic' or 'legendary' allusions, see, e.g., Boris Vian's allusion to the Isis myth in *L'Ecume des jours* or Goethe's in *Das Märchen* (*The Parable*). For an example of historical and mythic allusions working in conjunction, see the excellent study by David Lee Rubin, *Higher, Hidden Order: Design and Meaning in the Odes of Malherbe* (University of North Carolina Studies in the Romance Languages and Literatures [hereafter UNCSRLL] no. 117; Chapel Hill: U of North Carolina P, 1972). Fontanier, *Les Figures* 125–6, would add 'moral allusions' to historical and mythic allusions, by which he means reference

to social customs or opinions. Annick Bouillaguet, in *Marcel Proust: Le Jeu intertextuel* (Paris: Editions du Titre, 1990), includes categories based on intertextual reference to literature, to such genres as theater, or such media as music or painting (99–148).

22 I am grateful to René de Costa for the example of Sánchez.

23 E.g., Raúl H. Castagnino, *El Análisis literario: Introducción metológica a una estilística integral* (Buenos Aires: Nova, 1970) 242–4. Less commonly, critics focus on the alluding text to the exclusion of the external referent. Hebel points to numerous examples of critics interested in the location of the marker – title, epigraph, name, quotation: 'Towards a Descriptive Poetics of *Allusion*,' 145–53. Others stress the clarity of the allusion: Hebel differentiates between marked (explicit) and unmarked (implicit) (ibid. 142–4), while Rhonda L. Blair would distinguish between '(1) straightforward, obvious allusions; (2) straightforward allusions which are less obvious . . . ; (3) veiled allusions . . . ; (4) allusions through word play': 'Homo faber, homo ludens, and the Demeter-Kore Motif,' *Germanic Review* 56 (1981): 140–50. The quotation is from 141.

24 Paul Valéry, *Œuvres*, 2 vols, Bibliothèque de la Pléiade (Paris: Gallimard, 1957, 1960) 2.566.

25 J. Dubois, F. Edeline, J.M. Klinkenberg, P. Minguet, F. Pire, H. Trinon, *Rhétorique générale* (Paris: Larousse, 1970) 107.

26 Paul Ricoeur, *La Métaphore vive* (Paris: Seuil, 1975): 'Metaphor is . . . a semantic event which is produced at the point of intersection between several semantic fields' (127). Somewhat farther on, he says that the 'semantic event' is 'an event and a significance, a signifying event' (ibid.).

27 Michael Riffaterre, 'Discussions' [following the presentation of his paper] 'Sémantique du poème,' *Cahiers de l'Association Internationale des Etudes Françaises* 23 (1971): 355.

28 Ben-Porat, 'Poetics of Literary Allusion' 108; Perri, 'On Alluding' 299.

29 For Hickey, the reader needs 'a certain mental agility to translate his attention from one plane to another': Leo Hickey, 'El Valor de la alusión en literatura,' *Revista de Occidente* 88 (July 1970): 55.

30 While Ziva Ben-Porat would divide allusion into two groups: metaphoric and metonymic ('Poetics of Literary Allusion' 105–28), I shall argue that allusions are metaphoric, though the relationships that compose the metaphor may be anything from parallels to opposites, as long as the metaphoric relationship remains intact.

31 Ronald J. Christ, *The Narrow Act: Borges' Art of Allusion* (New York: New York UP, 1969) 39, 34.

32 Jorge Luis Borges, 'Preface,' in ibid. ix.

33 Philip A. Wadsworth, 'The Art of Allegory in La Fontaine's *Fables*,' *French Review* 45 (1972): 1125.

34 J.W. von Goethe, *Maximen und Reflexionen*, No. 1112, quoted from Kurt Weinberg, *On Gide's Prométhée* (Princeton: Princeton UP, 1972) 12.

35 E.M.W. Tillyard, *Poetry Direct and Oblique* (London: Chatto and Windus, 1934) 184.

36 Ibid. 184–5.

37 W.B. Yeats, *Collected Poems* (New York: Macmillan, 1951) 453.

38 Although I recognize that the problem touched on here is significant (Hans-Georg Gadamer's thought might offer a solution, however), I shall be content to posit as a working ploy that allusion exists in the text, whether or not it is recognized by a reader and completed. The difficulty is by no means new. I.A. Richards, for example, discusses the 'assumption that if we cannot see how a metaphor works, it does not work': *The Philosophy of Rhetoric* (1936; rpt New York: Oxford UP, 1965) 118.

39 In *A la recherche* 4.489–90, Proust merely notes that the book may be too difficult for naive readers. Elsewhere, he discusses those readers who will not understand his novel because they lack the faculties to which the book is addressed. He concludes that an auctorial explanation would not help and that he can therefore do nothing about them (Nouvelles Acquisitions Françaises [hereafter NAF] 16699, f. 1r, at the Bibliothèque Nationale of France). This notebook is written in the large, legible hand of Proust near the end of his life. He apparently meant to add the passage to his novel, for above it he reminded herself to intercalate the passage into the last volume (i.e., *Le Temps retrouvé*).

40 Roger Rosenblatt, 'The People versus Literature,' *The American Scholar* 43 (1974): 601. Many writers have said that ignorance of the tradition precludes understanding: e.g., Jurij Tynjanov, 'On Literary Evolution' (1927), in Ladislav Matejka and Krystyna Pomorska, eds, *Readings in Russian Poetics: Formalist and Structuralist Views* (Cambridge: MIT Press, 1971) 70. George Steiner offers little hope for allusion and other such sophisticated devices in his analysis of the current state of readers: 'The familiarity with Scripture, . . . with . . . liturgical allusion and ritual routine, which is presumptive in the speech and inference of English literature from Chaucer to Auden, is largely dissipated. Like the fabric of classical reference, citation, pastiche, parody, imitation, within which English poetry developed from Caxton's *Ovid* to T.S. Eliot's *Sweeney Among the Nightingales*, Biblical literacy is passing quickly into the deep-freeze of academicism': 'Text and Context,' *Salmagundi* 31–2 (1975–6): 178.

2 Ironic Interference and Allusion: 'Un Cœur simple'

1 Jonathan Culler, *On Deconstruction: Theory and Criticism after Structuralism* (Ithaca: Cornell UP, 1982) 7.
2 Paul de Man, *Blindness and Insight: Essays in the Rhetoric of Contemporary Criticism*, 2nd ed. (Minneapolis: U of Minnesota P, 1983) 224 for the quotation, but the entire section 208–28 is pertinent.
3 Gustave Flaubert, letter to Mme Roger des Genettes, 19 June [1876], *Correspondance*, vols 12–16, *Œuvres complètes* (Paris: Club de l'Honnête Homme, 1974–5) 15.974–5.
4 Grahame C. Jones, *L'Ironie dans les romans de Stendhal* (Lausanne: Grand Chêne, 1966) 66.
5 E.D. Hirsch, Jr, *The Aims of Interpretation* (Chicago: U of Chicago P, 1976) 23.
6 'pessimism': Enid Starkie, *Flaubert the Master: A Critical and Biographical Study (1856–1880)* (New York: Atheneum, 1971) 260; 'tenderness': Victor H. Brombert, *The Novels of Flaubert: A Study of Themes and Techniques* (Princeton: Princeton UP, 1966) 237, and Mariane Bonwit, *G. Flaubert et le principe d'impassibilité*, U of California Publications in Modern Philology, 33, no. 4 (1950) 394; 'love': Frederic J. Shepler, 'La Mort et la rédemption dans les *Trois Contes* de Flaubert,' *Neophilologus* 565 (1972): 415.
7 Brombert, *Novels of Flaubert* 241. See, e.g., for similar points of view, Anthony Thorlby, *Gustave Flaubert and the Art of Realism* (New Haven: Yale UP, 1957) 58–9; Ben Stoltzfus, 'Point of View in "Un Cœur simple,"' *French Review* 35 (1961): 20–1; François Marotin, 'Les Trois Contes: Un Carrefour dans l'œuvre de Flaubert,' in François Marotin, ed., *Frontières du conte* (Paris: Centre National de la Recherche Scientifique [hereafter CNRS], 1982) 116–17. More recently, Ian Reid pronounces Loulou 'a stuffed absurdity': 'The Death of the Implied Author? Voice, Sequence, and Control in Flaubert's *Trois contes*,' *Australian Journal of French Studies* 23, no. 2 (1986): 210. Jean-Louis Cabanès, in 'Désymbolisation, imitation et pathologie de la croyance,' *Littérature et pathologie* (Saint-Denis: PU de Vincennes, 1989) 133–48, considers 'Un Cœur simple' one of several 'secretly parodic narrations' (146), and 'the divine Word, as it appears with Loulou's traits, is the "glorified" projection of an alienated self' (144). See also René Jasinski, 'Le Sens des *Trois contes*,' in Raymond J. Cormier and Urban T. Holmes, eds, *Essays in Honor of Louis Francis Solano*, UNCSRLL 92 (Chapel Hill: U of North Carolina P, 1970) 117–28. Jasinski views the story both more negatively, as sarcasm (120, 123, 127), and more positively: 'Is not absurd Félicité in her way one of the elect, since

her renunciations sanctify her? And what difference does it make that the final miracle is only a supreme chimera, when the illusion uncovers the truest kind of reality?' (127). For Fredric Jameson, the theme of sainthood is 'a projection of the religion of other people which informs the nineteenth century's sense . . . of the mirage of value of precapitalist societies.' In particular, 'The sham endings of the tales – the Holy Spirit or Christ soaring, the severed head – by their own immobilization in the Imaginary, their sudden stasis as the reified images into which these narratives have been transformed offer testimony enough to the impossibility of closure here by their shift to a different discursive register, that of sheer decoration and of the impressionistic': 'Flaubert's Libidinal Historicism: *Trois Contes*,' in Naomi Schor and Henry F. Majewski, eds, *Flaubert and Postmodernism* (Lincoln: U of Nebraska P, 1984) 80.

8 English Showalter, Jr, '"Un Cœur simple" as Ironic Reply to Bernardin de Saint-Pierre,' *French Review* 40 (1966): 55. This, of course, was the position Flaubert took in his famous letter to Mme Roger des Genettes (quoted above). See, also, Starkie, *Flaubert the Master* 55; Maurice Bardèche, *L'Œuvre de Flaubert* (Paris: Les Sept Couleurs, 1974) 345, and Leonard Marsh, 'Visual Perception in Flaubert's "Un Cœur simple,"' *Studies in Short Fiction* 23, no. 2 (1986): 189.

9 Benjamin F. Bart, 'Women in the Novels of Flaubert,' in Sandro Sticca, ed., *Historical and Literary Perspectives; Essays and Studies in Honor of Albert Douglas Menut* (Lawrence: Coronado Press, 1973) 148.

10 Benjamin F. Bart, *Flaubert* (Syracuse: Syracuse UP, 1967) 695–6. I make this case for Félicité's intelligence while acknowledging Nathaniel Wing's demonstration that Félicité is incapable of comprehending metaphorically. All her understanding comes metonymically. '[C]ontiguity of association is accompanied by literal contiguity of the objects as the engraving of the Holy Ghost is placed *next* to Loulou': 'Reading Simplicity: Flaubert's "Un Cœur simple,"' *Nineteenth-Century French Studies* 21, nos 1–2 (1992–3): 88–101; the quotation is from 88. 'Simple' and 'intelligent' need not be contraries.

11 Gustave Flaubert, 'Un Cœur simple,' *Trois Contes*, *Œuvres*, 2 vols, Bibliothèque de la Pléiade (Paris: Gallimard, 1952) 2.595. Further references will be indicated parenthetically in the text by page only.

12 Wayne C. Booth's touchstones referred to here and below are posited in his *A Rhetoric of Irony* (Chicago: U of Chicago P, 1974) 47–76.

13 Jonathan Culler, *Flaubert: The Uses of Uncertainty* (Ithaca: Cornell UP, 1974) 210–11.

14 D.C. Muecke, 'Irony Markers,' *Poetics* 7 (1978): 363–75.

15 D.C. Muecke, 'The Communication of Verbal Irony,' *Journal of Literary Semantics* 2 (1974): 35.

16 Booth, *Rhetoric of Irony* 53.

17 While showing that 'Un Cœur simple' can be read as an ironic reply to the Pollyanna in Bernardin de Saint-Pierre (a point I do not reject, though I would point out that the possible irony is after the fact and that its potentially interesting inclusion in a reading does not change any relationship within the story itself), English Showalter mentions that Flaubert's Paul and Virginie, who leave Félicité without 'so much as a farewell,' do not share the warm feeling that Bernardin's eponyms have toward Mme de la Tour and Marguerite ('"Un Cœur simple" as Ironic Reply' 54). See also, Phillip A. Duncan, 'Paul and Virginia / Flaubert and Bernardin,' *Studies in Short Fiction* 24, no. 4 (1987): 436–8.

18 Prosper Mérimée, 'Tamango,' *Romans et nouvelles*, 2 vols, (Paris: Garnier, 1967) 1.287.

19 Gustave Flaubert, *Un Cœur simple: Nouvelle Edition avec les variantes intégrales des manuscrits* (Paris: Pensée Universelle, 1974) 54.

20 Gustave Flaubert, *Plans, notes et scénarios de 'Un Cœur simple,'* ed. François Fleury (Rouen: Lecerf, 1977), folio 388: 30.

21 C.H. Wake, 'Flaubert's Search for an Identity: Some Reflections on "Un Cœur simple,"' *French Review* 44, Special issue no. 2 (1971): 95.

22 External evidence in early drafts would not support such a view. George A. Willenbrink, after studying Flaubert's identification of the Holy Spirit with Loulou as it appears in the various drafts, argues – and I think convincingly – that the manuscripts make it seem probable Flaubert intended no irony in the bird: *The Dossier of Flaubert's 'Un Cœur simple'* (Amsterdam: Rodopi, 1976) 237–47.

23 For persuasive explanation of this widely sensed unity, see John R. O'Connor, 'Flaubert: *Trois contes* and the Figure of the Double Cone,' *PMLA* 95 (1980): 812–26; and Shelley Purcell, '"Hérodias": A Key to Thematic Progression in *Trois contes*,' *Romanic Review* 80, no. 4 (1989): 541–7. It has also been pointed out that the three stories are arranged in reverse chronology to move toward the past – see, e.g., Jasinski, 'Le Sens des *Trois Contes*' 119 – and that they correspond to Flaubert's tripartite conception of history: paganism, Christianity, loutishness (*muflisme*): William J. Beck, 'Flaubert's Tripartite Concept of History and *Trois contes*,' *College Language Association Journal* (1977): 75. Carla L. Peterson persuasively argues that Flaubert was thinking of Joachim of Flora's notions of historical repetition and progression and of periodization: he divided history into the time of the Old Testament, the New Testament,

and the period since 1240: 'The Trinity in Flaubert's *Trois Contes*: Deconstructing History,' *French Forum* 8, no. 3 (1983): 243–58. One might also suggest that 'Un Cœur simple' centers on the Holy Spirit, 'La Légende de saint Julien l'Hospitalier' on Jesus Christ, while Iaokanann or John the Baptist was the last of the preredemption prophets who spoke directly for God the Father. Ann L. Murphy has demonstrated that from 'Un Cœur simple' through the volume to 'Hérodias,' there is a gradual increase in chronological and spatial distance between speech and result: 'The Order of Speech in Flaubert's *Trois Contes*,' *French Review* 65 (1992): 402–14. Finally, though I do not agree that the structure of *Trois Contes* is nonlinear, Michael Issacharoff's study is excellent, full of helpful, penetrating insights into the unifying motifs and themes: *L'Espace et la nouvelle* (Paris: Corti, 1976) esp. 21–59. Jacques Neefs mentions the repetition of, for example, dove imagery throughout *Trois Contes* – 'Le Récit et l'édifice des croyances: *Trois Contes*,' in P.M. Wetherill, ed., *Flaubert: La Dimension du texte* (Manchester: Manchester UP, 1982) 124 – and continues the analysis of unifying spatial imagery initiated by Issacharoff (125–35).

24 Letter of 18 Mar. [1857] to Mlle Leroyer de Chantepie.

25 Edwin Stein, *Wordsworth's Art of Allusion* (University Park: Pennsylvania State UP, 1988) 123.

26 Félicité's saintliness has been widely recognized – e.g., Harry Levin, *The Gates of Horn: A Study of Five French Realists* (New York: Oxford UP, 1963) 291; Showalter, '"Un Cœur simple" as Ironic Reply' 55; Brombert, *Novels of Flaubert* 238. For Andrew Lytle, 'Félicité in offering Loulou offered herself, for to the parrot dead or alive she had given her full last love. So then the bird becomes not only the symbol of a simple heart's invincible charity': 'Three Ways of Making a Saint: A Reading of *Three Tales* by Flaubert,' *Southern Review* 20, no. 3 (1984): 527. K.D. Utti, in 'Figures and Fiction: Linguistic Deformation and the Novel,' *Kentucky Romance Quarterly* 17 (1970): 161–9, studies the tale's exploitation of the traditional hagiographic mode. I am, however, most indebted to William J. Beck's work cited in nn 27, 29, 30.

27 William J. Beck, 'Félicité and the Bull in Flaubert's *Un Cœur simple*,' *Xavier University Studies* 10, no. 1 (Spring 1971): 16–26; and his 'Félicité et le taureau: Ironie dans *Un Cœur simple* de Flaubert,' *Romance Quarterly* 37 (1990): 293–300.

28 E.g., Holger Steen Sørensen, *The Meaning of Proper Names with a Definiens Formula for Proper Names in Modern English* (Copenhagen: G.E.C. Gad, 1963).

29 William J. Beck, 'Flaubert's Félicité,' *Explicator* 35, no. 4 (1976): 3–4.

30 William J. Beck, 'Flaubert's *Un Cœur simple*: The Path to Sainthood?' *Xavier University Studies* 7, no. 2 (July 1968): 59–67; and his '"Un Cœur simple" de Flaubert: Le Chemin de la sainteté,' *University of Dayton Review* 20, no. 1 (Summer 1989): 109–15.

31 I have depended primarily on Sherman E. Johnson's and George A. Buttrick's glosses on Matthew in *The Interpreter's Bible* (New York: Abingdon-Cokesbury Press, 1951) vol. 7, though I have also looked at more popular explications by Roger L. Shinn, *The Sermon on the Mount* (Philadelphia: United Church P, 1954), and Knoffel Staton, *The Perfect Balance: A Study of Matthew 1–18* (Cincinnati: Standard Publishing, 1975).

32 Johnson and Buttrick, *Interpreter's Bible* 7.282.

33 The scene of Félicité's torment on the road to Honfleur has other functions as well. As Leonard Marsh points out in his fine consideration of repeating motifs and images, the passage prepares the final Corpus Christi procession and Félicité's vision: 'Félicité on the Road: A Synchronic Reading of "Un Cœur simple,"' *Romanic Review* 81, no. 1 (1990): 56–65.

34 Paul A. Mankin, 'Additional Irony in "Un Cœur Simple,"' *French Review* 35 (1962): 411. Culler claims that the '"crut voir" acts . . . as a distancing which challenges [the reader's] sympathy to overcome this coldness and estrangement' (*Flaubert: The Uses of Uncertainty* 210). Supporting his position with an example from *Bouvard et Pécuchet* ('Swedenborg. . . . a vu à Londres Jésus-Christ'), Stirling Haig argues that when such distancing as that provided by the 'crut' is absent from Flaubertian texts, one should beware. He also provides a brief history of the 'crut voir' controversy: 'The Substance of Illusion in Flaubert's "Un Cœur simple,"' *Stanford French Studies* 7 (1983): 309–10 and n17. The controversy continues: e.g., Ross Chambers suggests that the 'crut' reintroduces the realistic optic: 'Simplicité de cœur et duplicité textuelle: Etude d'*Un Cœur simple*,' *MLN* 96 (1981): 791n14. Raymonde Debray-Genette comments that the 'ultimate symbol remains completely motivated and, by that very fact, completely realistic': *Métamorphoses du récit: Autour de Flaubert* (Paris: Seuil, 1988) 187. Robert Griffin refers to 1 Cor. 13:10: 'But when that which is perfect is come, then that which is in part shall be done away,' and maintains that the 'crut voir' thus 'leaves her vision indeterminate' and 'sandwiches her private "theological" musings amid official Church views': *Rape of the Lock: Flaubert's Mythic Realism* (Lexington: French Forum, 1988) 292.

35 For a somewhat more detailed argument, see my *Balzacian Montage: Configuring 'La Comédie humaine'* (Toronto: U of Toronto P, 1991) 118.

There are, of course, exceptions, but as a general rule stories of the supernatural in nineteenth-century France took place somewhere between the 'Once upon a time' of fairy tales and the 'I was very young back then' of Gautier's 'Omphale: Histoire rococo,' between Sindbad's mysterious valley of the diamonds and the 'Horlà' imported from abroad for Maupassant's purposes.

36 See Antoine Compagnon's consideration of the way quotations function within literature, particularly in regard to the degree to which they bring external texts into the one being read: *La Seconde Main ou le travail de la citation* (Paris: Seuil, 1979).

3 From Translation, Imitation, and Plagiarism to Parallel Allusion: *Antigone*

1 Glyn Norton, *The Ideology and Language of Translation in Renaissance France and Their Humanist Antecedents* (Geneva: Droz, 1984). For this chapter, I also profited from Leonard B. Meyer's discussion of paraphrase, borrowing, and simulation: *Music, the Arts and Ideas: Patterns in Twentieth-Century Culture* (Chicago: U of Chicago P, 1967) 191–208.

2 Terence Cave, *The Cornucopian Text: Problems of Writing in the French Renaissance* (Oxford: Clarendon P, 1979) 61.

3 See my *The Color-Keys to 'A la recherche du temps perdu'* (Geneva: Droz, 1976), 39–55. Compare the pink of Proust's *A la recherche* 1.68, 415; 2.55, 83, 254, to the red of C.K. Scott-Moncrieff's translation, *Remembrance of Things Past*, 2 vols (New York: Random House, 1934) 1.52, 322, 526, 548, 675.

4 James J. Murphy, *Rhetoric in the Middle Ages: A History of Rhetorical Theory from Saint Augustine to the Renaissance* (Berkeley: U of California P, 1974) ix. Horace recommends taking 'familiar matter' and by 'order and arrangement' treating it in an original fashion. One thus avoids the dangers of appearing hackneyed or of 'introducing a subject unknown and hitherto unsung': 'The Art of Poetry,' tr. Edward Henry Blakeney, in *The Complete Works of Horace*, ed. Casper J. Kraemer, Jr (New York: Modern Library, 1936) 401–2. For a recent consideration of models, see Dominique Jullien's *Proust et ses modèles: Les 'Mille et Une Nuits' et les 'Memoirs' de Saint-Simon* (Paris: Corti, 1989).

5 Bernard Weinberg, *A History of Literary Criticism in the Italian Renaissance*, 2 vols (Chicago: U of Chicago P, 1961) 1:178–9.

6 Michael Worton and Judith Still, 'Introduction,' in Michael Worton and Judith Still, eds, *Intertextuality: Theory and Practices* (Manchester: Manchester UP, 1990) 7.

7 Jean Giraudoux, *Siegfried: Pièce en quatre actes*, act 1, scene 4, *Théâtre* (Paris: Grasset, 1958) 1.22–3.

8 Emile Zola, *Les Rougon-Macquart*, 5 vols, Bibliothèque de la Pléiade (Paris: Gallimard, 1960–7) 2.1561–2. The thought, of course, has a long and distinguished history. Montaigne put it this way: 'He will transform and mix the material taken from others, so as to make a work and a judgment that is entirely his own': 'De l'institution des enfans,' *Essais, Œuvres complètes*, Bibliothèque de la Pléiade (Paris: Gallimard, 1962) 1.26.151. And Seneca: 'To know is to make something one's own, without either depending on a model or looking often to a master': quoted and translated from Antoine Compagnon, *La Seconde Main ou le travail de la citation* (Paris: Seuil, 1979) 351.

9 Anouilh quoted by Jean Ferran, 'Ce Soir-là à Bordeaux Anouilh ressuscitait Molière,' *Paris Match* 531 (13 June 1959): 98.

10 John Harvey, *Anouilh: A Study in Theatrics* (New Haven: Yale UP, 1964) 16.

11 Paul Valéry, *Œuvres*, 2 vols, Bibliothèque de la Pléiade (Paris: Gallimard, 1957, 1960) 2.677.

12 Gustave Flaubert, letter to Louise Colet, [6–7 June 1853], *Correspondance 1850–1859, Œuvres complètes* (Paris: Club de l'Honnête Homme, 1974) 2.355.

13 Zola, *Les Rougon-Macquart*, 2.1561–2. The point has been made repeatedly through the ages, though in different guises and with differing emphases. Amado Alonso, for example, said, 'What has once been formed – an object of consciousness – can then return to the state of being material – mere sensation or incitation – from which a new poetic power can elicit a new form': 'Estilística de las fuentes literarias: Rubén Darío y Miguel Angel,' *Materia y forma en poesía*, 3d ed. (Madrid: Gredos, 1965) 326. More recently, Claude Ollier told Bettina L. Knapp, 'The one who writes invents new combinations from previous combinations': 'Interview avec Claude Ollier,' *French Review* 46 (1973): 973.

14 Henry James, 'The Art of Fiction' (1884), *The Future of the Novel: Essays on the Art of Fiction* (New York: Vintage, 1956) 12–13.

15 Leonard B. Meyer, *The Poetics of Quotation* (Princeton: Princeton UP, 1968) 101. Thomas Mallon's consideration of plagiarism is excellent: *Stolen Words: Forays into the Origins and Ravages of Plagiarism* (New York: Ticknor and Fields, 1989). Peter J. Rabinowitz takes a different tack and uses the reader's appreciation to identify plagiarism: 'if discovery of the source will diminish the effect, we have plagiarism.' '"What's Hecuba to Us?": The Audience's Experience of Literary Borrowing,' in Susan R. Suleiman

and Inge Crosman, eds, *The Reader in the Text: Essays on Audience and Interpretation* (Princeton: Princeton UP, 1980). The problems of plagiarism are complicated when 'borrowing' is legal, as it was, for example, for playwrights to help themselves to successful novels in the late eighteenth and early nineteenth centuries. See Marie-Pierre Le Hir, '*Indiana* on Stage: Questions of Genre and Gender,' *George Sand Studies* 11 (1992): 31–42; and her 'Authors vs. Playwrights: The Two Authorship Systems of the Old Regime in France and the Repercussions of Their Merger,' *Theatre Journal* 44 (1992).

16 Roland Barthes, *Le Plaisir du texte* (Paris: Seuil, 1973) 59.

17 Michel Tournier, *Le Vent Paraclet* (Paris: Gallimard, 1977) 52. Pierre-Jean Remy describes what is perhaps more traditional behavior. He 'simply tak[es] the trouble,' he says, 'to parody my sources so that, having so boldly admitted them, no one would reproach me for having turned to them': *Les Enfants du parc* (Paris: Gallimard, 1977) 32–3.

18 Quoted by E. Bergerat, *Souvenirs d'un enfant de Paris: Les Années de bohème*, 4 vols (Paris: Fasquelle, 1911–13) 1.400.

19 As Leonard Cabell Pronko indicates, Sophocles' play is not only the most likely basis of comparison, since Antigone is a minor character in the plays of Aeschylus, Euripides, and Seneca, but the most similar in plot and characterization: *The World of Jean Anouilh* (Berkeley: U of California P, 1968) 201–7, 225, and n16. As I shall point out, I believe Pronko sees more similarities than there are in actuality. The relationship between Anouilh and Sophocles has been frequently considered. See, e.g., Rosaire Bellemare, 'Deux Visages d'Antigone,' *Revue de l'Université d'Ottawa* 19 (1949): 335–9; Etienne Frois, '*Antigone*,' *Anouilh: Analyse critique*, Collection Profil d'une Œuvre (Paris: Hatier, 1972) 36–47; Elemér Hankiss, 'L'*Antigone* de Sophocle: Tragédie; L'*Antigone* d'Anouilh: Tragédie?' *Prometeu* (Porto, Portugal) 3 (1949–50): 137–41; W.D. Howarth, *Anouilh: 'Antigone'* (London: Edward Arnold, 1983) 12–46; Sister Emily Joseph, 'The Two Antigones: Sophocles and Anouilh,' *Thought* 38 (1963): 578–606; and Pierre-Henri Simon, 'Les Deux Antigone,' *Revue de Paris* 66 (Sept. 1959): 129–33. Clément Borgal comments cogently on the Sophoclean mysticism that is missing in Anouilh: *Anouilh: La Peine de vivre* (Paris: Centurion, 1966) 73–8. Philip Thody feels, however, that 'the substitution, in the central character, of Anouilh's pet obsessions for the dignity and piety of the Sophoclean original reduces a genuinely tragic conflict to a study of adolescent hysteria': *Anouilh* (Edinburgh and London: Oliver and Boyd, 1968) 31 – a position that has elicited an explicitly contrary view: Christopher Smith, *Jean Anouilh: Life, Work, and Criticism* (Fredericton,

N.B.: York P, 1985) 24–6. The emphasis on Sophocles should, of course, be tempered by a recognition of Seneca's influence; see, e.g., Lewis W. Leadbeater, 'Senecan Elements in Anouilh's *Antigone*,' *Classical and Modern Literature* 7, no. 2 (1987): 63–9.

20 This program, the earliest I have been able to find, has a penciled notation on the cover: 'Représent. à la lumière du jour juin 1944–) [perform. in daylight June 1944–)]': Arts du spectacle, coll. A. Barsacq, Bibliothèque Nationale. I am grateful to Mme Mengozzi of the Bibliothèque de l'Arsenal for her help in locating it.

21 Jean Anouilh, *Antigone* (Paris: La Table Ronde, 1947) 9.

22 Henri Peyre, *L'Influence des littératures antiques sur la littérature française moderne: Etat des travaux* (New Haven: Yale UP, 1941) 80–1.

23 Gabriel Marcel, 'De *Jézabel* à *Médée*: Le Tragique chez Jean Anouilh,' *Revue de Paris* 56 (1949): 105.

24 Sophocles, *Antigone*, *Seven Famous Greek Plays*, ed. Whitney J. Oates and Eugene O'Neill, Jr (New York: Random House, 1950) 203.

25 A point made by Murray Sachs, 'Notes on the Theatricality of Jean Anouilh's *Antigone*,' *French Review* 36 (1962): 7.

26 William Calin, 'Patterns of Imagery in Anouilh's *Antigone*,' *French Review* 41 (1967): 82; see also 83n9.

27 Michael Spingler, 'Anouilh's Little Antigone: Tragedy, Theatricalism, and the Romantic Self,' *Comparative Drama* 8 (1974): 228–38. I suspect that anyone who has taught this play regularly over the last twenty-five years knows the degree to which Anouilh has successfully balanced all these alternatives. In my own experience, students of the late sixties and early seventies identified so whole-heartedly with Antigone that they could not see Creon in any light but that of the death camps. For a belated but well-argued defense of this position, see Richard Hewitson, 'Anouilh's *Antigone*: A Coherent Structure,' *Australian Journal of French Studies* 17, no. 2 (1980): 167–80. In the eighties, however, Antigone came to be seen as a self-indulgent brat colored by anarchism and terrorism. Creon, on the other hand, was no longer considered an ill-intentioned collaborator but a balanced, sensible, and sensitive administrator involved in a dirty but necessary task. For one version of this view, see Redmond O'Hanlon, 'Metatragedy in Anouilh's *Antigone*,' *Modern Language Review* 75 (1980): 534–46. The pedagogical challenge, of course, rests in keeping both alternatives alive while wondering whether the play resolves the ambiguities.

28 Hubert Gignoux, *Jean Anouilh* (Paris: Temps Présent, 1946) 94.

29 Perhaps as a reaction to the play's insistent (over-insistent?) reiteration

that Antigone's death is inevitable, several critics have chosen to claim that the play permits suspense, that Antigone has a free choice. See Evan John, 'The Two Antigones,' *Drama* 26 (Autumn 1952): 15–17; H.G. McIntyre, *The Theatre of Jean Anouilh* (London: Harrap, 1981) 50; Thody, *Anouilh* 31. For the reasons I have given, I agree with the position articulated by the majority, for example by Paul Ginestier: 'Without Thésée, Phèdre could love Hippolyte without sin. Without Hippolyte, she could be a faithful wife. Without Aricie, she could not be prey to morbid jealousy. Without Œnone, she would have died without accusing Hippolyte. On the other hand, if Créon, or Ismène, or Hémon are withdrawn from Anouilh's tragedy, Antigone's destiny would not be altered one iota. . . . Phèdre's death can be explained; that of Antigone cannot': *Jean Anouilh* (Paris: Seghers, 1969) 74.

30 Peter Nazareth has accurately pointed out that 'Anouilh is one of the pioneers of what has been called the Theatre of the Absurd': 'Anouilh's Antigone: An Interpretation,' *English Studies in Africa* 6 (1963): 63; see also David J. DeLaura, 'Anouilh's Other "Antigone,"' *French Review* 35 (1961): 40–1. As Pol Vandromme has said, '[T]he absurd has replaced the gods': '*Antigone*' *de Jean Anouilh*, Coll. Lire aujourd'hui (Paris: Hachette, 1975) 20.

31 E.g., for W.N. Ince, Anouilh made a 'serious error of judgement which led to a basic flaw in *Antigone*'s structure' (277). 'Writing in the twentieth century, being the person he is, Anouilh cannot recreate a world of tragedy where events are really seen as irreversible and where real fatality counts. . . . If life evokes such complete hopelessness, where is the tragedy in leaving it? In disaster or in struggle, tragedy has implied the affirmation of some value or values and has to that extent never been utterly pessimistic' (282): 'Prologue and Chorus in Anouilh's *Antigone*,' *Forum for Modern Language Studies* 4, no. 3 (1968): 277, 282. For Nazareth, because Anouilh's play would not exist without that of Sophocles, it is 'not a finished work of art' (69).

32 For the Christ allusion in *Le Rouge et le noir*, see Richard B. Grant, 'The Death of Julien Sorel,' *L'Esprit créateur* 2 (1962): 26–30. For the Lear allusion, see Gretchen R. Besser, 'Lear and Goriot: A Reevaluation,' *Orbis Litterarum* 27 (1972): 28–36.

33 Literature is rife with such examples, though some authors are more prone than others to exploit onomastics, which has been an important part of my own work, e.g., *Balzacian Montage: Configuring 'La Comédie Humaine'* (Toronto: U of Toronto P, 1991) passim; 'Balzac's Second-Rate Muse,' *L'Esprit créateur* 31, no. 2 (1991): 67–77; 'Ursule through the Glass Lightly,' *French Review* 65, no. 1 (Oct. 1991), or 'The Artistry of Gide's

Onomastics,' written with Wilfrid J. Rollman, *MLN* 86 (1971): 523–31. Paolo Cherchi's considerations on Voltaire's use of names within the larger perspective of a parody of Genesis in *Candide* provides a further example: 'Alcune note per un commento al *Candide*,' *Zeitschrift für Französische Sprache und Literatur* 78 (1968): 44–53.

34 For other examples, see E. Ludovicy, 'Le Mythe grec dans le théâtre français contemporain,' *Revue des langues vivantes* 22 (1956): 387–418.

4 From Allegory to Parallel Allusion and Sources: 'Le Rideau cramoisi'

1 Using the short story as a vehicle, I have discussed the problems of definition at length in 'On Defining Short Stories,' *New Literary History* 22, no. 2 (1991): 407–22.

2 Pierre Fontanier, *Les Figures du discours* (1821–30; rpt Paris: Flammarion, 1968) 114.

3 The relevant passages of Dante's discussions in the letter to Can Grande della Scala and in the *Convivio* are quoted in John MacQueen, *Allegory* (London: Methuen, 1970) 54–7. For an example of typology applied to literature, see, Richard Goodkin's excellent 'T(r)yptext: Proust, Mallarmé, Racine,' in his *Around Proust* (Princeton: Princeton UP, 1991) 38–62.

4 I take the belief that allegory is a mode from C.S. Lewis, who argued, 'Symbolism is a mode of thought, but allegory is a mode of expression': *The Allegory of Love: A Study in Medieval Tradition* (London: Oxford UP, 1936) 48. I would rather say that allegory is both a mode of thought and of expression, as I shall argue below, but it is worth insisting that when allegorical readings are imposed on works that were not intended as allegories, the results are often unconvincing or even ludicrous. For a number of examples, see those provided by Lewis 60–3, and by Ernst Curtius, *European Literature and the Latin Middle Ages*, tr. W.R. Trask (1948; rpt Princeton: Princeton UP, 1967) 204–7. For discussions of allegory and narrative, see Gay Clifford, *The Transformations of Allegory* (London: Routledge and Kegan Paul, 1974) 7, 80; Edwin Honig, *Dark Conceit: The Making of Allegory* (1959; Cambridge: Walker-de Berry, 1960) 4. Jon Whitman, *Allegory: The Dynamics of an Ancient and Medieval Technique* (Cambridge: Harvard UP, 1987), has an excellent, short history of the term 'allegory,' 263–8. In respect to allegory as genre, see Honig, *Dark Conceit* 93, and Maureen Quilligan, *The Language of Allegory: Defining the Genre* (Ithaca: Cornell UP, 1979).

5 For commentaries on allegory and interpretation, see Northrop Frye, *Anatomy of Criticism: Four Essays* (Princeton: Princeton UP, 1957), which I

take up below; and Angus Fletcher, *The Theory of a Symbolic Mode* (Ithaca: Cornell UP, 1964). For a discussion of allegory in relation to symbol (and both Goethe's and Coleridge's contributions), see Fletcher, *Theory of a Symbolic Mode* 16–19 and passim; and Paul de Man, *Blindness and Insight: Essays in the Rhetoric of Contemporary Criticism*, 2nd ed. (Minneapolis: U of Minnesota P, 1983) 189–208.

6 Samuel Taylor Coleridge, *Miscellaneous Criticism*, ed. T.M. Raysor (Cambridge: Harvard UP, 1936) 99; see also 28–32.

7 Remy de Gourmont, 'La Vie de Barbey d'Aurevilly,' *Promenades littéraires*, 8th ed., vol. 1 (Paris: Mercure de France, 1919) 278.

8 Pierre Schneider, 'Barbey d'Aurevilly l'extrême,' *Les Temps Modernes* 6 (Mar. 1951): 1547, makes this point about Barbey's novels, but it is equally true of his short stories.

9 Marcel Proust, *A la recherche du temps perdu*, ed. Jean-Yves Tadié, 4 vols, Bibliothèque de la Pléiade (Paris: Gallimard; 1987–9) 3.877.

10 Jules-Amédée Barbey d'Aurevilly, *Œuvres romanesques complètes*, ed. Jacques Petit, 2 vols (Paris: Pléiade, 1964, 1966) 2.21. All further references to this edition will be found in the text, cited by volume and page. References to 'Le Rideau cramoisi' will be preceded by RC.

11 A. Le Corbeillier, *Les Diaboliques de Barbey d'Aurevilly* (Paris: Edgar Malfère, 1939) 84.

12 The passage might be compared to a similar scene in Proust's *A la recherche* (2.271–4). There the much older narrator tells of his younger counterpart's emotions when he held Albertine's hand (both Proust's and Barbey's girls have the same first name). For Proust's young protagonist, as for Brassard, Albertine's hand represents a spectacular, though hidden, reality. Of course, Proust's adolescent misinterpreted the experience, as he discovers to his embarrassment, whereas Brassard was apparently right. The point is, however, that Proust effectively communicates the young man's emotions without losing his grip on the narrator; Barbey was less successful. I shall return to these passages in the next chapter.

13 Dorothy Kelly, 'Seeing Albertine Seeing: Barbey and Proust through Balzac,' *Studies in Twentieth-Century Literature* 14, no. 2 (1990): 139–57; Eileen Boyd Sivert's earlier consideration of the story's equivalence of death and sex is equally interesting: 'Narration and Exhibitionism in *Le Rideau cramoisi*,' *Romanic Review* 70 (1979): 155–6.

14 Stendhal, *Le Rouge et le noir*, ed. Henri Martineau (Paris: Garnier, 1960) 457. All further references to this edition will be preceded by *RN*.

15 RC 2.28, 42, 45, 46, 49, 51.

16 *RN* 253, 363, 365.

17 *RN* 449–50. Jacques Petit asks, 'Would it be going too far to see an allusion to this image [of blood] in "the fascinating light" from "the crimson curtain" in "this empty, red and luminous square [of glass]"'': 'L'Imagination de la mort,' *Revue des Lettres Modernes* 189–92 (1968): 82. A Stendhalian would immediately make this association, for, as is widely recognized, Stendhal clearly associated blood with the curtains: 'On leaving, Julien thought he saw blood near the holy-water basin, but it was holy-water which had been spilled: the reflected light from the red curtains covering the windows made it look like blood' (*RN* 25); see, e.g., H. Martineau, *RN* n36; E.B.O. Borgerhoff, 'The Anagram in *Le Rouge et le noir*,' *MLN* 68 (1953): 383; André Le Breton, *Le Rouge et le noir de Stendhal: Etude et analyse* (Paris: Mellottée, 1934) 236–7. In addition to incorporating the Stendhalian features that I mention here and in an earlier version, as Sivert points out, 'Barbey recreates Stendhal's famous garden scene from *Le Rouge et le noir*, but in this passage Alberte plays Julien Sorel's role as she seizes the young officer's hand under the table': 'Narration and Exhibitionism' 153–4.

18 To the best of my knowledge, Maurice Hewlett was the first to recognize the Julien Sorel / Louis Jenrel anagram that so clearly foreshadows Julien's death: 'De Stendhal and *La Chartreuse*,' introduction to Mary Loyd's translation of *The Chartreuse of Parma*, by Stendhal (New York: P.F. Collier, 1901) xv. See also Borgerhoff, 'Anagram' 383–6; S. de Sacy, 'Le Miroir sur la grande route,' *Mercure de France* 306 (1949): 74-76; F.W.J. Hemmings, *Stendhal: A Study of his Novels* (Oxford: Clarendon P, 1964) 124–5.

19 Léon Blum, *Stendhal et le beylisme* (Paris: P. Ollendorff, 1914) 129–41. For others of similar persuasion, see e.g., Albert Thibaudet, *Stendhal* (Paris: Hachette, 1931) 120–2; or, more recently, Hemmings, *Stendhal* 117–19; his 'Stendhal relu par Zola au temps de "l'Affaire" (documents inédits),' *Stendhal Club* 4 (1962): 305–6; and Grahame C. Jones, *L'Ironie dans les romans de Stendhal* (Lausanne: Grand Chêne, 1966) 52–8.

20 Several critics have insisted on the story's role reversal and on Brassard's sexual ambiguity: e.g., Kelly, 'Seeing Albertine Seeing' 141; Sivert, 'Narration and Exhibitionism' 154; Timothy Unwin, 'Barbey d'Aurevilly conteur: Discours et narration dans *Les Diaboliques*,' *Neophilologus* 72, no. 3 (July 1988): 362.

21 The conclusion is Jacques Petit's (Barbey, *Œuvres* 2.1302) and is simply unacceptable. I would also disagree with Jean-Pierre Boucher, who believes that '[t]his diabolism . . . must not be taken literally': '*Les Diaboliques*' de Barbey d'Aurevilly: Une Esthétique de la dissimulation et de la

provocation (Montreal: P de l'U du Québec, 1976) 19. Elisabeth Cardonne-Arlyck's position is more acceptable: 'Most often, in fact, the Devil does not enter the text as an actant, but rather as an object of comparison': 'Nom, corps, métaphore dans *Les Diaboliques* de Barbey d'Aurevilly,' *Littérature* 54 (May 1984): 9. Even here, however, more emphasis should be placed on the textual suggestion of the reality of evil and of the devil.

22 Pierre Colla, *L'Univers tragique de Barbey d'Aurevilly* (Brussels: La Renaissance du Livre, 1965) 48–50.

23 Mario Praz, *The Romantic Agony* (New York: Meridian, 1956) 189–286.

24 E.T.A. Hoffmann, 'Le Choix d'une fiancée,' *Contes fantastiques*, tr. Loeve-Veimars, vol. 4 (Paris: E. Renduel 1830) 1–146. Elizabeth Teichmann, *La Fortune d'Hoffmann en France* (Geneva: Droz, 1961); Maurice Breuillac, 'Hoffmann en France,' *Revue d'Histoire Littéraire de la France* 13 (1906): 427–57; 14 (1907): 74–105. For Hoffmann and Barbey, see particularly Breuillac, 'Hoffmann en France' 14 (1907): 88, 95–8.

25 B.G. Rogers makes the very interesting suggestion that *Léa* alludes to the Sleeping Beauty legend: *The Novels and Stories of Barbey d'Aurevilly* (Geneva: Droz, 1967) 36–7. See also Alain Toumayan, 'Barbey d'Aurevilly and Flaubert: Engendering a Diabolique,' in Alain Toumayan, ed., *Literary Generations: A Festschrift in Honor of Edward D. Sullivan by His Friends, Colleagues, and Former Students* (Lexington: French Forum, 1992) 141–9; and Toumayan's 'Barbey d'Aurevilly's Intertextual Poetics of the Short Story,' Kentucky Foreign Language Conference, University of Kentucky, Apr. 1990.

26 J.-H. Bornecque, ed., 'Introduction' to Barbey d'Aurevilly, *Les Diaboliques*, (Paris: Garnier, 1963) ciii.

27 Hippolyte Taine, 'Stendhal (Henri Beyle),' *Nouveaux Essais de critique et d'histoire* (1864; rpt Paris: Hachette, 1905) 233.

28 Hippolyte Babou, 'Stendhal,' *Les Sensations d'un juré* (Paris: A. Lemerre, 1875) 21. For the summary in this paragraph, the following sources have been particularly helpful: the article by Babou 87–136; Adolphe Paupe, *Histoire des œuvres de Stendhal* (Paris: Dujarric, 1903) esp. 75–103; C.-A. Sainte-Beuve, 'M. de Stendhal: Ses Œuvres complètes, Causeries du lundi, 9th ser., 3rd ed. (Paris: Garnier, 1869) 301–41; Barbey's 'Stendhal et Balzac' (1853), *Romanciers d'hier et d'avant hier* (Paris: A. Lemerre, 1904) 1–16; his 'De Stendhal' (1856), 'Prosper Mérimée' (1874), and 'X. Doudan' (1876), all in *Littérature épistolaire* (Paris: A. Lemerre, 1893) 31–49, 211–25, and 291–304, respectively; Prosper Mérimée, 'Notes et souvenirs' (1855), in *Stendhal: Correspondance inédite* (Paris: Calmann Lévy, 1907), 1.v–xxiv; Paul Bourget, 'Stendhal (Henri Beyle),' in his *Essais de psychologie contemporaine*,

8th ed. (Paris: A. Lemerre, 1892) 251–323, first published in 1883, and his later (1923) 'L'Art du roman chez Stendhal,' in his *Quelques témoignages* (Paris: Plon, 1928) 41–55; Taine's 'Stendhal (Henri Beyle)' 223–57; E.-M. de Vogüé, 'De la littérature réaliste: A propos du roman russe,' *Revue des Deux Mondes*, 3, no. 75 (15 May 1886): 298; Emile Zola, 'Stendhal' (1880), in his *Les Romanciers naturalistes* (Paris: Fasquelle, 1906) 75–124.

29 Although he does not quote it exactly, Bourget refers to the passage, the night after Mathilde went to Opéra Bouffe, where Julien is filled with despair and his imagination is working furiously to paint his situation in even more somber colors. 'Dans cet état d'*imagination renversée* [In this state of *inverted imagination*]' (*RN* 358), Julien uses his imagination to judge his life. With the next reference, also not quite an exact quotation, Chapron refers to a conversation between an academician and Julien about the success of Hugo's play *Hernani* (*RN* 300).

30 Léon Chapron, *L'Evénement* (1 May 1882), quoted from Paupe, *Histoire des œuvres* 88–9.

31 Emile Zola, 'Stendhal' 123. See Emile Talbot, 'Perspectives sur la critique stendhalienne avant Bourget,' *Stendhal Club* 20 (1978): 343–55.

32 Pierre Brun, *Henry Beyle – Stendhal* (Grenoble: A. Gratier, 1900) 59.

33 Jean Canu, *Barbey d'Aurevilly* (Paris: R. Laffont, 1945) 413.

34 Philippe Berthier, 'Stendhal,' *Revue des Lettres Modernes* 234–7 (1970): 50. The episode appears in *Rome, Naples et Florence*, vol. 1 (Paris: Le Divan, 1927) 213–27.

35 Brantôme, *Les Dames galantes* (Paris: Garnier, 1960) 71. For similar adventures, see the story of the mortal risks run by Captain Beaulieu while enjoying the two daughters of the man holding him prisoner (101–2). For other such stories, though without excessive danger, see 145–50.

36 Gérard de Nerval, 'Angélique' (1850): *Les Filles du feu*, in *Œuvres*, Bibliothèque de la Pléiade, vol. 1 (Paris: Gallimard, 1960) 181–5, 193–200.

37 E.g., A.C. Lee, *The Decameron: Its Sources and Analogues* (London: David Nutt, 1909) 231–257, 294.

38 Robert J. Niess, *Zola, Cézanne, and Manet: A Study of l'Oeuvre* (Ann Arbor: U of Michigan P, 1969).

39 François-René de Chateaubriand, *Atala, René, Les Aventures, du dernier Abencérage*, ed. Fernand Letessier (Paris: Garnier, 1958).

40 Jean Plattard, *L'Œuvre de Rabelais (Sources, invention et composition)* (Paris: H. Champion, 1910) 37.

41 Octave Mirbeau, *Le Journal d'une femme de chambre* (Paris: Fasquelle, 1900) 166–204; Jean Bruce, *Les Espions du Pirée (OSS 117)* (Paris: Presses de la Cité, 1962) 104.

42 Henri Béraud, 'Les Sources d'inspiration du "Bateau ivre,"' *Mercure de France* 153 (1922): 104.

43 W.D. Redfern, 'The Prisoners of Stendhal and Camus,' *French Review* 41 (1968): 659.

44 See Frank Kermode, a welcome exception, who suggests that Meursault 'is clearly and literally an Antichrist, with the tradition of Christian heroism rendered absurd in him; we might say the careful meaningless-ness of his life is exactly antithetical to the fullness of the concordances found in the life of Jesus': *The Sense of an Ending: Studies in the Theory of Fiction* (New York: Oxford UP, 1967) 143. There seems little doubt that both Camus and Stendhal used allusion to suggest that their messianic characters represent a new breed that may bring a new world. Though I argued in chapter 2 that unintegrated irony should raise warning signals in the wise reader, this is easily integrated and should be accomplished. To suggest with Mary McCarthy that Stendhal's use of the Christ story is thereby a 'wicked analogy,' a 'little blasphemy,' or even 'a shaft of mockery' – *Ideas and the Novel* (New York: Harcourt Brace Jovanovich, 1980) 55–6 – shows a misunderstanding of the social thrust of Stendhal's work. It leaves the allusion outside the movements of the novel, thus pointless.

45 Earl Miner has written that allusion is 'found chiefly in periods setting value on tradition': 'Allusion,' in Alex Preminger, ed., *Princeton Encyclopedia of Poetry and Poetics* (Princeton: Princeton UP, 1974) 18. With the striking exception of Proust, however, neither the authors I have included nor, in general, the period they represent set much store by tradition. Allusion exists in all periods of western literature of which I have knowledge.

46 E.g., Henri Peyre, *L'Influence des littératures antiques sur la littérature française moderne: Etat des travaux* (New Haven: Yale UP, 1941) 80–1. For an example of vitally related divergences that have not been understood, there is C. Th. Dimaras's 'Gide et la Grèce,' *Revue d'Athènes* 2 (Apr. 1951): 42: 'In [Gide's] first period, that of symbolism, ancient Greece appears and reappears; you would almost say the recollections from high school, regis-tered by genius. Later he returned to it, dipping liberally into Hellenic literature for subjects which he renewed without paying much attention to their origin or their profound meaning. I do not believe that there can be any question of the tradition of ancient Greece in the work of André Gide.'

47 Amado Alonso makes this point with considerable force in 'Estilística de las fuentes literarias: Rubén Darío y Miguel Angel,' in his *Materia y forma en poesía*, 3rd ed. (Madrid: Gredos, 1965) 325–38.

48 Alain Robbe-Grillet, 'Mes Romans, mes films et mes ciné-romans,' *Magazine littéraire* 6 (Apr. 1967) 17. Susanne K. Langer's conclusion is worth remembering: 'Every successful work of literature is wholly a creation, no matter what actualities have served as its models, or what stipulations set up its scaffold': *Feeling and Form* (New York: Charles Scribner's Sons, 1953) 245.

49 T.S. Eliot, 'Philip Massinger' (1920), in his *Selected Essays* (New York: Harcourt, Brace, 1950) 182.

5 Allusive Complex: *A la recherche du temps perdu*

1 Both Albert Feuillerat, *Comment Marcel Proust a composé son roman* (New Haven: Yale UP, 1934), and Robert Vigneron, 'Structure de *Swann*: Combray ou le cercle parfait,' *Modern Philology* 45 (1948): 185–207, argued that Proust's uncontrolled additions compromised the order of the original text. Though the position has been refuted many times by critics who have considered Proust's manuscripts and proofs, variations on the view continue to surface in critics. For a brief consideration of Feuillerat, see Jean-Yves Tadié, *Lectures de Proust* (Paris: Armand Colin, 1971) 211–15.

2 See my *The Color-Keys to 'A la recherche du temps perdu'* (Geneva: Droz, 1976), but perhaps more accessibly in my *Novel Configurations: A Study of French Fiction*, 2nd ed. (Birmingham: Summa, 1994) 151–72.

3 Marcel Proust, *Contre Sainte-Beuve*, ed. Pierre Clarac, Bibliothèque de la Pléiade (Paris: Gallimard, 1971) 176–7.

4 Marcel Proust, *A la recherche du temps perdu*, ed. Jean-Yves Tadié, 4 vols, Bibliothèque de la Pléiade (Paris: Gallimard, 1987–9) 2.802. For this chapter the abbreviation *R* will precede references to Tadié's edition.

5 Gérard Genette, 'Proust et le langage indirect,' in his *Figures II* (Paris: Seuil, 1969) 243.

6 Such nuclei have been studied by numerous scholars. I have particularly appreciated Jean-Yves Tadié's splendid consideration of the way characters establish a web of relationships: *Proust et le roman* (Paris: Gallimard, 1971); William Stewart Bell's analysis of dream: *Proust's Nocturnal Muse* (New York: Columbia UP, 1962); the views of cathedrals of Serge Doubrovsky, *La Place de la Madeleine* (Paris: Mercure de France, 1974) and Jean Ricardou, ' "Miracles" de l'analogie: Aspects proustiens de la métaphore productrice,' *Etudes Proustiennes* 2, *Cahiers Marcel Proust* 7 (Paris: Gallimard, 1975) 11–39; and Richard Goodkin's perception of 'avuncular' relationships: *Around Proust* (Princeton: Princeton UP, 1991) 17–37. In addition, Roger Shattuck's description of the novel's structure

remains well worth rereading: *Marcel Proust* (New York: Viking, 1974) 25–55.

7 Despite an ill-considered propensity to term many of Proust's allusions plagiarisms, and without apparent knowledge of the early version of this chapter published by *Romanic Review* in 1971, Annick Bouillaguet, in *Marcel Proust: Le Jeu intertextuel* (1990), has usefully studied the way multiple allusions work together in *A la recherche* to add meaning.

8 Roland Barthes, 'Proust et les noms,' *To Honor Roman Jakobson: Essays on the Occasion of His Seventieth Birthday: 11 October 1966*, in *Janua Linguarum* 31 (1967): 1.152.

9 Part three of *Du côté de chez Swann* is entitled 'Noms de pays: le Nom [Names of Regions: The Name]' and part two of *A l'ombre des jeunes filles en fleurs* is 'Noms de pays: le Pays [Names of Regions: The Region].' As is well known, Proust also planned a chapter entitled 'Noms de personnes: la Duchesse de Guermantes [Names of People: The Duchess de Guermantes].' See my forthcoming 'Reading the Age of Names in *A la recherche du temps perdu*,' *Comparative Literature* 46 (1994).

10 R 4.45–6; Anna Louise Frey refers to several versions, including Wagner's *Lohengrin*, where the Swan Knight leaves the ring: *The Swan-Knight Legend* (Nashville: George Peabody College, 1931) 13, 49, 55, 76, 116. Albertine's rings may indicate that she was having an affair with one of the Swan Knight's descendants, since the rings, which are inscribed with what Françoise makes out as an eagle (or could it be a swan?), were perhaps given to her by her lover.

11 Dorothy Kelly is drawn to other portions of the protagonist's saga, especially *La Prisonnière* with Albertine, particularly in respect to the similarities in the role reversal of the two heroines, the gender ambiguity, and the images of warfare: 'Seeing Albertine Seeing: Barbey and Proust through Balzac,' *Studies in Twentieth-Century Literature* 14, no. 2 (1990): 139–57.

12 Marcel Proust, *Albertine disparue: Edition originale de la dernière version revue par l'auteur*, ed. Nathalie Mauriac and Etienne Wolff (Paris: Grasset, 1987) 76.

13 Victor E. Graham, *The Imagery of Proust* (Oxford: Basil Blackwell, 1966) 123; and his 'Water Imagery and Symbolism in Proust,' *Romanic Review* 50 (1959): 122–3. Bernard Brun in Jean Milly's edition of *A la recherche du temps perdu*, 10 vols (Paris: Garnier-Flammarion, 1984–7) 1.594–5n109, and Jacques Nathan, *Citations, références et allusions de Marcel Proust dans 'A la recherche du temps perdu'* (Paris: Nizet, 1969) 17 and passim, trace the priest's etymologies to Jules Quicherat's *De la formation française des anciens*

noms de lieux (1867), though Graham argues that Auguste Longnon constitutes Proust's principal source: 'Proust's Etymologies,' *French Studies* 29 (1975): 300–12. Antoine Compagnon disagrees with Graham, arguing indeed that for most of the etymologies Longnon is an unlikely source: *Proust entre deux siècles* (Paris: Seuil, 1989) 231n2; 245–55.

14 A belief held, for example, by Louis Félicien de Saulcy, *Voyage autour de la Mer Morte et dans les terres bibliques exécuté de décembre 1850 à avril 1851, par F. de Saulcy*, vol. 2 (Paris: Gide et J. Baudry, 1853) 631. Since the discovery of the Ras Shamra texts in 1929, this opinion has been disputed. See Arvid S. Kapelrud, *Baal in the Ras Shamra Texts* (Copenhagen: G.E.C. Gad, 1952) esp. 93–145.

15 Michel Butor mentioned this in reference to Proust's Balbec: *Les Œuvres d'art imaginaires chez Proust* (London: Athlone, 1964) 24. The information appears in works that were available in Proust's time: e.g., Saulcy, *Voyage* 2.609, 621, 627, 635, 636; *Nouveau Larousse illustré: Dictionnaire universel encyclopédique*, vol. 1 (Paris: Librairie Larousse, 1898) 687. Alphonse de Lamartine mentions that the sun was worshipped at Baalbek: *Souvenirs, Impressions, Pensées et Paysages pendant un voyage en Orient; ou notes d'un voyageur*, vol. 2 (Paris, 1861) 169.

16 Henri Dontenville, ed., *La France mythologique: Travaux de la Société de Mythologie Française* (Paris: Tchou, 1966) 46–56; Harold Bayley, *The Lost Language of Symbolism: An Inquiry into the Origin of Certain Letters, Words, Names, Fairy-Tales, Folklore, and Mythologies* (1912; New York: Citadel, nd) 150. Bayley also points out that the *Bel* of Cymbeline (Celtic for 'Lord of the Sun') 'is identical with the *Bel* of Belenus, the Celtic Apollo; and with the *Bal* of Balder, the Sun god of Scandinavia' (ibid.). *Bal* until recently was still found in such related languages as Gaelic with the meaning of 'the sun' and 'the Lord.' Following this line of thought, it seems reasonable to assume that the *Bal-* of Proust's Balbec would derive from the Indo-European **bhel* ('white' or 'to shine'). If so, there is an evident relationship to Albertine, probably derived from the Indo-European **alhg* ('white' or 'becoming shiny') or the Latin *albus*. Proust's knowledge of related words is indicated when M. de Bréauté says, 'Albius . . . means white' (*R* 2.806), and when Brichot finds 'l'aubier [sapwood]' in M. Alberet (*R* 3.322). For the derivations suggested, I have consulted numerous sources, including Walter von Wartburg, *Französisches etymologisches Wörterbuch*, 25 vols (Bonn-Leipzig-Basel: Helbing und Lichtenhahn, 1928–82); and A. Ernout and A. Meillet, *Dictionnaire étymologique de la langue latine: Histoire des mots* (Paris: Klincksieck, 1932).

The Indo-European etymons were taken from Jan de Vries, *Altnordisches etymologisches Wörterbuch* (Leiden: Brill, 1957–61).

Still, we know that Proust's interest in names did not stop at etymology. His love of puns attests to an interest in the phonic texture. See, e.g., Marcel Proust, *Lettres à Reynaldo Hahn*, ed. Philip Kolb (Paris: Gallimard, 1956) passim; *R* 1.335–6. With this in mind, it is difficult to ignore the associations of the French word *bal* ('dancing, youth, mating,' etc.) and of the ornithological *bec* ('beak'). All of these associations are important to the concerns of the Balbec sequences.

17 Incarville does not appear in the extract from *A l'ombre des jeunes filles en fleurs* published in the *NRF* 11.66 (1 June 1914): 921–69. In the passage: 'Every few minutes the little railroad stopped at one of the preceding stations, whose very names (Criqueville, Equemauville, Couliville) seemed strange to me' (926), Proust later changed the names of the towns. In the final version they became 'Incarville, Marcouville, Doville . . . Hermonville, Maineville' (*R* 2.22). Both Albertine and Incarville were apparently added after May 1914. See n29 below.

18 *R* 3.501n3, 503; 4.7n1. It is also interesting to note that the sole mention of the town Apollonville ('The names of these stations, Apollonville...') appears in conjunction with the protagonist's reminiscing about Albertine and Balbec (*R* 3.518). 'Proust,' add Clarac and Ferré, 'noted for himself: "Copy the names"': *A la recherche*, ed. Pierre Clarac and André Ferré, Bibliothèque de la Pléiade (Paris: Gallimard, 1954) 3.1104n3 for p. 518. Apollo was the Greek god of light, and the Celts equated him with their sun god, Belenus: Dontenville, *La France mythologique* 46. By this late introduction of Apollonville, Proust may have wished to support further the sun allusions, or it may be that he had forgotten which names evocative of sun imagery he had actually employed. There is then good reason to believe that Proust's recent editors working under Tadié were mistaken when they deleted Apollonville before adding the original list of names: *R* 4.1075na for p. 100.

19 Ovid, *Metamorphoses*, tr. Frank Justus Miller, vol. 8 (Cambridge: Harvard UP, 1956) 203–6, 220–30. Although Cottard's quotation from Ovid is irrelevant to the conversation taking place, it may be considered as an adumbration of the allusive episode discussed below: 'Os homini sublime dedit coelumque tueri [iussit et erectos ad sidera tollere voltus]' (He gave to man an uplifted face and bade him stand erect and turn his eyes to heaven: *R* 3.459; Ovid, *Metamorphoses* 1.185–6).

20 E.g., *Le Livre des mille nuits et une nuit*, tr. J.C. Mardrus, vol. 9 (Paris:

Fasquelle, 1920) 8. Further references to this edition of the *Arabian Nights* will be preceded by *AN*.

21 In his stimulating but not completely convincing book, Claude Vallée has argued that the creative processes apparent in *A la recherche* are similar to the figuration of the *Arabian Nights*: *La Féerie de Marcel Proust* (Paris: Fasquelle, 1958). Jean Rousset, *Forme et signification* (Paris: Corti, 1962) 158–63; P.-E. Robert, *Marcel Proust, lecteur des Anglo-Saxons* (Paris: Nizet, 1976) 79–81; Jan Hokenson, 'Proust in the Palace of Sheriar,' *Far-Western Forum* 1 (May 1974): 187–98; Alain Buisine, 'Marcel Proust: Le Côté de l'Orient,' *Revue des Sciences Humaines* 90, no. 214 (1989): 123–44; and Dominique Jullien, *Proust et ses modèles: Les 'Mille et une Nuits' et les 'Memoires' de Saint-Simon* (Paris: Corti, 1989), argue more persuasively for deep-seated influence on Proust's masterpiece.

22 The direct references to the *Arabian Nights* are frequent enough to keep this Oriental fairyland in the reader's mind. For other examples of unequivocal references to the *Arabian Nights*, see *R* 1.56; 2.98, 257–8; 2.406, 740; 3.638; 4.229, 560–1. Although less direct, one might also mention 'the family spirit [*le Génie de la famille*]' (*R* 2.733) and the 'Roc bird' (*R* 2.694). For a much more complete index of these references, see Jullien, *Proust et ses modèles* 233–8.

23 *AN* 10.7–159; esp. 21–159. Another version of this story, 'Aventures de Mazen du Khorassan,' appears in the 'Contes supplémentaires' of A. Loiseleur-Deslongchamps' edition of *Les Mille et une nuits, contes arabes, traduites en français par Galland* (Paris: A. Desrez, 1838) 729–47. This version lacks the bird and flower imagery as well as Splendeur's significant name.

24 E.g., *R* 2.180, 189, 230; 2.656; 3.575–6.

25 E.g., *R* 2.199, 244, 285. I have discussed the changes that occur in the physical traits of Albertine in *Color-Keys* 25–37.

26 Charlotte M. Yonge, *History of Christian Names* (London: Macmillan, 1884) 410.

27 The importance of nonbiographical considerations has been argued in an excellent fashion by Carlos Lynes, Jr, 'Proust and Albertine: On the Limits of Autobiography and of Psychological Truth in the Novel,' *Journal of Aesthetics and Art Criticism* 10 (1952): 328–37. 'Albertine' also serves other functions. Like the 'M' Gide used to relate Michel, Marceline, Ménalque, and Moktir, Albertine joins Andrée and Aimée through the 'A.' Similarly the *bert* links those characters whom Jean-Pierre Richard calls 'creatures of desire' (*Proust et le monde sensible* [Paris: Seuil, 1974] 236) by means of the seme *bert*: Gilbert le Mauvais, Gilberte Swann, Robert de Saint-Loup,

Albertine. For those sensitive to etymologies, it might even be interesting to recall that *bert* derives from *bericht* meaning 'bright' or 'famous.' The *bert* supports such phrases as: 'I could almost believe that Gilberte's sensual and willful personality had emigrated into Albertine's body, somewhat different it is true, but presenting, now that I thought after the fact about it, profound analogies' (*R* 4.83–4). Surely one should couple Charlus and Charlie. Given the narrator's recognition that homosexuals may mentally transform the young women into young men (*R* 3.489), and Albertine's lesbian proclivities, it may even be appropriate to remember that Andrée derives from the Greek *andros* meaning 'male' (Goodkin, *Around Proust* 80).

28 E.g., Philip Kolb, ed., 'Préface,' *Marcel Proust: Lettres retrouvées* (Paris: Plon, 1966) 24–5; André Germain, *Les Clés de Proust: Suivi de portraits* (Paris: Editions Sun, 1953) 61–76; Justin O'Brien, 'Albertine the Ambiguous: Notes on Proust's Transposition of the Sexes,' *PMLA* 44 (1949): 946. Albertine's debt to Agostinelli has been frequently mentioned. See, e.g., Robert Vigneron, 'Genèse de *Swann*,' *Revue d'Histoire de la Philosophie et d'Histoire Générale de la Civilisation* 5 (1937): 100–15; Richard H. Barker, *Marcel Proust: A Biography* (New York: Grosset and Dunlap, 1962) 225; Harold March, *The Two Worlds of Marcel Proust*, Perpetua (New York: A.S. Barnes, 1961) 116–18.

29 According to Albert Feuillerat, 'In the Grasset galley proofs [of what became *A l'ombre des jeunes filles en fleurs* in 1918], Albertine is not mentioned. Mme Bontemps simply has a daughter whose name is not given, and it is of this daughter that she says, "And my daughter is like me," a phrase that was changed in the definitive version to: "And my niece Albertine is like me"': *Comment Marcel Proust a composé* 42. Let me repeat that her name does not occur in the extract from *A l'ombre des jeunes filles en fleurs* published in the *NRF* of 1 June 1914 (see n17 above). To the best of my knowledge, the first mention of 'Albertine' in a source susceptible of being dated occurs in Proust's letter of early November 1915 to Madame Scheikevitch: Philip Kolb, ed., *Correspondance*, 20 vols (Paris: Plon, 1970–92) 14.281. It would seem, then, that Proust decided on the name 'Albertine' between May 1914 and Nov. 1915. Maurice Bardèche states that she did not appear before May 1913, though he does not justify his conclusion: *Marcel Proust: Romancier*, 2 vols (Paris: Les Sept Couleurs, 1971) 1.299.

The references to the *Arabian Nights* in Proust's early correspondence are in hyperboles typical of his complimentary letters and indicate neither a very strong interest nor a recent reading. See, e.g., the letter of April

1904 to Robert de Flers, *Correspondance* 4.113; the letter of 20 June 1905 to Countess de Noailles, *Correspondance* 5.241–2; the letter of 6 March 1905 to Robert de Montesquiou, *Correspondance* 5.66. It was not until May or June of 1916 that Proust wrote to ask Daudet whether he should read the tale of Sinbad in the Mardrus or Galland translation (*Correspondance* 15.150), and he does not mention Mardrus in any way that would indicate a familiarity with his translation until mid-December of that same year (*Correspondance* 15.337). Apparently Proust's reading of Mardrus occurred some time in 1916. This evidence is insufficient for firm conclusions. Nonetheless, it does seem likely that 'Albertine' came first and that the discovery of 'Les Aventures de Hassân' and the exploitation of its imagery is an example of Proust's serendipity. Dominique Jullien believes the Mardrus translation of secondary importance, though she does not justify her position: *Proust et ses modèles* 8n3.

30 E.g., *R* 1.102–5; 3.280–4; Lucien Daudet, ed., *Autour de soixante lettres*, Les *Cahiers Marcel Proust* 5 (Paris: Gallimard, 1929) letter 9, 108–9.

31 For one variation of such an argument, see Charles N. Clark, 'Elstir: The Roles of the Painter in Proust' (PhD diss., Yale University 1952), 286–307.

32 Jean-Jacques Nattiez, 'Le Septuor de Wagner,' *Magazine Littéraire* 210 (Sept. 1984): 48. Gurnemanz is not the only explanation for Proust's choice. Graham has discussed the etymology of Guermantes: 'The probable origin of the root *Germ* or *Guerm* is a Celtic form of the Indo-European **ghwerm* which gives Greek *termos* and English *warm*, etc. Knowing Proust's interest in philology and in the light of evidence to be presented later it is not unreasonable to suggest that we have here the motivating cause for the particular choice of imagery drawn from heat or flame' (*Imagery* 70). Philip Kolb points out, however, that there are serious problems with the chronology. Proust chose the name Guermantes 'around the month of May 1909,' according to Philip Kolb, ed., *Le Carnet de 1908*, *Cahiers Marcel Proust* 8 (Paris: Gallimard, 1976) 141n61; 185n392. Anthony R. Pugh believes that the relevant leaf of this notebook (Nouvelles Acquisitions Françaises [hereafter NAF] 16637.35) was written in April of 1909: *The Birth of 'A la recherche du temps perdu'* (Lexington: French Forum, 1987) 64. In March of 1909, Proust asked Georges de Lauris whether the Guermantes name were free for artistic use: *Correspondance* 9.102. It was not until more than a decade later, in 1922, that he wrote to Martin-Chauffier to ask about its etymology. See, Philip Kolb, review of Victor E. Graham's *The Imagery of Proust*, *Modern Language Quarterly* 29 (1968): 119. Of course, Proust was, and had long been, a rather accomplished amateur philologist in his own right, and these

etymologies may have influenced his choice of imagery around the name, as Graham suggests, and moreover his choice of the name itself. We cannot say with certainty. Another possible motivation for the choice of Guermantes exists. Graham has pointed to the importance of the German ancestry and sympathy of the Guermantes (*Imagery* 70). The Verdurins claim to believe that Charlus is, in fact, either Austrian or Prussian (*R* 4.346–7). Perhaps it is not too far-fetched to see G()erm(ain)-antes. This might explain Proust's peculiar syllabic division: Guerm-antes (*R* 1.169).

33 NAF 16697.13, quoted from Henri Bonnet and Bernard Brun, eds., *Matinée chez la Princesse de Guermantes: Cahiers du 'Temps retrouvé'* (Paris: Gallimard, 1982) 318.

34 Florence Hier, *La Musique dans l'œuvre de Marcel Proust* (New York: Columbia UP, 1933) 45; Georges Piroué, *Proust et la musique du devenir* (Paris: Denouël, 1960) 107–8. Danièle Gasiglia-Laster goes into some detail in respect to the parallels between Wagner's 'flowering girls' and those of Proust in the Milly edition (2.40–1). J.-J. Nattiez argues convincingly that '[l]ike *Parsifal*, *A la recherche* is a work whose hero is on a quest for redemption': *Proust as Musician*, tr. Derrick Puffett, rev. ed. (1984; Cambridge: Cambridge UP, 1989) 32. Margaret Mein makes the point that Proust thought for a time of insisting on the parallels between the redemption of Amfortas, the Fisher King, and Swann in *Le Temps retrouvé*: 'Proust and Wagner,' *Journal of European Studies* 19 (1989): 205–22. Rina Viers says twice, 'The Narrator is identified with Parsifal': 'La Signification des fleurs dans l'œuvre de Marcel Proust,' *Bulletin de la Société des Amis de Marcel Proust et des Amis de Combray* 25 (1975): 158–9. Jean-Marc Rodrigues shows conclusively that Proust's love of Wagner must be distinguished from the shallow *fin-de-siècle* Wagnerism: 'Genèse du wagnérisme proustien,' *Romantisme* 17, no. 57 (1987): 75-88. Of Proust's many epistolary references to Wagner, the following seems particularly telling: 'The more Wagner is legendary, the more I find him human. His most splendid artifices of the imagination seem to me nothing but the symbolic and gripping language of human truths' (*Correspondance* 1.383, letter of May 1895 to Hahn).

35 The manuscripts raise the question of why the author revised his text to obscure the stranger's identity. An early version indicates that the fisherman might have been a friend of Mme Putbus's maid (NAF 16675.4r–5r). By deleting any indication of recognition, Proust emphasized the strange fact that the boy did not ask the expected question. Cf, however, Marcel Muller, who believes that the 'anonymousness of this fisherman may be taken as symbolical of the unknowable aspect of all

Proustian characters': *Les Voix narratives dans la 'Recherche du temps perdu'* (Geneva: Droz, 1965) 56. Georges Matoré and Irène Mecz link Perceval's failure to ask the appropriate questions to Swann's 'forgetting' to ask Vinteuil whether the creator of the sonata was related to him: *Musique et structure romanesque dans 'La Recherche du temps perdu'* (Paris: Klincksieck, 1973) 97–8. Furthermore, as Marie Miguet-Ollagnier points out in her *La Mythologie de Marcel Proust*, Annales Littéraires de l'Université de Besançon, no. 276 (Paris: Les Belles-Lettres, 1982), like Perceval, the protagonist abandons his mother (139), though the latter's betrayal is submerged and diffused across several thousand pages.

36 Patrick Brady has perceptively considered the linkage: 'Farms, Trees, and Bell-Towers: The "Hidden Meaning" of Triads in Proust's *Recherche*,' *Neophilologus* 61, no. 3 (1977): 371–7.

37 Frey, *The Swan-Knight Legend* 5–6.

38 *R* 2.219; 4.485,488.

39 Marcel Proust, *Lettres à la NRF*, Les Cahiers Marcel Proust 6 (Paris: Gallimard, 1932) 103–4.

40 Emeric Fiser, *Le Symbole littéraire: Essai sur la signification du symbole chez Wagner, Baudelaire, Mallarmé, Bergson et Marcel Proust* (Paris: Corti, 1941) 169.

6 Oppositional Allusion: *Electre, La Symphonie pastorale, Eugénie Grandet*

1 Herman Meyer's *Poetics of Quotation* (Princeton: Princeton UP, 1968) is an important exception to which I am indebted. While he does not distinguish between the various forms of parallels and oppositions occurring in alluding texts, or between satire and allusion, he manifests great insight into the interpretive problems that arise when texts make use of quotations from external sources. There are, as well, numerous cases of critics who recognize specific instances of an author calling up a contrastive text for reasons that are neither satirical nor ironic. See, e.g., Jan H. Logan, 'Flannery O'Connor and Flaubert: A French Connection,' *Notes on Contemporary Literature* 13, no. 5 (Nov. 1983): 2–5.

2 Lise Gauvin, *Giroudoux et le thème d'Electre*, Archives des Lettres Modernes, 108 (Paris: Lettres Modernes, 1969) 8.

3 My definition owes much, of course, to C.G. Jung (e.g., his 'The Archetypes of the Collective Unconscious,' *The Archetypes and the Collective Unconscious* [Princeton: Princeton UP, 1969] 6) and little to Sartre, for whom an archetype is more conventionally a preceding model or pattern

that determines succeeding forms. See, J.-P. Sartre, 'M. Jean Giraudoux et la philosophie d'Aristote, à propos de *Choix des élues*' (Mar. 1940), *Situations I* (Paris: Gallimard, 1947) 82–98.

4 Raymond Williams, *Drama from Ibsen to Eliot* (London: Chatto and Windus, 1952) 200.

5 Gay Clifford, *The Transformations of Allegory* (London: Routledge and Kegan Paul, 1974) 49–50. Parody, like other terms, has recently been subjected to the play that obscures conventional meaning. Michel Butor, for example, says that 'The most literal quotation is already to some degree a parody': *Répertoire III* (Paris: Minuit, 1968). He means that, depending on the new context, a quotation can be made to take on a completely different meaning. Of course, as Laurent Jenny points out, '[I]f parody is always intertextual, intertextuality is not limited to parody': 'La Stratégie de la forme,' *Poétique* 27 (1976): 260.

6 Lionel Duisit, *Satire, parodie, calembour: Esquisse d'une théorie des modes dévalués*, Stanford French and Italian Studies, 11 (Saratoga: Anma Libri, 1978) 8–86. This position should be tempered somewhat, since there are cases of burlesque serving less to ridicule than to elevate. I think of Rabelais's burlesque of Genesis to make Pantagruel larger than life, thus capable of bearing his significance as an exemplar of the Renaissance. See, Raymond C. La Charité's discussion in *Recreation, Reflection and Re-Creation: Perspectives on Rabelais's Pantagruel* (Lexington: French Forum, 1981) 28–31. Michael Issacharoff's detailed analysis of several examples of parody at work is also very useful: 'Theatrical Intertextuality,' in his *Discourse as Performance* (Stanford: Stanford UP, 1989) 28–51.

7 Harold Bloom, *The Anxiety of Influence: A Theory of Poetry* (London: Oxford University Press, 1973) 11.

8 André Gide, *La Symphonie pastorale, Romans, récits et soties, œuvres lyriques*, ed. Yvonne Davet and J.-J. Thierry, Bibliothèque de la Pléiade (Paris: Gallimard, 1958) 877 (hereafter cited as *Récits*).

9 See, though for a much more positive example, Philip Hallie's description of Le Chambon: *Lest Innocent Blood Be Shed* (New York: Harper, Torchbook 1979).

10 André Gide, *Journal: 1889–1939*, Bibliothèque de la Pléiade (Paris: Gallimard, 1958) 132.

11 Ibid. And as Gide did in *Numquid et tu...* A number of critics have consequently seen *La Symphonie pastorale* as Gide's effort at self-correction, e.g., Klaus Mann, *André Gide and the Crisis of Modern Thought* (New York: Creative Age Press, 1943) 155–6; Justin O'Brien and M. Shackleton, eds.,

'Introduction,' *La Symphonie pastorale*, by André Gide (Boston: D.C. Heath, 1954) xxviii; Claude Martin, ed., 'Introduction,' *La Symphonie pastorale*, by André Gide (Paris: Minard, 1970) cvii.

12 Henri Maillet, *'La Symphonie pastorale' d'André Gide* (Paris: Hachette, 1975) 90.

13 For Gide, of course, Jacques's solution is but another unacceptable extreme, as is clear from his correspondence with Paul Claudel.

14 Gérard Genette, *Figures II* (Paris: Seuil, 1969) 103.

15 Pierre Citron, 'Préface,' *Eugénie Grandet* (Paris: Garnier-Flammarion, 1964) 11.

16 Maurice Bardèche, 'Notice,' *Eugénie Grandet, Œuvres complètes de Balzac*, vol. 5 (Paris: Club de l'Honnête Homme, 1956) 244. See also, in this regard, Balzac's letter to Mme Hanska of 10 Feb. 1838, and Nicole Mozet's comments in her introduction to *Eugénie Grandet* in the Pléiade edition that I use for all references to Honoré de Balzac's *La Comédie humaine*, ed. Pierre-Georges Castex, 12 vols, Bibliothèque de la Pléiade (Paris: Gallimard, 1976–81) 3.991. As just one example of a suggestive objection to the novel's widely perceived simplicity, see John T. Booker, 'Starting at the End in *Eugénie Grandet*,' *L'Esprit Créateur* 31, no. 3 (1991): 38–59.

17 Percy Lubbock, *The Craft of Fiction* (1921; New York: Viking, 1966) 203.

18 Nicole Mozet, *La Ville de province dans l'œuvre de Balzac: L'Espace romanesque: Fantasmes et idéologie* (Paris: Société d'Edition et d'Enseignement Supérieur, 1982) 151.

19 See my *Balzacian Montage: Configuring 'La Comédie humaine'* (Toronto: U of Toronto P, 1991) 22–45.

20 L.-F. Hoffmann, and the Princeton Balzac Seminar, 1974, 'Thèmes religieux dans *Eugénie Grandet*,' *L'Année Balzacienne* (1976): 201–29.

21 Harry Levin, *The Gates of Horn: A Study of Five French Realists* (New York: Oxford UP, 1963) 192. I am grateful to J. Wayne Conner, who provided me with the source of this insight.

22 Alexander Fischler, 'Eugénie Grandet's Career as Heavenly Exile,' *Essays in Literature* (1989): 271. In regard to the novel's religious themes and images, see, in addition to this article (271–80), Fischler's 'Show and Rumor: The Worldly Scales in Balzac's *Eugénie Grandet*,' *International Fiction Review* 8, no. 2 (1981): 98–105; and his 'The Temporal Scale and the Natural Background in Balzac's *Eugénie Grandet*,' in Will L. McLendon, ed., *L'Hénaurme siècle: A Miscellany of Essays on Nineteenth-Century French Literature* (Heidelberg: Carl Winter Universitätsverlag, 1984) 35–45.

23 Joan Dargan's interesting comparison of Grandet to a basilisk adds further
support for the belief that the miser becomes a perverted, monstrous god:
'[T]he root *basileus* (Greek, king) is also that of *basilica*, incorporating in a
single image Grandet's sovereignty in his household and religious
devotion to his fortune. . . . And finally, the legendary basilisk, with that
calm, devouring and also fatal gaze, is a heraldic monster, an emblem of
this tale of inheritance': *Balzac and the Drama of Perspective: The Narrator in
Selected Works of 'La Comédie humaine'* (Lexington, KY: French Forum, 1985)
137.

24 Cf modern French: *nantir, nantissement.*

25 The fact that the 1843 version of *Eugénie* minimized the previously much
more salient association of Eugénie to the Virgin Mary, which Fischler
skillfully elicits in his already mentioned 'Eugénie Grandet's Career as
Heavenly Exile,' may perhaps be explained by the traditional emphasis of
Mary as linked to Jesus rather than as linked to the church. Balzac's
earlier allusions were doubtless to emphasize Eugénie's saintliness, but at
some point he must have realized that they raised dissonances with his
central reference to the Second Coming.

26 Pierre-Georges Castex, 'Introduction,' *Eugénie Grandet* (Paris: Garnier,
1965) lxv; Maurice Bardèche, *Balzac, romancier* (Paris: Plon, 1940) 466–7.

27 Jacobus de Voragine, *La Légende dorée*, tr. Teodor de Wyzewa (Paris:
Perrin, 1923) 537.

28 Louis Réau, *Iconographie de l'art chrétien*, tome 3 (Paris: Presses
Universitaires de France, 1958–9) 1.462.

7 Allusive Oxymoron: *La Faute de l'abbé Mouret*

1 Jules-Amédée Barbey d'Aurevilly, 'Zola: *La Faute de l'abbé Mouret*' (1875),
rpt in Jacques Petit, ed., *Le XIXe Siècle: Des œuvres et des hommes*, vol. 2
(Paris: Mercure de France, 1966) 254–6; and Henri Guillemin, *Présentation
des Rougon-Macquart* (Paris: Gallimard, 1964) 92, 102, respectively.

2 Philip Walker, 'Prophetic Myths in Zola,' *PMLA* 74 (1959): 444–7. For
Pierre Ouvrard, Zola describes Serge 'as a place of conflict between the
call of life and the mortal negation of life, which is religious celibacy in
his eyes': *Zola et le prêtre* (Paris: Beauchesne, 1986) 70.

3 Guy Robert, *Emile Zola: Principes et caractères généraux de son œuvre* (Paris:
Belles Lettres, 1942) 97. Similar positions are taken by Louis Kamm, *The
Object in Zola's Rougon-Macquart*, Studia Humanitas (Madrid: José Porrúa
Turanzas, 1978) 134, and Colette Becker, 'Introduction,' *La Faute de l'abbé
Mouret*, by Emile Zola (Paris: Garnier, 1972) 19.

4 Barbey, 'Zola' 257–9.

5 F.W.J. Hemmings, *Emile Zola*, 2nd ed. (Oxford: Oxford UP, 1966) 107; cf Angus Wilson, *Emile Zola: An Introductory Study of His Novels* (London: Secker and Warburg, 1952) 48, 77, 94, 98.

6 Guillemin, *Présentation* 85–6, 101–2.

7 A.A. Greaves, 'Mysticisme et pessimisme dans *La Faute de l'abbé Mouret*,' *Les Cahiers Naturalistes* 36 (1968): 148–55.

8 Richard B. Grant, 'Confusion of Meaning in Zola's *La Faute de l'abbé Mouret*,' *Symposium* 13 (1959): 284–9. This article gives an excellent summary of the problems that have confronted readers of Zola's novel and of the solutions suggested.

9 Letter dated 20 Apr. [1875] by Hippolyte Taine, quoted in John C. Lapp, 'Taine et Zola: Autour d'une correspondance,' *Revue des Sciences Humaines* 87 (1957): 325; Guy de Maupassant, 'Emile Zola' (1883), in Maupassant's *Chroniques, études, correspondance*, ed. René Dumesnil, rpt (Paris: Grund, 1938) 79; Joris-Karl Huysmans, 'Note sur Emile Zola et *L'Assommoir*' (1876), rpt in Huysmans' *Œuvres complètes*, vol. 2 (Paris: Crès, 1928) 172.

10 Henri Mitterand, ed., *La Faute de l'abbé Mouret*, by Emile Zola, vol. 1 in his *Les Rougon-Macquart*, 5 vols, Bibliothèque de la Pléiade (Paris: Gallimard, 1960–7) 1677–8. Further references to this edition will be cited by page only. Page references to other of Zola's novels in the *Rougon-Macquart* will be preceded by the volume number.

11 Janet L. Beizer argues that the Artauds, as incestuous people of the soil, provide an important key to *La Faute*, and to Zola as well: 'This Is Not a Source Study: Zola, Genesis, and *La Faute de l'abbé Mouret*,' *Nineteenth-Century French Studies* 18, nos 1–2 (1989–90): 186–95.

12 Honoré de Balzac, *La Comédie humaine*, ed. P.-G. Castex, 12 vols, Bibliothèque de la Pléiade (Paris: Gallimard, 1976–81) 1.1001.

13 Edgar Quinet, *Le Génie des religions* (1842; rpt Paris: Hachette, nd) 380. Quinet may have served as a source for some of the information, themes, and images apparent in *La Faute*. I shall mention a number of suggestive parallels as this chapter progresses.

14 Mario Maurin, 'Zola's Labyrinths,' *Yale French Studies* 42 (1969): 89, is probably correct in concluding, 'The labyrinth is fundamentally ambiguous: it is the locus of love, and its meanders insure protection as they lead to a central refuge. But it is also a realm of danger. Within its narrow lanes lurk fear and death. In Zola as in other labyrinthine writers, it preserves this double character. For them, love and death are the two faces of a single reality, a single experience.' Of course, the labyrinth is but one part of Zola's incredibly powerful and widely recognized personi-

fication of the garden/park and nature. See, e.g., Jules Lemaître, 'Emile Zola' (14 Mar. 1885), *Les Contemporains: Etudes et portraits littéraires*, 1st ser. (Paris: Boivin, nd) 261–2; Philippe Hamon, *Le Personnel du roman: Le Système des personnages dans les 'Rougon-Macquart' d'Emile Zola* (Geneva: Droz, 1983) 253; Henri Mitterand, *Zola et le naturalisme*, 2nd ed., Que sais-je (Paris: Presses Universitaires de France, 1989) 74.

15 Marcel Cressot, 'Zola et Michelet: Essai sur la genèse de deux romans de jeunesse: *La Confession de Claude, Madeleine Férat*,' *Revue d'Histoire littéraire de la France* 35 (1928): 382–9; John C. Lapp, *Zola before the Rougon-Macquart* (Toronto: U of Toronto P, 1964) esp. 121–4, 136–7, 157–8; Guy Robert, 'Zola et le classicisme,' *Revue des Sciences Humaines* 49 (1948): 14.

16 Roger Ripoll, 'Le Symbolisme végétal dans *La Faute de l'abbé Mouret*: Réminiscences et obsessions,' *Les Cahiers Naturalistes* 31 (1966): 12–16, cites *La Montagne* (1868), the *Bible de l'humanité* (1864), *L'Amour* (1858), and *La Femme* (1860), to which should perhaps be added *La Sorcière* (1862) and *Nos fils* (1870). For a broader discussion of Michelet's influence on Zola, see Ripoll's *Réalité et mythe chez Zola*, 2 vols (Lille: Atelier Reproduction des Thèses, Université de Lille III, 1981) 1.50–60

Zola's 'Causerie' in question here has been reprinted in Henri Mitterand's edition: Emile Zola, *Œuvres complètes*, 15 vols (Paris: Cercle du Livre Précieux, 1966–9), 13.112–17. All further references to this edition will be cited as *OC*. The reviews to which I shall refer somewhat farther on are to be found in vol. 10 of the *OC*, printed chronologically. I also quote from several of Zola's letters, published in Emile Zola, *Correspondance*, 2 vols (Paris: Bernouard, 1928–9), likewise printed in chronological order.

17 Jules Michelet, *La Femme* (Paris: Calmann Lévy, 1884) 65.

18 Jules Michelet, *L'Amour* (Paris: Calmann Lévy, 1878) 119–20.

19 Michelet, *L'Amour* 84, 89; *La Femme* 279.

20 Michelet, *La Femme* 273; *L'Amour* 13, 196, 404.

21 Michelet, *L'Amour* 77, 119; *La Femme* 347.

22 Michelet, *L'Amour* 118–30; *La Femme* 187, 286, 296, 236–42, 254–60.

23 Zola, *La Faute* 1351, 1353. According to Alphonse Karr, 'The odor of tuberoses used to be considered mortal for women in labor': *Voyage autour de mon jardin* (1845; Paris: Calmann Lévy, 1882) 21. Hyacinths are merely associated with death, since they are said to have been formed from the blood of a young man that Apollo loved (Karr, *Voyage* 194). This, of course, does not impugn Ripoll's argument that Albine's death surrounded by flowers indicates her complete union with nature: *Realité et mythe* 374–7.

24 But perhaps that is better than simply abandoning the post, as Quinet's

angels did in the garden Merlin finds: Edgar Quinet, *Merlin, l'enchanteur*, 2 vols (1860; rpt Paris: Hachette, nd) 2.139–40.

25 Zola, *La Faute* 1220, 1222, 1224, 1230.

26 Ibid. 1343, 1344, 1479–80.

27 Ibid. 1308; see also 1441, 1492.

28 Jerome, in *Patrologiae cursus completus* (Paris: Migne, 1845) 25.220.

29 Smaragdus, in *Patrologiae cursus completus* (Paris: Migne, 1865) 102.182.

30 Leviticus 21:18–23; see also F. Vigouraux, *Dictionnaire de la Bible*, vol. 4 (Paris: Letouzy, 1912) 1362.

31 Nouvelles Acquisitions Françaises (hereafter NAF), 10294.35.

32 D'Holbach took pains to show that his system of morality did not contravene the world of nature, but he was equally explicit in stating that to consider human beings alone in a nature isolated from men was a useless abstraction: Paul Henri Thiry, Baron d'Holbach, *La Morale universelle ou Les Devoirs de l'homme fondés sur sa nature*, 3 vols (Amsterdam: Marc-Michel Rey, 1776) 1.69–70. For d'Holbach, humanity's nature was not the jungle, it was civilized society. He would never advocate turning children loose to run free and unguided in absolute liberty. Over and over again, he insisted that children must be taught virtue, e.g., in *Système de la nature ou Des lois du monde physique et du monde moral*, 2 vols (Hildesheim: Georg Olms, 1966) 2.411, 435, 437. Jeanbernat's faulty philosophical undergirding notwithstanding, I agree with David Baguley's suggestion that *La Faute* may 'be read as a novelized philosophical tale': *Naturalist Fiction: The Entropic Vision* (Cambridge: Cambridge UP, 1990) 131. *La Faute* uses an extended allusion to Voltaire's comic masterpiece, *Candide*, to highlight its denigration of philosophy and theology in favor of what might be called a common-sense 'philosophy of life.'

33 Zola, *La Faute* 1239–40, 1278.

34 Ibid. La Teuse: 1228, 1229; Pascal: 1247.

35 The quotation is from 'Etudes sur la France contemporaine' (1878), *OC* 14.358–9. In all Zola's ideas about education, Michelet is apparent. Zola mentions him in 'Catherine' (1870): 'Yesterday, as I watched Catherine getting dressed, I remembered the beautiful book by Michelet: *Nos fils*. All mothers should certainly read this work. They will find the great law of child rearing in it. Michelet laid down the new principle: action. A child must act, create. Education is teaching to act and to create': *OC* 13.275. For the other passages used in this summary, see, 'Au couvent' (1870), *OC* 9.929, 931; 'Causerie' (1868), *OC* 13.184–8; 'Etudes sur la France con-temporaine' (1878), *OC* 14.362–3, 365, 368–9, 373–4, 681–5. Some of Zola's

prescriptions remain acceptable, others do not, but it is important to recognize that none were original. Robert Debré is overly enthusiastic when he claims that in respect to raising children, Zola 'is an innovator or rather a precursor': 'Emile Zola et l'enfant,' *L'Education Nationale* 33 (10 Dec. 1953): 11. Almost all the opinions that Zola expressed on child rearing and education, including many of the examples, are to be found in Michelet's far more comprehensive treatment in *Nos fils, La Femme,* and *L'Amour.* For a considerably more general consideration of Zola's ideas about education, see, Jacques Durin, 'Zola éducateur,' *Cahiers Naturalistes* 57 (1983): 5–17. In respect to sexual education, see Jean-Marie Paisse, 'L'Education sexuelle de Pauline Quenu dans *La Joie de vivre,' Cahiers Naturalistes* 41 (1971): 35–41.

36 For Zola's other allusions to Sleeping Beauty, see, e.g., 'Un Bain' (1873), *OC* 9.353, 355, 359; 'Lili' (1868), *OC* 9.385–6; and 'Causerie' (1868), *OC* 13.187.

37 NAF 10294.4. Some references for Zola's educational ideas are given in my n35, above. Elsewhere Zola also attacked the cruelty that took place in some church schools: 'Causerie' (1868), *OC* 13.211–15.

38 NAF 10294–4.

39 Cf 'Remember what it was like in high school. Vice grew luxuriantly, we lived in the middle of Roman rottenness. Any cloistered association of people of the same sex is bad for morals. In schools for girls, the same things take place. And here the consequences are heartbreaking. Our customs make of a man a fighter who must know everything; it is for him to construct his own virtue, dignity, upright and happy life; he is the protector, the man of experience; he can brush against all kinds of dirt and occasionally be only the stronger for it. But a girl is not raised for the struggles of life. She must be ignorant when she is put into her husband's arms, receive her knowledge from him and bring with her no memories of the heart or of the flesh': 'Au couvent,' *OC* 9.929.

40 Ovid, *Fasti,* tr. J.G. Frazer (London: Heinemann, 1931) bk 4, vv 227–8.

41 This summary of the Cybele-Attis myth, as well as the information below concerning her attributes and her cult were drawn from many sources. The following were particularly helpful: Henri Graillot, *Le Culte de Cybèle: Mère des dieux à Rome et dans l'Empire Romain* (Paris: Fontemoing, 1912); J.G. Frazer, *Adonis, Attis, Osiris,* pt 4 of *The Golden Bough,* 3rd ed. (London: Macmillan, 1907) 217–65; Frédéric Creuzer, *Religions de l'antiquité, considérées principalement dans leurs formes symboliques et mythologiques,* tr. J.D. Guigniaut, tome 2, pt 1 (Paris: Treuttel et Würtz, 1829) 56–75; L.F. Alfred Maury, *Histoire des religions de la Grèce antique depuis leur origine*

jusqu'à leur complète constitution, 3 vols (Paris: Librairie Philosophique de Ladrange, 1857–9) 3.79–102, 110–23; Larousse's *Grand Dictonnaire universel* under the rubrics 'Atys' and 'Cybèle'; Ovid's *Fasti* 4.179–372 and his *Metamorphoses*, tr. Rolfe Humphries (Bloomington: Indiana UP, 1955) bk 10, vv 103–05; Arnobius of Sicca, *The Case against the Pagans* [*Adversus Gentes*], tr. George E. McCracken (Westminster: Newman, 1949) bk 5, pars 6–7, 14; 7.49–50; Pausanias, 'Achaia,' *Description of Greece*, tr. J.G. Frazer, 5 vols, Loeb Classical Library, (London: Macmillan, 1898) vol. 3, bk 17, pars 10–12; Julian, 'Oration 5,' *The Works of the Emperor Julian*, tr. Wilmer Cave Wright, vol. 1 (Cambridge: Harvard UP, 1930) 439–503.

Ripoll has mentioned some of the ramifications of Zola's Cybele: 'Symbolisme végétal' 18–20.

42 Jules Michelet's mention of the Phoenician god Desire is perhaps pertinent: *Bible de l'humanité* (Paris: Calmann Lévy, 1876) 319. Desire, with Darkness, begot a whole pantheon of gods.

43 There is, however, one striking difference between this statue and Cybele. The stone face of the latter was dark in color: Arnobius, *Case against the Pagans* 7.49–50; Prudentius, *Peristephanon Liber*, tr. M. Lavarennes, 2nd ed., vol. 4 (Paris: Belles Lettres, 1955), hymn 10 v. 156. If Zola knew this fact, he might have decided nonetheless to make the statue's featureless visage white to emphasize the continuing, though quiescent, life that may break out again in a new form. Both Marcel Girard, 'L'Univers de Germinal,' *Revue des Sciences Humaines* 69 (1953): 61–3, and A.A. Greaves, 'Mysticisme' 149, have a differing opinion about the significance of Zola's white. For Girard, and afterwards for Greaves, it represents hopeless exhaustion immediately preceding death or, simply, nothingness (*néant*). My interpretation of the connotations of white may not seem so extreme if one considers that the white-covered coron of Germinal is only apparently dead. It will soon break forth even more violently. Similarly, the main thrust of Father Caffin's white tombstone is as a marker for the place where the good priest produces magnificent fodder for Désirée's animals (Zola, *La Faute* 1454–5).

44 Ferdinand Loise, *De l'influence de la civilisation sur la poésie, ou Histoire de la poésie mise en rapport avec la civilisation* (Brussels: Académie Royale, 1862) 45. Zola's note appears at NAF 10294.60. That firs are associated with bloody rites was, of course, known and used by other nineteenth-century writers. See, e.g., Baudelaire's 'Les Phares' vv 25–32.

45 Zola, *La Faute* 1349. This passage, and the one below, might recall the words of Viviane when Merlin picks some flowers and presents them to her: 'What are you doing?' she said. "You are hurting me! These are my

sisters. When you tear them from their stems, you are wounding me."
And she pointed to a drop of reddish blood which shone on her cheek':
Quinet, *Merlin* 1.35. The latter's Eden, abandoned and overrun with lush
vegetation, strangely resembles Paradou (2.140–6).

Doubtless, from the standpoint of recurring figures in Zola's work, it is
more important to recall that in the *Contes à Ninon*, Lois and Odette were
changed into sweet marjoram ('La Fée amoureuse,' *OC* 9.65) and Fleur-
des-Eaux into the flower *Anthapheleia limnaia* ('Simplice' *OC* 9.40). Zola's
editor points out that, although the latter flower is apparently imaginary,
one may recognize the Greek *anthos* 'flower,' and *limnaios* 'which grows in
marshes' (*OC* 9.196n1). Zola reedited the *Contes à Ninon* in 1874. A more
interesting variant to the whole Paradou love story occurs in 'Un Bain,'
probably written in 1873 and included in the *Nouveaux Contes à Ninon*
(1874). Zola not infrequently took the same images, themes, and settings
that appear in one of his *Rougon-Macquart* novels and made a very
different story – cf., e.g., 'Madame Sourdis' (1880) and *L'Œuvre* (1886). The
trivial 'Un Bain' seems designed for the newspaper audience Zola
professed to disdain (see, e.g., the Goncourts' *Journal* entry for 14 Dec.
1868), but it provides an excellent example. The story takes place in a
large park (*jardin*) of untended, luxurious greenery surrounding a
tumbledown château, 'Sleeping Beauty's château' (*OC* 9.353). A legendary
lord had once enclosed there a local farm girl whom he loved. Every so
often, Zola's heroine, Adeline, comes to visit and 'humanizes this land of
wolves' (*OC* 9.355). There, 'always searching,' Adeline passes her time
with an armless cupid, a grotto, the sun, some thick leaves, and the
flowers. On one occasion she is compared to Diana (*OC* 9.356). But she
marries her prince, and apparently lives happily ever after. And, if one is
willing to accept F.W.J. Hemmings's suggestion of Hugo's 'House on
Plumet Street' in *Les Misérables* as a possible source for *La Faute*: ('The
Secret Sources of *La Faute de l'abbé Mouret*,' *French Studies* 13 [1959]: 227–
31), I suppose, in reference to recurring themes in Zola, one could
mention the no-less-similar abandoned house and vast, untended yard of
Zola's 'Angeline ou la maison hantée' (1899; *OC* 9.1153). For an Edenic
dream, spoiled by man's bloodthirstiness, see, 'Le Sang' (1863; *OC* 9 esp.
69–70). Paradou, we learn in *Le Docteur Pascal*, was ruined by greed. It
was eventually cleared and subdivided. For other parallels between *La
Faute* and Zola's earlier or later efforts, see Lapp, *Zola before the Rougon-
Macquart* 6–7, 32–3, 38–40, 44–5, 154–6; and Hemmings, *Émile Zola* 15.

46 Zola had originally thought of calling her Blanche, the French word for
white: NAF 10294.2, 4, 6, 7.

47 Zola, *La Faute* 1511–12; the story of Leucothoe and Sun is told in Ovid's
Metamorphoses 4.190–270. Ovid says nothing about her being pregnant. Still,
knowing the potency of the gods, and of Sun in particular, it would be surprising if she were not. Hyginus's mention of a son by Helios and Leucothoe would even suggest that somehow the child was saved: *The Myths of
Hyginus*, tr. Mary Grant (Lawrence: U of Kansas P, 1960) nos 2, 4, 5.

48 The first account of the legendary lord and lady given in *La Faute*
corresponds to the Numa legend much better than the details Albine later
adds. At first we are told only: 'In the time of Louis XV, a lord had built
a superb palace there, with immense gardens, basins, running water,
statues, a whole little Versailles lost in the rocks beneath in the big sun of
the Midi. But he had only come to spend one season there, in the
company of an adorably beautiful woman, who doubtless died there, for
no one had ever seen her come out' (1248). This very faint allusion joins
with many others like it to suggest a mythic realm. Cf, for Numa:
Plutarch, 'Numa,' *Lives,* tr. Bernadotte Perrin, vol. 1, Loeb Classical
Library (Cambridge: Harvard UP, 1914) 306–401; Livy, *Ab urbe condita,* tr.
B.O. Foster, vol. 1,. Loeb Classical Library (London: Heinemann, 1922) bk
1, par. 21, line 3; Ovid, *Metamorphoses* 15.479–96, 547–51.

49 For the material on Diana, see Robert Graves, *The Greek Myths,* 2 vols
(Harmondsworth: Penguin, 1962) s. 27, no. 2; Antonini Liberalis,
Metamorphoses, ed. Edgar Martini, in *Mythographi Graeci*, vol. 2, fasc. 1
(Leipzig: Teubner, 1896) 107–8, par. 28, s. 3; Creuzer, *Religions* 2.1.106–8,
120; Ovid, *Metamorphoses* 2.409–507; 5.330; 15.531–46; and *Fasti* 2.153–92;
3.263–72; 6.739–62; Herodotus, *The History,* tr. David Grene (Chicago: U of
Chicago P, 1987) bk 2, pars 59, 67, 137, 156; Higgins, *L'Astronomie*, tr.
André Le Bœffle (Paris: Belles Lettres, 1983) bk 2, s. 1, par. 2; s. 28;
Maury, *Histoire des religions* 1.150–3, 454; Catullus, *Works*, tr. Francis Warre
Cornish (Cambridge: Harvard UP, 1988), no. 34; Arnobius, *Case against the
Pagans* 3.34; Virgil, *The Æneid, An Epic Poem of Rome,* tr. L.R. Lind
(Bloomington: Indiana UP, 1963); Pausanius, 'Corinth,' *Description of
Greece,* 3.37.4; Strabo, *The Geography,* tr. Horace Leonard Jones, vol. 3, Loeb
Classical Library (Cambridge: Harvard, 1924) bk 5, pt 1, par. 12; Larousse,
Grand Dictionnaire under the rubrics 'Diane,' 'Endymion,' 'Actéon,' and
'Hécate'; and, of course, the famous argument by J.G. Frazer, *The Magic
Art and the Evolution of Kings,* pt 1 of *The Golden Bough,* 3rd ed., 2 vols
(New York: Macmillan, 1935) 1.1–43; 2.380–2.

50 Hesiod, *Theogony,* in *The Homeric Hymns and Homerica,* tr. Hugh G.
Evelyn-White, Loeb Classical Library (Cambridge: Harvard, 1936) vv
674–86, 702–8, 713–20. Zola would use the Titanomachy again in *Germinal;*

see, Philip Walker: 'Prophetic Myths in Zola,' *PMLA* 74 (1959): 450–1; and
my own *Novel Configurations: A Study of French Fiction*, 2nd ed.
(Birmingham: Summa, 1994) 73–93.

51 Zola, *La Faute* 1454. Although some of Zola's characters reliably reflect the
overriding attitudes of the entire work and, indeed, of the author himself
(see, e.g., my 'The Failure of *L'Œuvre*,' *L'Esprit Créateur* 9 [1971]: 45–55),
this is most frequently not the case. In all instances the comments and
conclusions of the author's creations should be tested against the whole
work, plot, themes, and images. For example, Pascal's decision in favor of
the moron Désirée should not be accepted uncritically as the key to this
novel's meaning. Such an interpretation will simply not construe without
deforming the rest of *La Faute*. Especially in the case of Pascal, there is the
temptation to view him as the author's spokesman. As we shall see
farther on, there is ample evidence that, although if there were no
alternatives Zola would opt for a Désirée over a Serge, he would not in
any sense agree with Pascal that a world populated uniquely with brutes
could be beautiful.

52 G. Belèze, *Dictionnaire des noms de baptême* (Paris: Hachette, 1863) 129.

53 See, for example, pl. 28 in J.E. Cirlot, *A Dictionary of Symbols* (New York:
Philosophical Library, 1962). In his 'dossier' of material and thoughts for
the novel (NAF 10294.119), Zola wrote:

Matthew	man
Mark	lion
Luke	ox
John	eagle

54 Jacobus de Voragine, *La Légende dorée*, tr. Teodor de Wyzewa (Paris:
Perrin, 1923) 704. The information also appears in Pierre Larousse's *Grand
Dictionnaire universel* and in Justin Sabatier's *Encyclopédie des noms propres*
(Paris: Librairie du Petit Journal, 1865) 251.

55 Plutarch, "Alexander," *Moralia*, tr. Frank Cole Babbitt, vol. 4, Loeb
Classical Library (Cambridge: Harvard UP, 1922) 407, pt 331, s. A. He
attributes the statement to poets, rather than to Alexander.

56 Zola, *La Faute* 1236. Ripoll calls attention to the suggestive name of the
Solitaire and to the symbolic implications of the cypress: 'Symbolisme
végétal' 15. I do not dispute Louis Kamm's suggestion that '[t]he tree . . .
becomes a symbol of Serge's position as a priest': *Object* 45. I merely feel
that the priest and the tree are a part of the novel's symbolic representation of death. For the cypress as a symbol, see also Ovid, *Metamorphoses*
10.134–42; Grant Allen, *The Attis of Caius Valerius Catullus* (London: David
Nutt, 1892) 64.

57 Quinet, *Merlin* 2.305–7. In reference to regarding Paradou's tree as a tree of life, Philip Walker has suggested that it 'may recall not so much the tree of the knowledge of good and evil, perhaps, as the equally legendary tree of life, symbol of a fertile and beneficent Nature': *Emile Zola* (New York: Humanities Press, 1968) 28.

58 This is Michelet's interpretation of Solomon's Sulamite: *Bible de l'humanité* 387–409. If one is familiar with his reading, Zola's reference to her is appropriate to the context. It appears in the description of the rocks where Albine and Serge experience lust: 'The air slept, without a breath of wind. . . . A perfume of oriental love, the perfume of the Sulamite's painted lips, was exhaled from the fragrant woods' (1388).

   For historical background into the oppositions Zola establishes, Michelet's *Bible de l'humanité* and Quinet's *Le Génie des religions* are essential. I cannot prove that they constitute 'sources' or that Zola followed them, though it seems likely given a number of similarities.

59 As any reader of Michelet knows. See *Bible de l'humanité* 469, or *La Sorcière* (Paris: Lacroix, 1865) 38. References to Archangias's 'doigts velus' occur at 1239, 1280.

60 Zola, *La Faute* 1426, 1438, 1440.

61 Gen. 9:4–6; Lev. 17:10–14; Deut. 12:23.

62 Zola, *Le Roman expérimental*, *OC* 10.1263.

63 Zola, *Nos auteurs dramatiques*, *OC* 11.605.

64 Zola, 'Etudes sur la France contemporaine' (1878), *OC* 14.358.

65 Zola, *La Faute* 1290. Noted by Lapp, *Zola before the Rougon-Macquart* 13–14. Cf, 'In the evening it is the devil *Venus* that leads me into temptation with its soft gleams': Michelet, *La Sorcière* 30.

66 E.g., Zola, *La Faute* 1218, 1227. In reference to the Artauds, Zola wrote in the dossier that they represented 'an almost Biblical group': NAF 10294.11. A more universal conception appears subsequently (e.g., ibid. 13–14 and in the novel itself.

67 NAF 10294.6. One might even suggest that this portion of Zola's novel resembles a fictionalized version of Quinet's *La Création*, which Zola enthusiastically reviewed on 16 Feb. 1869.

68 Chantal Bertrand-Jennings argues that the life-death opposition of *La Faute* is picked up again in *Le Docteur Pascal*, though with reversed values. Rather than the death that reigns in the early novel, Zola paints triumphant life: 'Zola ou l'envers de la science: De *La Faute de l'abbé Mouret* au *Docteur Pascal*,' *Nineteenth-Century French Studies* 9, nos 1–2 (1980–1): 93–107. Cf, Ripoll, who argues that *Le Docteur Pascal* reverses the imagery of the entire *Rougon-Macquart*: *Réalité et mythe* 915–20.

69 In Walter Langlois, ed., *The Persistent Voice: Essays on Hellenism in French Literature since the 18th Century in Honor of Professor Henri M. Peyre* (New York: New York UP, 1971) 61–77.

70 Robert, 'Zola et le classicisme' 2. For a list of Zola's awards for scholastic achievement while at Aix, see *Correspondance* 2.634–5n1. Cf, however, Zola's 'Chronique' of 16 July 1868, where he claims to have forgotten his classics the minute he left school: *OC* 13.135. In the notes still available of Zola's preparation for *La Faute* (NAF mss 10294.1–164 and 10271.218–33), the unequivocal indications of the myths apparent in the novel itself are limited to the notation 'Désirée, Cybele' (ibid. 219). As already mentioned, he repeats the simile in the novel, 1261. Of course, as is widely recognized, Zola's preliminary sketches and notes never explain everything. Often the most creative work appears to have occurred subsequent to his note taking; see, for similar comments or more detailed discussion: Philip Walker, 'The *Ebauche* of *Germinal*,' *PMLA* 80 (1965): 571, 582, 583; Martin Kanes, '*Germinal*: Drama and Dramatic Structure,' *Modern Philology* 61 (1963): 22; Hemmings, 'Secret Sources' 227; Elliott M. Grant, *Zola's Germinal: A Critical and Historical Study* (Leicester: Leicester UP, 1962) 52; Guy Robert, *Emile Zola: Principes* 58.

71 See Charly Clerc, *Le Génie du paganisme: Essais sur l'inspiration antique dans la littérature française contemporaine* (Paris: Payot, 1926); E. Egger, *L'Hellénisme en France*, vol. 2 (Paris: Didier, 1869) 397–484; Henri M. Peyre, *L'Influence des littératures antiques sur la littérature française moderne: Etat des travaux* (New Haven: Yale UP, 1941) 55–74. For background on the first half of the nineteenth century, see as well René Canat, *La Renaissance de la Grèce antique (1820-1850)* (Paris: Hachette, 1911).

72 The notes he took remain in the dossier: NAF 10294.64. A few notes from a commentary on Genesis appear, f. 118. For Zola's investigation of church and theology, see Mitterand's conclusions, cited below, n74.

73 Robert Couffignal, '*Aux premiers jours du monde...*': *La Paraphrase poétique de la Genèse de Hugo à Supervielle*, Bibliothèque des Lettres Modernes, no. 16 (Paris: Minard, 1970) esp. 7–111. For Zola, of course, Eden was rather special, in that it was, as Ripoll puts it, 'a myth of origins, a myth that is perpetually offered for living once again': *Réalité et mythe* 366. This is perhaps the place to say that, although I have found Ripoll's work extraordinarily helpful, I disagree with one of his focal thoughts. In discussing the different traditions from which Zola took various elements, he concludes, 'It is not a question of allusions, but of a remaking and a transposition' (*Réalité et mythe* 532). As should be clear, I believe that what Zola creates depends upon the allusions to the independent systems.

74 Many other sources have been suggested for *La Faute de l'abbé Mouret*: works by Victor Hugo, Charles Hugo, Louis Ulbach, Léon Gozlan, Louis Bouilhet, Ernest Daudet and Michelet, as well as Zola's memories of Aix and the surrounding countryside. For these and other possibilities, see Hemmings, 'Secret Sources' 226–39; Guillemin, *Présentation* 73–6; Mitterand, '*La Faute de l'abbé Mouret*: Etude' 1.1680–1, 1684–6; Ripoll, 'Symbolisme végétal' 12–16. Quinet's works should be added to this list as well.

75 E.g., 'In the Indian Paradise, where the river Ganges . . . originates, there was a marvelous tree, whose fruit would have given immortality, if it had been permitted to eat it. This tradition proves how old the Garden of Eden allegory is. Could it have come from India? Did its constituent elements come from the ancient Scythians?': Pierre Lacour, *Æloïm, ou Les Dieux de Moïse*, vol. 2 (Bordeaux: Jules Teycheney, 1839) 198. Lacour takes particular trouble to show the degree to which Egyptian rites parallel his reading of Genesis.

76 Alexander Heidel, *The Gilgamesh Epic and Old Testament Parallels*, Phoenix Book (Chicago: U of Chicago P, 1963) 2.

77 *Catalogue de livres modernes: Auteurs contemporains en éditions originales: Revues, romans, poésies, dictionnaires… composant la bibliothèque de feu M. Emile Zola* (Paris: 9 Mar. 1903) 10, item 42. I am grateful to Philip Walker, who shared his copy of the catalog with me.

78 Henri Mitterand, after reading Zola's notes for this section, observes, 'As the names of the flowers, with the corresponding description, passed into the text of the novel, Zola crossed them off the list he had previously made' (Zola, *La Faute* 1345n1).

8 Allusive Permutations: *La Nausée, Les Gommes*

1 James W. Mileham, *The Conspiracy Novel: Structure and Metaphor in Balzac's 'Comédie humaine'* (Lexington: French Forum, 1982) 137n10.

2 Honoré de Balzac, *La Comédie humaine*, ed. P.-G. Castex, 12 vols, Bibliothèque de la Pléiade (Paris: Gallimard, 1976–81) 6.337.

3 J.D. Hubert, *Molière and the Comedy of Intellect* (Berkeley: U of California P, 1962) 71.

4 Emile Zola, *La Faute de l'abbé Mouret* (1.1251) and *Le Docteur Pascal* (5.960) in *Les Rougon-Macquart*, ed. Henri Mitterand, 5 vols (Paris: Pléiade, 1960–7).

5 Gérard Genette, *Palimpsestes: La Littérature au second degré* (Paris: Seuil, 1982) 14.

6 See, e.g., Robert Greer Cohn, 'Sartre versus Proust,' *Partisan Review* 28, nos 5–6 (1961): 633–45; Eugenia Noik Zimmerman, 'The Metamorphoses of Adam: Names and Things in Sartre and Proust,' in George Stambolian, ed., *Twentieth-Century French Fiction: Essays for Germaine Brée* (New Brunswick: Rutgers UP, 1975): 54–71; Sandra Teroni Menzella, 'Sartre lecteur de Proust: Sensation et mémoire dans *La Nausée*,' *Studi francesi* 27, no. 1 (1983): 44–52; Albert Mingelgrün, 'L'Air de jazz dans *La Nausée*: Un cheminement proustien,' *Revue de l'Université de Bruxelles* 1 (1972): 55–68; and the studies listed below in notes 6–11. Pierre Bost is particularly sensitive to Proust in the final pages of *La Nausée*: 'Proust devant une sonate, Sartre devant un air de jazz entendent une seul voix,' *Figaro Littéraire* (8 Jan. 1949) 1.3.

7 David I. Grossvogel, *Limits of the Novel: Evolutions of a Form from Chaucer to Robbe-Grillet* (Ithaca: Cornell UP, 1968) 226.

8 Pauline Newman-Gordon, 'Sartre, lecteur de Proust ou le paradoxe de *La Nausée*,' *Bulletin de la Société des Amis de Marcel Proust* 29 (1979): 103–14; and 'Sartre, lecteur de Proust ou le style de *La Nausée*,' *Bulletin de la Société des Amis de Marcel Proust* 31 (1981): 323–30.

9 Jean-Paul Sartre, *La Nausée*, in his *Œuvres romanesques*, ed. Michel Contat and Michel Rybalka, Bibliothèque de la Pléiade (Paris: Gallimard, 1981) 24–9. Page references in the text to this edition will be preceded by the abbreviation *N*. References to Proust's *A la recherche du temps perdu* are to the edition edited by Jean-Yves Tadié, 4 vols, Bibliothèque de la Pléiade (Paris: Gallimard, 1978–9), and page references in the text will be preceded by the abbreviation *R*. Contat and Rybalka tell us, however, that 'Sartre denies having intentionally referred to Proust in naming the waitress "Madeleine"': *La Nausée*, 1801, note to p. 204. As I argue, the textual evidence stands nonetheless strongly against Sartre's retrospective and, finally, incredible claim.

10 Critics have regularly pointed to Sartre's and Beauvoir's passion for this sort of music: e.g., E.N. Zimmerman, '"Some of These Days": Sartre's *Petite phrase*,' *Contemporary Literature* 11, no. 3 (1970): 378–81. Such enthusiasm for popular music does not annul Sartre's ability to use conventional understandings of 'serious' as opposed to popular music. In *La Nausée*, 'Some of These Days' joins with numerous other elements to suggest a debunking of Proust's 'high' aesthetic experience.

11 As Frank Kermode put it, '[H]is book, though it surrounds the hero with images of formlessness, inhumanity, nausea, must not itself be formless or viscous or inhuman': *The Sense of an Ending: Studies in the Theory of Fiction* (New York: Oxford UP, 1967) 146. Terry Keefe develops the thought in

'The Ending of Sartre's *La Nausée*,' *Forum for Modern Language Studies* 12, no. 3 (1976): esp. 228–32.

12 Geneviève Idt has specifically, though briefly, defended Sartre from the thought that the Christian vocabulary of 'the final pages contrasts with the whole of the text and seems superfluous, like a conventional solution in which the author no longer believes,' by suggesting that a few earlier passages indicate Roquentin's drift toward the novel genre: *'La Nausée,' Sartre: Analyse critique*, Collection Profil d'une Œuvre (Paris: Hatier, 1971) 34–5. Gerald Prince wonders whether the projected novel 'may paradoxically signal the possibility of [Roquentin's] return to history, society, the world. Perhaps: *La Nausée* does not dispense certainty': *Narrative as Theme* (Lincoln: U of Nebraska P, 1992) 103. The central question is, of course, not whether he would write a novel, but whether he could seriously believe after his gradual discovery of his own contingency and superfluity that writing a novel could do more for him than any other endeavor. As Keith Gore points out, 'A writer has no special prestige'; Roquentin repeats the 'bad faith' of Sartre's boyhood self, as described in *Les Mots: Sartre: 'La Nausée' and 'Les Mouches'* (London: Edward Arnold, 1970) 67. The difficulties raised by numerous scholars considering this conclusion have been summarized by Keefe, 'Ending,' 217–35. Contrary to Denis Hollier, in *The Politics of Prose: Essay on Sartre*, tr. J. Mehlman (1982; Minneapolis: U of Minnesota P, 1986) 5, and others, Keefe argues that we simply do not know whether Sartre would have subscribed to Roquentin's 'solution' at the time he composed *La Nausée*, though Sartre's later thought would definitely find any such resolution inauthentic. Of course, for those willing to ignore the problems raised by an author's retrospective conclusions and posthumous publications, Sartre has resolved the controversy: he claims that it was a belief in salvation by means of art that brought him out of depression in 1935, though he shortly lost the faith: *Les Carnets de la drôle de guerre: Novembre 1939–Mars 1940* (Paris: Gallimard, 1983) 100–2. For myself, I wonder whether the scanty preparation for *La Nausée*'s last few pages might not indicate Sartre's perhaps still unconscious realization that such a conclusion simply would not construe with Roquentin's discoveries encapsulated by the symbol of nausea. However that may be, it is perhaps best to recognize simply that *La Nausée* is fiction, not philosophy – a point made, e.g., by Georges Raillard, *'La Nausée' de J.-P. Sartre*, Collection Poche Critique (Paris: Hachette, 1972) 42–4; and, especially, by Claude-Edmonde Magny's 'Sartre ou la duplicité de l'être: Ascèse et mythomanie,' in her

Les Sandales d'Empédocle: Essai sur les limites de la littérature (Neuchâtel: La Baconnière, 1945) 105–72.

13 Gerald Prince, 'La Nausée and the Question of Closure,' *Yale French Studies* 67 (1984): 182–90; the quotation is from 183.

14 The quotation is from ibid. 188. Raillard uses similar expressions in discussing the same phenomena, but he views them differently, as ways *La Nausée* enhances verisimilitude, by attempting to give the text the look and sense of a diary: *'La Nausée'* 45–51.

15 Leo Spitzer, 'Linguistics and Literary History,' in his *Linguistics and Literary History: Essays in Stylistics* (1948; rpt New York: Russell and Russell, 1962) 11–15.

16 Roquentin's antipathy toward the bourgeois that dominate the town gives weight to Margaret Church's suggestion: 'Bouville echoes, as does Bovary, that which is bovine. *Bouvier* (cowherd), *bouvillon* (steer), *bouc* (goat) all come to mind as well as the Latin *bos, bovis*. . . . Bouville represents a reality beyond which a transcendence is impossible': *Time and Reality: Studies in Contemporary Fiction* (Chapel Hill: U of North Carolina P, 1963) 262.

17 See, my *Novel Configurations: A Study of French Fiction*, 2nd ed. (Birmingham: Summa, 1993) 104–6.

18 Philip R. Wood, *Understanding Jean-Paul Sartre* (Columbia: U of South Carolina P, 1990) 79. Suzanne Lilar's monograph, *A propos de Sartre et de l'amour* (Paris: Grasset, 1967), argues that the author's attitude toward love reveals deep-seated misogyny.

19 See, e.g., Alain Robbe-Grillet's essay, 'Nature, humanisme, tragédie' (1958), in his *Pour un nouveau roman* (Paris: Minuit, 1963) 45–67. The quotation is from p. 64.

20 Uri Eisengweig, 'Entretien [avec Robbe-Grillet],' *Littérature* 49 (1983): 16.

21 Alain Robbe-Grillet, *Les Gommes* (Paris: Minuit, 1953) 70.

22 Charlotte M. Yonge, *History of Christian Names* (1884; rpt Detroit: Gale, 1966) 316–17, 367–71. Still, as Martha Onan rightly points out, one would more normally consider Wallas as a derivation of Old Norse, Anglo-Saxon, and Welsh words for 'foreigner or stranger': 'The Riddle of Names in Robbe-Grillet's *Erasers,' Literary Onomastics Studies* 10 (1983): 154.

23 *Œuvres complètes d'André Gide*, ed. L. Martin-Chauffier, vol. 6 (Paris: NRF, 1934) 361–2.

24 André Gide, *Journal: 1889–1939*, Bibliothèque de la Pléiade (Paris: Gallimard, 1951) 760.

25 Bruce Morrissette, 'Oedipus or the Closed Circle: *The Erasers* (1953),' in his *The Novels of Robbe-Grillet* (1st French ed. 1963; rev. tr. Ithaca: Cornell UP,

1975) 38-74. Although Morrissette gives the credit of first mentioning Oedipus in the context of *Les Gommes* to Samuel Beckett, his analysis remains the most thorough and convincing. (I follow his argument, which is considerably more extended and complete than my own.) When critics wish to suggest other possibilities, they have little choice but to bank their argument against that of Morrissette.

26 Morrissette mentions Leon Roudiez's suggestion of Didier (*Novels of Robbe-Grillet* 63–4n9). Robert R. Brock suggests that it might be the word *radier* (erase): 'From *Les Gommes* to *Dans le labyrinthe*: or, Play it again, Alain,' *Romance Quarterly* 33 (1986): 44. A.R. Chadwick and Virginia Harger-Grinling consider that '[a]nother, more suggestive, possibility centers on the letters *di* which Wallas remembers seeing on an eraser of the type he is looking for. . . . [W]hen reversed they form *id*, the unconscious part of Wallas's character upon which he is unable to focus': 'Mythic Structures in Alain Robbe-Grillet's *Les Gommes*,' *International Fiction Review* 11, no. 2 (1984): 103.

27 Jean Ricardou, *Le Nouveau Roman* (Paris: Seuil, 1973) 32-7.

28 See my *Novel Configurations* 174-5.

29 I follow Tremewan closely, without however repeating all his evidence: P.J. Tremewan, 'Allusions to Christ in Robbe-Grillet's *Les Gommes*,' *AUMLA: Journal of the Australasian Universities Modern Language Association* 51 (1979): 40-8.

30 For Adam and lizardlike serpents, see, e.g., Georges Duby, *History of Medieval Art: 980–1440*, vol. 1 (New York: Rizzoli, 1986) 73-9. For the figural relationship of Adam and Apollo, see, e.g., James Snyder, *Northern Renaissance Art: Painting, Sculpture, the Graphic Arts from 1350 to 1575* (Englewood Cliffs: Prentice-Hall, 1985) 316-17. I am grateful to L.R. Lind for help with the Greek, and to Sheri Valentine for assistance with art history.

31 Morrissette, *Novels of Robbe-Grillet* 57-60; Bruce Bassoff, 'Freedom and Fatality in Robbe-Grillet's *Les Gommes*,' *Contemporary Literature* 20 (1979): 445-7;

32 The books and pamphlets concerning the Tarot are legion. Good introductions and bibliography are to be found in: Richard Cavendish, ed., *Encyclopedia of the Unexplained: Magic, Occultism, and Parapsychology* (New York: McGraw-Hill, 1974); J.E. Cirlot, *A Dictionary of Symbols*, tr. Jack Sage (New York: Philosophical Library, 1962); and Jean Chevalier and Alain Gheerbrant, eds, *Dictionnaire des symboles: Mythes, rêves, coutumes, gestes, formes, figures, couleurs, nombres* (Paris: Robert Laffont, 1969). I have found the following books particularly helpful: Gareth Knight, *The Magical World*

of the Tarot: Fourfold Mirror of the Universe (London: Aquarian Press, 1991);
Rosemary Ellen Guiley, *The Mystical Tarot* (New York: Signet, 1991);
Stewart R. Kaplan, *The Encyclopedia of Tarot*, 3 vols (Stamford: U.S. Games
Systems, 1978–90); Oswald Wirth, *Le Tarot des imagiers du moyen âge* (Paris:
Tchou, 1966).

33 Jean Alter, *La Vision du monde d'Alain Robbe-Grillet* (Geneva: Droz, 1966) 8–
19; Olga Bernal, *Alain Robbe-Grillet: Le Roman de l'absence* (Paris: Gallimard,
1964), 91, 101, and passim; Ann Jefferson, *The Nouveau Roman and the
Poetics of Fiction* (Cambridge: Cambridge UP, 1980) 18–30.

34 Allusive relationships that resist integration are by no means uncommon.
Thomas Pynchon's *V* provides another illustration. See, David H. Richter,
Fable's End: Completeness and Closure in Rhetorical Fiction (Chicago: U of
Chicago P, 1974) 130–1.

35 I would also disagree with Heinrich F. Plett in regard to the frequency of
intertextuality: 'Intertextuality is not a time-bound feature in literature
and the arts. Nevertheless, it is obvious that certain cultural periods
incline to it more than others': 'Intertextualities,' in Plett, ed.,
Intertextuality (Berlin: Walter de Gruyter, 1991) 26.

Index